Atlassian Confluence 5 Essentials

Learn how to install, configure, and manage
Atlassian Confluence 5 to build an enterprise-grade
collaboration platform

Stefan Kohler

BIRMINGHAM - MUMBAI

Atlassian Confluence 5 Essentials

First published: June 2013

Production Reference: 1030613

Published by Packt Publishing Ltd.
Livery Place
35 Livery Street
Birmingham B3 2PB, UK.

ISBN 978-1-84968-952-6

www.packtpub.com

Cover Image by Eugenio Dal Monte (e_dm@fastwebnet.it)

Credits

Author
Stefan Kohler

Reviewers
Gregory Kneller
Alek Lotoczko
Jurriaan van Reijsen
Emma Rush

Acquisition Editor
Andrew Duckworth

Lead Technical Editors
Amey Varangaonkar
Savio Jose

Technical Editors
Jalasha D'costa
Pushpak Poddar
Amit Ramadas

Project Coordinator
Leena Purkait

Proofreader
Chris Smith

Indexer
Tejal Soni

Graphics
Abhinash Sahu

Production Coordinator
Shantanu Zagade

Cover Work
Shantanu Zagade

About the Author

Stefan Kohler is senior Atlassian consultant for 42, a company that specializes in Atlassian and is known for its expertise in the field. Stefan was in a big way responsible for setting 42 on Atlassian's path and making sure the company has a solid plugin development, consultancy and support offering. Stefan is a much sought-after consultant, requiring his agenda to be planned months ahead.

Within the community, Stefan is a person of some renown, having set up the Dutch chapter of the Atlassian User Group in 2010. He has written a number of award-winning add-ons for Confluence and Stash, and has scored an Atlassian prize for the best website. On Atlassian Answers, Stefan is a highly appreciated contributor with his useful answers and suggestions.

Stefan has extensive experience with designing and deploying Atlassian solutions. He has got Atlassian solutions working for many customers, in various industries, such as Software Engineering, Healthcare, Government, and Finance.

I would like to thank my family and friends for all their support and understanding during this project. A special thanks goes to Eric Meijer and 42 for making it possible for me to take on this project. I would also like to thank all the editors and reviewers for their efforts and much appreciated feedback.

About the Reviewers

Gregory Kneller started as a software developer in 1991, focusing on developing and implementing order-, task- and content-management systems for business customers. Before 200x, the main instruments for such kind of tasks were MS Access, Turbo C, and Borland Delphi. In 2000, he changed to web development and created a couple of custom CMS and data management systems with a web interface that were used by his customers.

Gregory's main concerns are usability, value for business, and team collaboration. He started implementing DHTML and XMLHttpRequest for developing frontends in 2003. These technologies were very new at that time; however, they promised rich user interfaces and communication features for project teams.

During that time, Gregory was looking for the best tool that has a web interface, which provides good usability, enough flexibility in order to adjust it to a variety of business requirements, and which does not require deep development at its customization. He probed many web tools such as Drupal, Typo3, Mambo-Joomla!, Tikiwiki, and a few others.

In 2007, being a Front Office Support Engineer in Deutsche Bank, he got acquainted with the Atlassian tools, JIRA and Confluence, and he decided that they are exactly the instruments he was looking for.

Since 2010, Gregory works as an independent contractor and he provides services of business customization, technical change management, enterprise integration, technical project management, and advanced administration for JIRA and Confluence. Alstom, UNFCCC, and ZDF are a few names among his clients.

Alek Lotoczko is an IT professional with more than 30 years' experience. For the last decade, Alek has specialized in the field of intranet and digital workplace solutions, with an emphasis on exploiting social networking elements within the corporate firewall environment.

Alek has worked with global companies in the banking, marine transportation, manufacturing, and logistics sectors.

Jurriaan van Reijsen has an M.Sc. degree (1982), and is a learning technology consultant at The Courseware Company in the Netherlands. He has implemented Confluence in several of the top 100 Dutch companies and helped those organizations to devise their knowledge strategy. Moreover, Jurriaan is a Ph.D. researcher at Utrecht University. His research focuses on the influence of knowledge networks on organizational learning, and his papers have been published in the proceedings of several leading international conferences. Jurriaan studied Information Science at Utrecht University and graduated on the topic of Knowledge Management.

Emma Rush is an Atlassian product specialist. She began as a developer, and now works as a consultant and technology evangelist, helping organizations to use applications to manage their development life cycle and business processes.

www.PacktPub.com

Support files, eBooks, discount offers and more

You might want to visit www.PacktPub.com for support files and downloads related to your book.

Did you know that Packt offers eBook versions of every book published, with PDF and ePub files available? You can upgrade to the eBook version at www.PacktPub.com and as a print book customer, you are entitled to a discount on the eBook copy. Get in touch with us at service@packtpub.com for more details.

At www.PacktPub.com, you can also read a collection of free technical articles, sign up for a range of free newsletters and receive exclusive discounts and offers on Packt books and eBooks.

http://PacktLib.PacktPub.com

Do yout need instant solutions to your IT questions? PacktLib is Packt's online digital book library. Here, you can access, read and search across Packt's entire library of books.

Why Subscribe?

- Fully searchable across every book published by Packt
- Copy and paste, print and bookmark content
- On demand and accessible via web browser

Free Access for Packt account holders

If you have an account with Packt at www.PacktPub.com, you can use this to access PacktLib today and view nine entirely free books. Simply use your login credentials for immediate access.

Instant Updates on New Packt Books

Get notified! Find out when new books are published by following @PacktEnterprise on Twitter, or the *Packt Enterprise* Facebook page.

Table of Contents

Preface   **1**

Chapter 1: Getting Started with Confluence   **7**

Understanding the architecture   **7**

High-level architecture   8

Supported browsers   8

Data storage   9

Confluence Installation directory   9

Confluence Home directory   9

Installation options   **11**

Standalone and WAR distributions   11

Operating systems   11

Databases   12

Application servers   12

Installing Confluence   **12**

Installing Java   13

Installing PostgreSQL   15

Creating a user and a database   16

Installing Confluence   18

Unpacking Confluence   18

Configuring Confluence Home   19

Configuring the port   19

Configuring e-mail JNDI resource   20

Configuring HTTPS   21

Configuring Confluence as a service   23

Starting Confluence   **25**

Installation wizard   26

Setting up the e-mail server   30

Summary   **32**

Chapter 2: User Management   **33**

  Understanding authentication   **33**

    Password authentication   34

    Seraph   34

  Adding users   **34**

    Manually adding users   35

    Open registration   37

    Inviting users   38

  Managing groups   **39**

    Creating groups   39

    Adding users to groups   40

      Editing group membership from the user details screen   40

      Editing group membership via the group management screen   41

  Administrating users   **42**

    Searching for users   42

      Using the simple user search   43

      Using the membership search   43

    Editing user details   44

    Resetting the password   46

  Public signup   **47**

  External user directories   **49**

    The effect of directory order   50

    Limitations when using external directories   51

      Build-in user management   51

      Editing directories   51

    Connecting to an LDAP directory   52

      Connecting to LDAP   52

      Server settings   52

      LDAP schema settings   53

      LDAP permissions   53

      Advanced settings   54

      User schema settings   55

      Group schema settings   56

      Membership schema settings   57

    Connecting to a Crowd directory   57

      Connecting to Crowd   58

      Server settings   58

      Crowd permissions   59

      Advanced settings   59

    Connecting to JIRA for user management   59

      Connecting to JIRA   59

      Server settings   61

      JIRA server permissions   61

      Advanced settings   61

  Summary   **62**

Chapter 3: Creating Content   63

The basic concepts   63
Spaces   63
Pages   64
Blog posts   64
Comments   65
Adding global spaces   65
Adding pages   66
Adding a new page to Confluence   67
Creating a page from another page   68
Setting the location of a page   68
The Confluence editor   69
The toolbar   70
Formatting and autocomplete   71
    Autoformatting   71
    Autocomplete   71
    Autoconverting   72
Drag-and-drop   73
Adding content   73
Styling   73
Macros   75
    The macro browser   76
    Editing macros   76
    Macro keyboard shortcut   78
Panels   78
Page layouts and sections   78
    Using page layouts   79
    Using Section and Column macros   80
Tables   81
    Editing a table   82
    Keyboard shortcuts   82
    Sorting the table   83
Attachments   83
    Attaching files to a page   83
    Attachment version management   84
    Downloading attachments   85
    Embedding attachments   85
Images   89
    Displaying an attached image   89
    Displaying an attached image on a different page   90
    Displaying an image from a remote web page   90
    Changing the image's appearance   91
    Displaying images in a gallery   93
Links   94
    Linking to Confluence pages   94

Linking to web pages	96
Linking to an anchor	96
Linking to a heading	98
Linking to an undefined page	98
Drafts	**98**
Changing the draft interval	99
Resuming editing a draft	99
Viewing unsaved changes	100
Working with content history	**101**
Viewing the page history	101
Importing content	**103**
Importing a Word document	103
Importing a Word document as a single page	104
Importing a Word document into multiple pages	106
Exporting content	**107**
Exporting a single page	107
Exporting a space	107
Summary	**109**
Chapter 4: Managing Content	**111**
Organizing your spaces	**111**
Changing the order of pages	111
Setting the page order to alphabetical	113
Orphaned pages	113
Archiving a space	114
Using Confluence labels	**116**
Content labels	116
Attachment labels	117
Using space categories	118
Viewing labels	119
Using labels to display content	120
The Content by Label macro	120
Tracking content	**123**
Watching content	123
Setting notification options	123
Watching a page or a blog post	125
Watching a space	125
Managing your watches	126
Favorites	127
Adding favorites	127
Viewing favorites	128
Searching Confluence	**129**
Quick navigation aid	129
Full and advanced search	131
"Did you mean"	132

Filtering results	132
Searching labels	133
The search syntax	134
Summary	**135**
Chapter 5: Collaborating in Confluence	**137**
Collaborating with other people	**137**
Mentions	138
Share content	139
Like	140
Status updates	140
Updating your status	141
Managing status updates	142
Displaying status updates	142
Working with notifications	**143**
Managing your notifications	144
Included notifications	145
Configuring workbox notifications	146
Enabling workbox notifications	146
Including notifications from JIRA	148
Sending notifications to another Confluence server	148
Working with tasks	**149**
Working with personal tasks	149
Working with tasklists	151
Managing tasks on a page	152
Confluence on your mobile device	**152**
Viewing	153
User profiles	155
Searching	156
Notifications and tasks	156
Notes about the mobile interface	157
Summary	**157**
Chapter 6: Securing Your Content	**159**
Accessing the content	**159**
Global permissions	160
Updating global permissions	162
Overview of the global permissions	164
Comparing the administration roles	165
Notes on global permissions	167
Space permissions	167
Overview of the permissions	167
Managing space permissions	168
Setting default space permissions	170

Page restrictions 171
Confluence security **174**
Secure administrator sessions 175
Atlassian security advisory 176
Limiting access to Confluence administration 178
Best practices 180
Summary **181**
Chapter 7: Customizing Confluence **183**
The Confluence dashboard **183**
The Confluence home page 184
The welcome message 184
Restoring the default welcome message 185
Removing the Get Started text 186
Including content from another page 187
Themes **188**
The Default Theme 190
Configuring the theme 191
The Documentation Theme 192
Configuring the theme 193
Look and feel **196**
Confluence logo 196
Space logo 198
Color schemes 200
Advanced customizing **201**
The default space content 201
Custom HTML 202
Custom stylesheets 203
Site layouts 206
Summary **207**
Chapter 8: Advanced Confluence **209**
Templates **209**
Using templates 210
Creating templates 211
Space templates 212
Global templates 212
Adding content to your template 213
Importing templates 217
Checking installed template bundles 217
Making templates available for usage 218
User Macros **218**
Managing user macros 218
Writing user macros 220

Writing a user macro template   223
  A descriptive header   223
  Parameters   224
  Template code   226
The Page Properties macro   **228**
Shortcut links   **231**
Creating a shortcut link   231
Using shortcut links   232
Summary   **233**
Chapter 9: General Administration   **235**
Working with add-ons   **235**
The Marketplace   236
The Universal Plugin Manager   238
  Online and offline modes   238
  Finding new add-ons   241
  Installing add-ons   242
  Updating add-ons   244
  Removing installed add-ons   245
  User requests for add-ons   247
Content indexing   **249**
Rebuilding the indexes   249
Changing the indexing language   251
Application links   **251**
Adding an application link   252
Editing an application link   255
Space project links   256
Configuring authentication   257
  Trusted applications authentication   257
  OAuth authentication   260
  Basic HTTP authentication   260
Using Application Navigator   **261**
Adding a new link   262
Managing links   262
Getting support   **263**
Atlassian Answers   264
Atlassian Support   265
  Atlassian Support tools   265
  Raising a support ticket   266
Atlassian experts   268
Summary   **270**

Chapter 10: Extending Confluence   271

The Atlassian Plugin SDK   271
Installing the Atlassian Plugin SDK   272
    Prerequisites   272
    Setting up the Atlassian SDK   275
Commands   276
    Creating a new plugin   276
    Adding a new module to your plugin   277
    Running a plugin in an application   277
    Running a specific version of an application   277
    Using the Maven Command Line Interface (CLI) plugin   277
    Running a standalone application   278
    The help command   278
    Maven   278
    The plugin descriptor   279
    Using a development environment   280

Building your first plugin   284
Creating the plugin project   284
Updating the generated code   285
    Adding plugin metadata to the POM file   286
    Verifying your Confluence version   286
    Cleaning up the plugin skeleton   286
Adding a new macro module   287
    Implementing the macro interface   287
    Implementing the getBodyType and getOutputType methods   288
    Implementing the execute method   288
Building, installing, and running your plugin   289
Adding resources   291
Releasing your plugin   292
    Setting distributionManagement   293

Plugin module types   294
Generic module types   294
Confluence-specific module types   296
The plugin module types in detail   296
    XWork   297
    Web Sections   299
    Web Items   300

Online resources   301
Summary   302
Index   303

Preface

Atlassian Confluence 5 Essentials is a practical hands-on guide introducing you to Atlassian Confluence, a powerful enterprise collaboration tool for teams to create, share, and discuss their content.

This book will show you how to install and manage your own Confluence installation. You will learn how to configure and customize Confluence to adapt it to your organization and add value to your business. The chapters in this book are structured to guide you through all the key aspects of managing and using Confluence.

You will start by setting up your own Confluence installation and will be introduced to all the key features in subsequent chapters. With each chapter, you will learn important concepts such as creating engaging content, sharing information, and engaging users to collaborate with each other.

This book is an in-depth guide to all the essential aspects of Atlassian Confluence. Packed with examples and step-by-step instructions, this book will help you become a Confluence expert.

What this book covers

Chapter 1, Getting Started with Confluence, will guide you through the installation process of Confluence and will give you a local installation, which will be used throughout the book. By the end of the first chapter you should have a running Confluence installation.

Chapter 2, User Management, covers how you can invite and register new users to join you in the content collaboration process. We will also go over how to connect Confluence to an existing user directory such as LDAP.

Chapter 3, *Creating Content*, is maybe the most important chapter, as content is king. We will go through the concepts of spaces, pages, and blog posts to explain how to add content to Confluence. Confluence's rich text editor has many features and in this chapter we will learn to master a large part of those by creating our first pages.

Chapter 4, *Managing Content*, focuses on how to find relevant content and how to use watches to keep track of you content. Confluence comes with a powerful search engine, which we will know all about by the end of this chapter.

Chapter 5, *Collaborating in Confluence*, goes into Confluence on a day-to-day basis. We will go into how to involve people in the content creation process using mentions and shares, and how to keep track of things using tasks. If you are on the road, Confluence mobile will keep you in touch with the latest content, tasks, and notifications.

Chapter 6, *Securing Your Content*, covers the options available for keeping your private information private. Confluence allows permissions to be set on a global, space, and content-specific level, giving us the fine-grained security an enterprise solution needs.

Chapter 7, *Customizing Confluence*, will go over the different features for changing the look and feel of Confluence so that we can add some company branding to our instance or just to a space.

Chapter 8, *Advanced Confluence*, covers many different advanced topics such as content templating, and working with metadata and keyboard shortcuts.

Chapter 9, *General Administration*, goes in-depth to find and manage add-ons to Confluence. Add-ons can add extra functionality or integrations. If you have problems with your Confluence installation and need support, this chapter will guide you to getting support from Atlassian or a local expert.

Chapter 10, *Extending Confluence*, focuses on some basics and possibilities of add-on development. By the end of the chapter you should know where to start if you would like to build an add-on, and on which level we can extend Confluence.

What you need for this book

The Confluence installation used in this book will be the Windows standalone distribution (ZIP), which you can get directly from Atlassian at www.atlassian. com/software/confluence/download.

At the time of writing, the latest version of Confluence was 5.1.1.

You will also need several additional software libraries including Java SDK, which you can get from `http://www.oracle.com/technetwork/java/javase/downloads/index.html` and PostgreSQL, which you can get from `http://www.postgresql.org/download/`.

Who this book is for

If you have just started with Confluence, as a user or administrator, this book will give you a running start and teach you everything you need to know. Even if you have been using Confluence for a while now, this book can give you new insights and tricks on how to use Confluence even more efficiently.

Conventions

In this book, you will find a number of styles of text that distinguish between different kinds of information. Here are some examples of these styles, and an explanation of their meaning.

Code words in text are shown as follows: "Create a file called `local_machines_only.conf` in your Apache configuration directory."

A block of code is set as follows:

```
<linklinkId="config-link">/plugins/config/alpha.action</link>

<icon height="16" width="16">
<link>/images/icons/config.gif</link>
</icon>
```

Any command-line input or output is written as follows:

```
netstat -a | find /I "1990"
```

New terms and **important words** are shown in bold. Words that you see on the screen, in menus or dialog boxes for example, appear in the text like this: "Clicking the **Next** button moves you to the next screen".

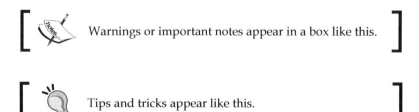

> Warnings or important notes appear in a box like this.

> Tips and tricks appear like this.

Reader feedback

Feedback from our readers is always welcome. Let us know what you think about this book—what you liked or may have disliked. Reader feedback is important for us to develop titles that you really get the most out of.

To send us general feedback, simply send an e-mail to feedback@packtpub.com, and mention the book title via the subject of your message.

If there is a topic that you have expertise in and you are interested in either writing or contributing to a book, see our author guide on www.packtpub.com/authors.

Customer support

Now that you are the proud owner of a Packt book, we have a number of things to help you to get the most from your purchase.

Downloading the example code

You can download the example code files for all Packt books you have purchased from your account at http://www.packtpub.com. If you purchased this book elsewhere, you can visit http://www.packtpub.com/support and register to have the files e-mailed directly to you.

Errata

Although we have taken every care to ensure the accuracy of our content, mistakes do happen. If you find a mistake in one of our books—maybe a mistake in the text or the code—we would be grateful if you would report this to us. By doing so, you can save other readers from frustration and help us improve subsequent versions of this book. If you find any errata, please report them by visiting http://www.packtpub.com/submit-errata, selecting your book, clicking on the **errata submission form** link, and entering the details of your errata. Once your errata are verified, your submission will be accepted and the errata will be uploaded on our website, or added to any list of existing errata, under the Errata section of that title. Any existing errata can be viewed by selecting your title from http://www.packtpub.com/support.

Piracy

Piracy of copyright material on the Internet is an ongoing problem across all media. At Packt, we take the protection of our copyright and licenses very seriously. If you come across any illegal copies of our works, in any form, on the Internet, please provide us with the location address or website name immediately so that we can pursue a remedy.

Please contact us at `copyright@packtpub.com` with a link to the suspected pirated material.

We appreciate your help in protecting our authors, and our ability to bring you valuable content.

Questions

You can contact us at `questions@packtpub.com` if you are having a problem with any aspect of the book, and we will do our best to address it.

1
Getting Started with Confluence

Atlassian started back in 2002 and they set out to create software that would be inexpensive, easy to use, and would take little effort to install and maintain. Thanks to these principles, the installation process of Confluence is relatively easy and straightforward; there is even a one-click installation wizard available. In this chapter, we will start with a high-level overview of Confluence, looking at the different components that make the application. We'll take a look at the different deployment options available, including distribution choices, application servers, and databases. Finally, we will install our own Confluence application from scratch.

By the end of the chapter, you will have learned about:

- The overall architecture of Confluence
- Platforms and applications supported by Confluence
- Installing Confluence and all of the required software
- Configuring database connections
- Running Confluence, safely

Understanding the architecture

Installing Confluence is simple and straightforward. However, it is important for us to understand the components involved in the installation process and the options that are available to us. This understanding will help you to make informed decisions and be better prepared for troubleshooting and future updates.

High-level architecture

Atlassian has a comprehensive overview of the technical components of Confluence, available at `https://developer.atlassian.com/display/CONFDEV/Confluence+Architecture`. However, this overview is mainly interesting for those who are developing some custom add-ons and not so much for day-to-day administration and usage of Confluence. For this reason, we have created a high-level overview that highlights the most important components in the architecture, and how our users will connect to Confluence:

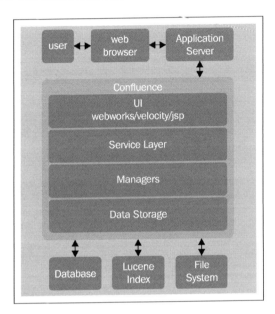

Supported browsers

Confluence is a web application, so the only thing our users need for accessing it is a compatible web browser. This can be on a desktop system, laptop, or even a mobile device such as a smartphone or tablet. The more recent versions of Confluence depend heavily on some new web technologies and standards. For this reason, older versions of Internet Explorer and Firefox are no longer fully compatible.

The following table summarizes the browser requirements for Confluence 5.1:

Browsers	Compatibility
Microsoft Internet Explorer (Windows)	8, 9 (drag-and-drop not completely supported because Internet Explorer doesn't fully support the related HTML5 feature)
Mozilla Firefox (all platforms)	10+
Safari (Windows and Mac)	5, 6
Google Chrome (Windows and Mac)	17+
Mobile Safari (iOS)	iOS 5.1, 6.0 (editing is not supported on mobile devices)

Data storage

The configuration files, attachments, indexes, and add-ons are stored, by default, in the Confluence Home directory that is configured when Confluence is first installed. All other data resides in the configured database. Optionally, attachments can be configured to be stored in the database instead of the Confluence Home directory.

You can choose to store the attachments in the database for ease of backup (all data in one single location) or to cope with characters that are invalid on your file system. Be aware: storing your attachments in the database increases the size of your database drastically. In a clustered environment where data is shared between several Confluence installations, you need to store the attachments in the database.

Confluence Installation directory

The directory where you install Confluence is called the Installation directory. It contains all the executable and configuration files of the application server. Confluence does not modify or store any data in this directory. This directory is primarily used for execution. For the remainder of the book we will be referring to this directory as CONF_INSTALL.

Confluence Home directory

The Confluence Home directory is the folder where Confluence stores its configuration, search indexes, attachments, and add-ons, specific to one Confluence installation. This means that every Confluence installation must, and can, have only one Confluence Home directory, and each Confluence Home directory can serve only one Confluence installation. If you're evaluating Confluence and using the embedded HSQLDB database, the database files are also stored in this directory. For the remainder of this book we will refer to this directory as CONF_HOME.

It's recommended that CONF_HOME is created separately from the Confluence installation. This separation of data and application makes tasks such as maintenance, back ups, and future upgrades easier. Keep in mind that the Confluence Home directory can grow quite large on an intensively used site.

Within CONF_HOME there are several important files and subdirectories:

File/Directory	Description
confluence.cfg.xml	Confluence's core configuration file; includes the configuration for connecting to its database and license key.
Attachments/	All file attachments in the Confluence site are stored under this directory. This is the place Confluence keeps attachment files if those are not stored in the database.
Backups/	If Confluence is configured to produce daily backups, these are stored in this directory. Administrators should occasionally delete old backups from this directory to prevent it from growing too large.
Bundled-plugins/	Add-ons bundled with the Confluence installation are stored here. User-installed plugins are not kept in this directory.
Config/	Miscellaneous global and per-space configuration files are kept in this directory.
Index/	The full-text search index is kept in this directory. Removing or modifying files in this directory may cause search to no longer function. A re-index operation from the Administration console will rebuild the files in this folder.
Logs/	The application log file is kept here.
Plugins-osgi-cache/	Plugins installed using the Confluence interface are downloaded and kept in this directory.
Temp/	Confluence stores temporary files in this directory, especially during backups and exports. A daily job within Confluence deletes files that are no longer needed.
Thumbnails/	Stores temporary files for image thumbnails. The contents of this directory can be safely deleted, as Confluence will regenerate thumbnails as required.

Installation options

Confluence is a Java-based web application, developed using many open standards and libraries. For this reason, it is able to run on many different operating systems, databases, and application servers. We will take a closer look at the options we have, and make an informed decision on what would work best in our situation.

Standalone and WAR distributions

First, we need to decide on the distribution. Confluence comes in three distributions:

- One-click installer
- Standalone bundled with Apache Tomcat
- WAR/EAR distribution

With regard to the application, there is no difference between the three distributions. The installer and standalone distributions are bundled with Apache Tomcat, which means we don't have to install and configure an application server ourselves. These distributions also come with an embedded in-memory database that can be used for evaluation purposes.

The installer is a very handy wrapper around the standalone bundle, automating all the steps we normally would have to perform manually. This is great when evaluating Confluence, but it doesn't give us much insight into the steps involved in maintaining our installation. For this reason, we will use the standalone distribution later, when we're going to install Confluence ourselves.

If you already have a running J2EE application server, or are experienced in installing and tuning one, the WAR distribution could be something for you. Due to differences between application servers, you are required to build the final deployment artifact with the provided build scripts. Once the artifact is built, you can deploy Confluence just like any other Java web application.

Operating systems

Confluence officially supports Microsoft Windows and Linux (all the distributions). Mac OS is supported only as a client platform. The choice of which operating system to run Confluence on is mostly a matter of preference based on expertise, and in most cases, there is an existing IT infrastructure with specific requirements.

If you do not have any preferences and would like to keep the initial costs down, Linux would be a good choice as there are no license fees involved. If you have more then 4 GB of memory on your server, make sure to pick a 64-bit version.

Databases

Confluence stores all its data in a relational database. The embedded in-memory HSQLDB database is only available for evaluation purposes, and should never be used in production environments. To limit the risk of data corruption, it's important that we use an enterprise database for production systems.

Confluence supports most relational databases available today. There will be no noticeable differences during the installation and configuration of Confluence. Just like the operating systems, your choice of database will come down to personal preference or IT standards within your organization. If you are using Windows as your operating system, the most likely choice would be Microsoft SQL Server. If you are using Linux, then you should consider PostgreSQL, MySQL, or Oracle.

The following table summarizes the list of databases currently supported by Confluence 5.1. It's worth mentioning that both PostgreSQL and MySQL are available as open source (free) products, making them excellent options if you are looking to minimize your initial investments.

Database	Supported version
PostgreSQL	8.4, 9.0
MySQL	5.1, 5.5
Microsoft SQL Server	2005, 2008, 2008 R2
Oracle	11.1, 11.2
HSQLDB	(for evaluation purposes only)

Application servers

Confluence requires a J2EE-compatible application server. The only officially-supported application server is Apache Tomcat. Fortunately, Apache Tomcat is an open source product and available for every operating system.

Confluence 5.1 will only support Tomcat 6.0.

Installing Confluence

Now that we have a good understanding of the overall architecture of Confluence and the various installation options, we are ready to install our own Confluence instance.

In the following exercise, we will be installing and configuring a fresh Confluence instance that will be ready for production. We will be using the standalone bundle, and the installation will be based upon the Windows platform. If you are planning on using a different operating system, please refer to `https://confluence.atlassian.com/display/DOC/Installing+Confluence` for details on installing Confluence on that specific platform.

In this exercise we will:

- Install a fresh instance of Confluence
- Configure Confluence to use a relational database
- Configure Confluence to send e-mail notifications
- Configure Confluence as an auto-start Windows service so that it starts automatically

We will continue to use this Confluence instance in other chapters and exercises as we prepare Confluence for usage within your own organization.

For our implementation, we will be using:

- Confluence standalone distribution 5.1.0
- PostgreSQL 9.0
- Java Development Kit 7 update 9
- Microsoft Windows Server 2008 R2

Installing Java

Confluence requires Java to be installed on the system, so this is our first step. Confluence 5.1 requires the latest update of JDK 7. If you are installing a different version of Confluence, make sure if JDK 7 is supported. Your choice between a 32-bit or 64-bit version depends on the amount of memory you want to allocate to Confluence; if it's more then 4 GB, pick the 64-bit version as 4 GB is the upper limit for the 32-bit version.

Currently, it is only possible to install Confluence as a Windows service if it is running on a 32-bit Java version.

Perform the following steps to install Java on your system:

1. Download the latest version of 32-bit JDK 7 from `http://www.oracle.com/technetwork/java/javase/downloads/index.html`.
2. Double-click on the downloaded installation file to start the installation wizard.

3. Select where you would like to install Java; or you can simply accept the default values. The location where you install the JDK will be referred to as JAVA_HOME for the rest of the book.

4. Create a new environmental variable named JAVA_HOME with the path where you just installed Java, as shown in the following screenshot:

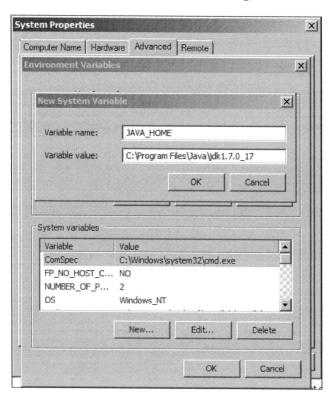

5. Test if installation was successful by typing the following command in the command prompt:

```
java -version
```

This should display the version of Java installed:

```
C:\>java -version
java version "1.7.0_17"
Java(TM) SE Runtime Environment (build 1.7.0_17-b02)
Java HotSpot(TM) Client VM (build 23.7-b01, mixed mode, sharing)
```

Installing PostgreSQL

The next step is to prepare a database for our Confluence installation.

To install PostgreSQL, simply perform the following steps:

1. Download PostgreSQL from
   `http://www.postgresql.org/download/windows/`.

    At the time of writing, the most recent version of PostgreSQL was not supported by Confluence. We will be using PostgreSQL Version 9.0.12.

2. Double-click on the downloaded installation file to start the installation wizard.

3. Select where you would like to install PostgreSQL and want to store the data. We'll be using the default settings during this exercise.

4. Choose a password for the root user; keep in mind that this is not the password for our Confluence database. I used `p0stgre$`, to keep it simple and easy to remember during this exercise and confirm to the Windows 2008 password security rules.

5. If you choose a different port number, please make sure it doesn't conflict with any other services running on your machine. Also remember the port number, as we'll need it later.

6. Uncheck the checkbox to make sure Stack Builder isn't launched at the completion of the installation process. We don't need it.

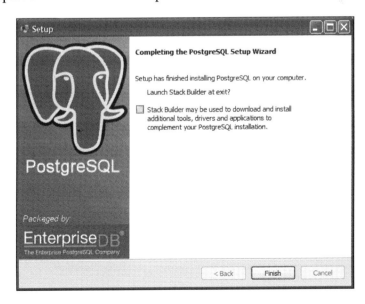

Creating a user and a database

Now that PostgreSQL is installed on our machine, we need to create a dedicated user and database for Confluence to use. This will prevent other users of the application from accessing Confluence data.

Perform the following steps to create a new user and a database:

1. Start the **pgAdmin III** administration tool, which has just been installed by the installer. We will be using this administration tool to create the Confluence user and database.

2. Connect to the PostgreSQL server running at localhost, by double-clicking on the server name. Enter the root password you just picked, when prompted:

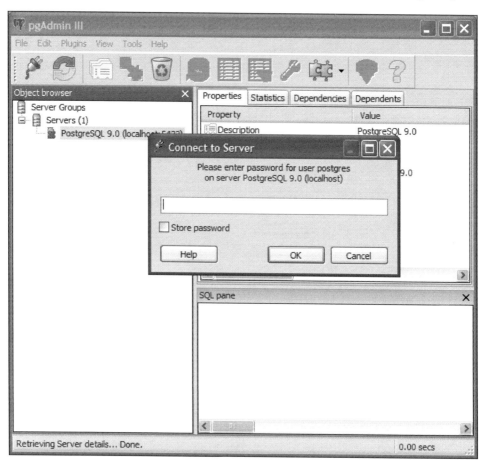

3. Create a new user, or "login role," as PostgreSQL calls it. Right-click on **Login Roles** in the object browser (on the left) and select **New Login Role...**:

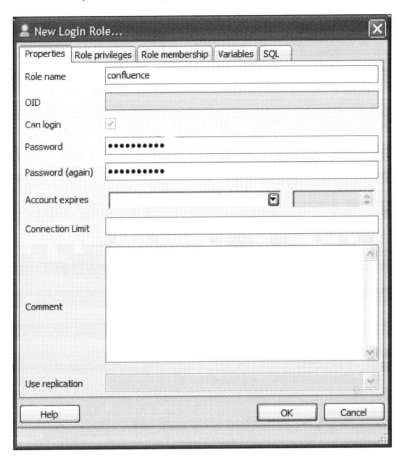

1. Enter the username: confluence.

2. Enter the password: confluence.

3. Do not select any role privileges.

4. Confirm the creation of the role.

4. Create a new database; right-click on **Databases** and select **New Database**.

1. Enter the database name: **confuencedb**.

2. Set the owner of the database to the user we just created.

3. Select **UTF-8** for encoding.

4. Confirm the creation of the database.

5. That is it. We have installed PostgreSQL and created a user and database for our Confluence installation to use.

Installing Confluence

Now that we have the JDK and database prepared, we have met all the conditions required to install Confluence on our machine. In order to get Confluence installed we have to:

- Unpack Confluence
- Configure the Confluence Home directory
- Check the ports Confluence uses
- Configure e-mail

Optionally, we can configure Confluence to use HTTPS and run as a Windows service.

Unpacking Confluence

Perform the following steps to unpack Confluence:

1. Download the latest version of Atlassian Confluence from www.atlassian.com/software/confluence/download.

2. The Atlassian website will detect the operating system you are using and will suggest a distribution accordingly. If you intend to install Confluence on a different system than the one you are currently on, make sure you select the correct distribution.

3. As mentioned before, there are one-click installers available for both Windows and Linux. For the purpose of this exercise we will be using the ZIP archive, as it will provide us with an insight of the steps that are normally hidden by the installation process.

4. Extract the downloaded ZIP file to c:/confluence/. It is recommended to use a third-party unzip software, such as 7-Zip or WinZip, as there are known issues with the unzip application provided with Windows. You can choose a different installation path; just make sure that you don't use spaces in your directory path.

5. C:\confluence\atlassian-confluence-5.1 will now be known as CONF_INSTALL. Next, we will define the Confluence Home directory.

Configuring Confluence Home

Next we have to define and configure CONF_HOME. Remember that we want to keep our data separated from our installation data.

1. Create c:\confluence\data; this directory will now be known as CONF_HOME.
2. Open CONF_INSTALL and open the file confluence\WEB-INF\classes\confluence-init.properties in your favorite text editor.
3. Locate the following line; it's usually at the end of the file.

   # confluence.home=c:/confluence/data

4. Remove the # and the space at the beginning of this line, so that Confluence no longer regards it as a comment.
5. If you have selected a different directory for CONF_HOME, then change the path accordingly. Please note the following:
   1. Avoid spaces in the directory path.
   2. Use forward slashes / to define the path.

Configuring the port

By default, Confluence runs on port 8090 with no context path. This means that after starting Confluence it will be available at http://localhost:8090/. If you have another application running on your machine that is using the same ports, you may need to change the port Confluence will use. Changing the context path is useful when you are running your applications behind a proxy and want to access them with the same domain, for example, http://example.com/jira and http://example.com/confluence. For this exercise we will be changing the context Confluence is running on to /confluence.

To change the ports for Confluence, open the file conf/server.xml under your CONF_INSTALL directory. An extract from that file is shown here:

```
<Server port="8000" shutdown="SHUTDOWN" debug="0">
<Connector className="org.apache.coyote.tomcat4.CoyoteConnector"
  port="8090".... />
<Context path="/confluence" docBase="../confluence" debug="0"
  reloadable="false" useHttpOnly="true">
```

Downloading the example code

You can download the example code files for all Packt books you have purchased from your account at http://www.packtpub.com. If you purchased this book elsewhere, you can visit http://www.packtpub.com/support and register to have the files e-mailed directly to you.

Line 1: This line specifies the port for the command to shut down Tomcat. By default this port is 8000. If you already have an application running on that port, you can change this to another port.

Line 2: This line specifies on which port Confluence/Tomcat will be running. By default this is port 8090. If that port is unavailable for some reason, you can change it to another available port.

Line 3: This line allows you to change the context path on which Confluence will be available. By default the path is empty, meaning Confluence will be available on `http://hostname:portnumber/`.

For this exercise we will change the context path to `/confluence`, as shown in the previous file.

Configuring e-mail JNDI resource

In order to use the share and notification features from Confluence an e-mail account has to be set up. Normally, we could do this using the Confluence interface, but there is an exception if you want to use SMTPS, with your Gmail account for example. So for this exercise we will be configuring Confluence to use your Gmail account for sending e-mail notifications to the users.

1. Move (*don't copy*) `activation-1.0.2.jar` and `mail-1.4.1.jar` from `CONF_INSTALL/confluence/WEB-INF/lib` to `CONF_INSTALL/lib`.

2. Add the following resource to your `CONF_INSTALL/conf/server.xml`; make sure to add it just before the `</Context>` tag.

```
<Resource name="mail/GmailSMTPServer"
auth="Container"
type="javax.mail.Session"
mail.smtp.host="smtp.gmail.com"
mail.smtp.port="465"
mail.smtp.auth="true"
mail.smtp.user="yourEmailAddress@gmail.com"
password="yourPassword"
   mail.smtp.starttls.enable="true"
   mail.transport.protocol="smtps"
mail.smtp.socketFactory.class="javax.net.ssl
   .SSLSocketFactory"
/>
```

3. Replace `yourEmailAddress@gmail.com` and `yourPassword` with the proper values for your account.

4. Remember or write down the resource name. When we are configuring Confluence and asked for an e-mail server the JNDI location will be:

```
java:comp/env/mail/GmailSMTPServer
```

Note that the name is case-sensitive.

Configuring HTTPS

By default, Confluence runs with a standard, non-encrypted HTTP protocol. This is acceptable if you are running Confluence in a secured environment, such as an internal network. However, if you are planning to open up access to Confluence via the Internet, you need to tighten the security. We will be doing this by configuring Confluence to run over HTTPS (HTTP over SSL), so that login information and data are encrypted during transport over the Internet.

For a standalone installation, we need to perform the following tasks:

* Create or request a new SSL Certificate
* Enable HTTPS on our application server
* Redirect traffic to HTTPS

First, we need to get a digital certificate. This can be one from a Certification Authority such as VeriSign or StartSSL (CA certificate), or a self-signed certificate generated by you. A CA certificate will not only encrypt your data, but also identify your copy of Confluence to users. A self-signed certificate is useful when you do not have a valid CA certificate and you are only interested in setting up HTTPS for encryption.

Because a self-signed certificate is not signed by a Certificate Authority, users may receive a message that the site is not to be trusted and may have to perform several steps to accept the certificate before they can access the site. This usually will only occur the first time they access the site. A self-signed certificate is great for evaluation purposes, but I would recommend a CA certificate for your production environment.

For the purpose of this exercise we will create a self-signed certificate. If you already have a CA certificate you can, of course, use that certificate.

Generating a certificate

Follow these steps to generate a certificate using Java's keytool utility. This tool is included in the JDK and can be found in JAVA_HOME/bin.

1. Run the following command in the command prompt:

```
"%JAVA_HOME%/bin/keytool.exe" -genkeypair -alias tomcat -keyalg
RSA
```

2. When asked for a password:

    1. Specify the password you want to use for the certificate. Note that the password text will not appear as you type.

    2. Make a note of the password you choose; we will need it in the next step when editing the Tomcat configuration.

    3. In this exercise we will be using the default password `changeit`.

3. Follow the prompts to specify your domain name, organization, and location. This information is used to construct the X.500 Distinguished Name (DN) of the entity. To the question **What is your first and last name?** (CN), don't give your actual name. The CN must match the fully-qualified hostname of the server running Confluence. Tomcat will not be able to use the certificate for SSL otherwise.

    For example, for our Confluence, running on localhost:

    CN = `localhost`, OU = `Confluence Essentials`, O = `Packt`, C = `UK`

4. Enter `y` to confirm the details.

5. When asked for the password for `tomcat` (the alias you entered in the keytool command), press the *Enter* key. You *must* use the same password here as the one that was used for the keystore password. This is a restriction of the Tomcat implementation.

6. Your certificate is now ready.

Our self-signed certificate is now available in Java's keystore. If you are using a previously generated certificate or a CA certificate, you will need to import that certificate into Java's keystore. This can be done with the following command:

```
keytool -importcert -alias tomcat -file <MY_CERTIFICATE_FILENAME>
```

Configuring Tomcat

To enable HTTPS, open the `CONF_INSTALL/conf/server.xml` file in a text editor. Locate and uncomment the following lines:

```
<Connector port="8443" maxHttpHeaderSize="8192"
    maxThreads="150" minSpareThreads="25" maxSpareThreads="75"
    enableLookups="false" disableUploadTimeout="true"
    acceptCount="100" scheme="https" secure="true"
    clientAuth="false" sslProtocol="TLS" SSLEnabled="true"
    URIEncoding="UTF-8" keystorePass="<MY_CERTIFICATE_PASSWORD>"/>
```

This connector will enable HTTPS for Confluence on port 8443. We will have to replace `<MY_CERTIFICATE_PASSWORD>` with the password we specified when creating our certificate. In our case this would be `changeit`.

By default, Tomcat expects the keystore file to be named `.keystore` and be located in the user home directory under which Tomcat is running. This could be a different account than your own, and therefore, can be another directory. If your certificate is not in the default location, you will have to update the server configuration to include `keystoreFile="<MY_CERTIFICATE_LOCATION>"` in the connector element.

Redirecting traffic to HTTPS

Although HTTPS is now active and available, the old HTTP URLs are still available. We will have to set up Confluence so that it will redirect automatically from an HTTP to an HTTPS request. We will need to do this by adding a security constraint in `web.xml`.

Open `CONF_INSTALL/confluence/WEB-INF/web.xml` and add the following snippet to the end of the file, before the `</web-app>` tag:

```
<security-constraint>
  <web-resource-collection>
    <web-resource-name>Restricted URLs</web-resource-name>
    <url-pattern>/</url-pattern>
  </web-resource-collection>
  <user-data-constraint>
    <transport-guarantee>CONFIDENTIAL</transport-guarantee>
  </user-data-constraint>
</security-constraint>
```

This will cause Tomcat to redirect all requests that come in on a non-SSL port. The first part will make sure all URLs are checked by this security constraint. The second part will guarantee that HTTPS is used for transportation.

Configuring Confluence as a service

Under Windows, Confluence can be configured to run as a Windows service, thus starting up automatically when the operating system reboots. This is recommended, as the alternative is having a console window open on the machine, which could be accidentally closed, thus shutting down Confluence.

To configure Confluence as a Windows service, simply perform the following steps:

1. Start a new command prompt as administrator, and browse to the `CONF_INSTALL/bin` directory.

2. Run the following command:

   ```
   service.bat install Confluence
   ```

3. This will install Confluence as a Windows service. The service will be called Apache Tomcat Confluence.

4. Verify the configuration by going to the Services console by going to **Start | Administrative Tools | Services**.

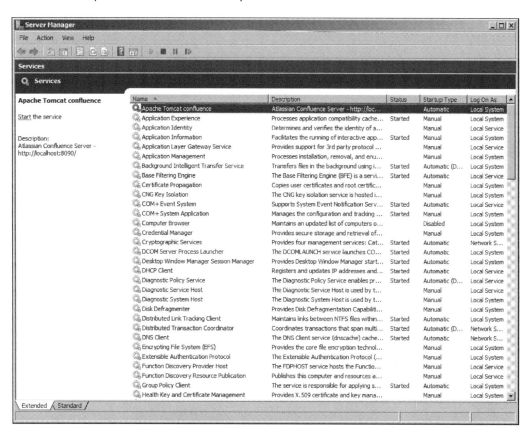

You can now start, stop, and restart Confluence from the Windows service panel.

Starting Confluence

Everything is in place to start our installation of Confluence. So let us start Confluence using the Services console in Windows. Once the server is running, you can access Confluence using your Internet browser. The URL to your Confluence is `https://localhost:8443/confluence`. If you didn't add the HTTPS or context path to your installation, you can find Confluence at `http://localhost:8090/`.

If you used a self-signed certificate, you will get a prompt that there is a certificate error, similar to the one shown in the following screenshot:

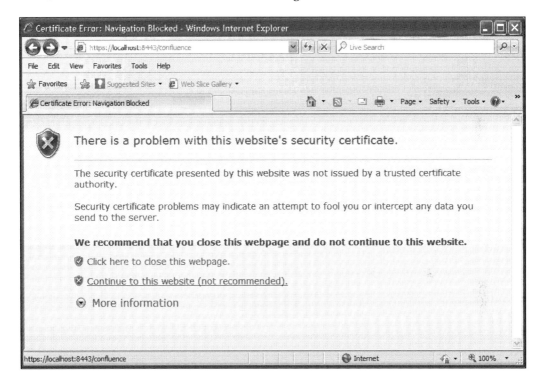

The first page you will see is the first step in the configuration wizard, which will finalize your Confluence installation.

Installation wizard

The first step in the wizard is providing a valid license. This can be either a full license or an evaluation license. If you have already obtained a license from Atlassian, you can cut and paste it into the **License Key** textbox. If you don't have a license, you can generate an evaluation license by clicking on the **generate an evaluation license online** link. Once you have filled in the license key, you have to choose your installation type. We are going to install a **Production Installation**, so choose that option.

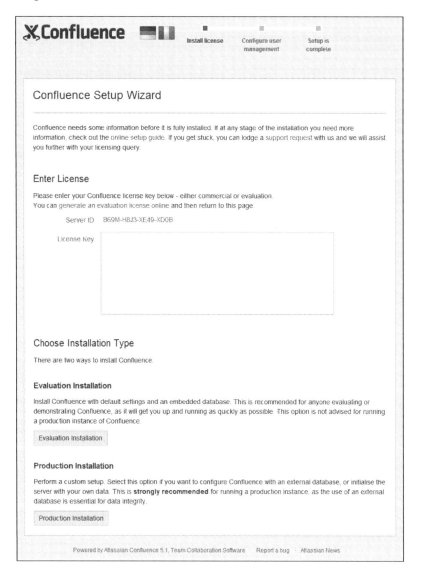

Step 2 is to configure our database connection. Select **PostgreSQL** from the drop-down list at the bottom and click on **External Database**. You will get the choice on how to connect to the database. This is either through JDNI or Direct JDBC. The difference is that JNDI is configured and managed on the application server, just like the SMTPS e-mail server. Direct JDBC is configured within the application.

For this exercise, we'll be using the Direct JDBC option.

On this screen we have to fill out our database configuration:

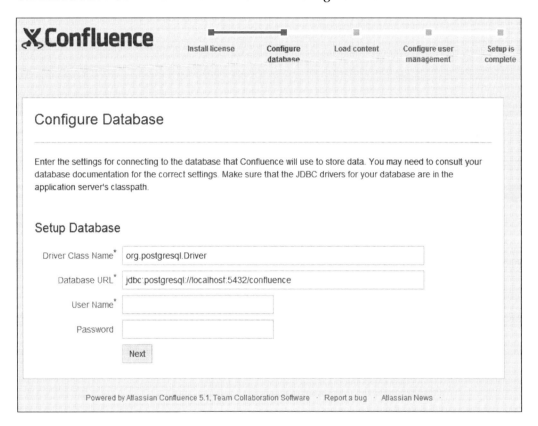

Enter the details for your database configuration according to the fields explained here:

Property	Value
Driver Class Name	`org.postgresql.Driver`
Database URL	`jdbc:postgresql://localhost:5432/confluencedb`
	If you configured a different port number for PostgreSQL, be sure to also change it in this URL.
User Name	`confluence`
Password	`confluence`

Click on **Next** to start the initialization of the database. This could take a while, so hold on.

After the database is initialized, you will get to the next screen (shown in the next screenshot), where you can choose how you would like to load content:

- **Example Site**: This will load a demonstration space into Confluence, showing some of the features Confluence has to offer. Great if you want to evaluate Confluence.

- **Empty Site**: A clean Confluence installation, without any space or content. Perfect if you are already familiar with Confluence and want to get started quickly.

- **Restore From Backup**: If you already have a Confluence installation and a backup from that installation, you can import it using this option. Make sure that the backup data is from the same major version as the target Confluence.

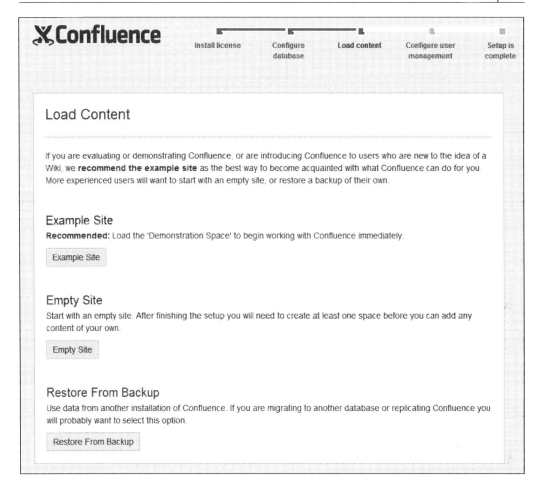

For our installation we will pick **Example Site**, as this gives us some exposure on how we could use Confluence.

Once **Example Site** is loaded, it is time to set up user management. Choose to set up user management within Confluence. Connecting user management to an external source is discussed in *Chapter 2, User Management*.

Set up the System Administrator account and make sure you remember the username/password, because Confluence only stores the hashed value of your password. You will not be able to retrieve it.

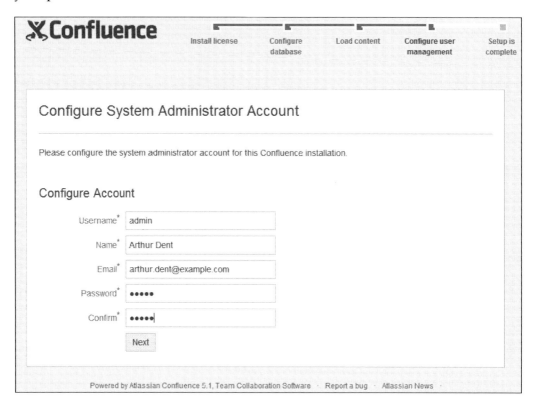

Confluence is now ready for use; you can either start using it or continue configuring. As for this exercise, we want to continue and set up the e-mail server, so choose **Continue configuration**. After logging in with your system administrator account, you will see the Confluence Administrator console.

Setting up the e-mail server

Log in to Confluence and go to the **Administration Console** by going to **Administration | Confluence Admin**. You might have to log in another time due to Confluence's **WebSudo**. WebSudo prevents other people from accessing the administrator console, if you left your machine unattended, for example.

In **Administration Console**, select **Mail Servers** in the left menu. Select **Add a new SMTP mail server** to add a new SMTP mail server that Confluence will use to send notifications and password resets.

Property	Description
Name	The name of the SMTP server used for reference within Confluence.
From address	Enter the e-mail address the e-mail is sent from. In most cases this must be the same address as the e-mail account you're using.
From Name	Enter the name that will be displayed in the `from` field for e-mail messages originating from this server. This field accepts the following variables, which reference specific details defined in the relevant Confluence user's profile: • `${fullname}`, The user's full name • `${email}`, The user's e-mail address • `${email.hostname}`, the domain name of the user The default is `${fullname} (Confluence)`.
Subject Prefix	Enter some text to appear at the beginning of the subject line.

Enter *either* the hostname and credentials of your mail server, or the JDNI resource. As we set up a Gmail account earlier, we will be using that one:

The JNDI location will be **java:comp/env/mail/GmailSMTPServer**.

Submit the configuration, and try to send a test e-mail to yourself to verify the settings.

Summary

We have seen that getting started with Confluence is fairly straightforward; it is also very flexible with regard to options you can choose from, when installing your copy of Confluence. You can mix these options to suit your situation best, or to comply with your IT department's requirements. If you wish to keep initial costs as low as possible, you can install Confluence completely with open source software, such as Linux and PostgreSQL, which are available for free.

Now that we have installed Confluence and gone through the set up wizard, we will start to dive deeper into the various aspects of Confluence. In the next chapter, we will go into how to manage your users and groups, as Confluence is not intended to be used alone.

2
User Management

A collaboration tool such as Confluence is nothing without its users, using the tool for collaboration. In this chapter we will learn different ways to add users to our Confluence instance and learn how to manage those users.

We will also learn that in a corporate situation, where user management often already exists, it is very easy to configure Confluence to make use of that existing user infrastructure.

In this chapter we will cover:

- Manually adding users to Confluence
- Inviting users
- Administrating your users
- Managing user groups
- Connecting to an external user directory

Understanding authentication

Authentication in Confluence takes place at different levels within the application, for example, when retrieving information from the database or when displaying this information on a Confluence page. The technology that is used depends on the request made to Confluence or your configuration. The following are a few examples of authentication technologies.

Password authentication

Password authentication is, by default, delegated from Seraph to the user management system. If you use a **Single sign-on (SSO)** system this might not be necessary. The authenticator gets all the necessary credentials from your SSO provider.

Seraph

Seraph is an open source framework developed by Atlassian and almost all authentication in Confluence is done using this framework. The goal of Seraph is to provide a simple, extensible authentication system that can be used on any application server.

Seraph is implemented as a filter. Filters dynamically intercept every authentication request and response to your application and use and transforms the information in the request or response. The purpose of Seraph is to associate the request with a particular user (or no user if the request is anonymous). Seraph supports HTTP Basic Authentication and form-based authentication, and can look up credentials already stored in the user's session.

Seraph itself isn't used for user management. It only checks the credentials of the incoming requests and delegates any user management functions, including finding the users and checking a user's password.

If you want to integrate Confluence with your own SSO infrastructure, you can write your own Seraph authenticator. See `http://docs.atlassian.com/atlassian-seraph` for more information on Seraph.

Adding users

There are a couple of options available for adding users to your Confluence installation. The options do not exclude each other so it's possible to use them all, depending on your installation and how open your Confluence should be to the outside world.

Manually adding users

As you are just getting started with Confluence, adding users manually is probably the way you want to go. Adding users is an option only available to Confluence administrators or system administrators.

To add a user, navigate to the Administration Console in Confluence (**Administration | Confluence Admin**) and select **users** from the left menu. As shown in the following screenshot, click on the **Add Users** tab:

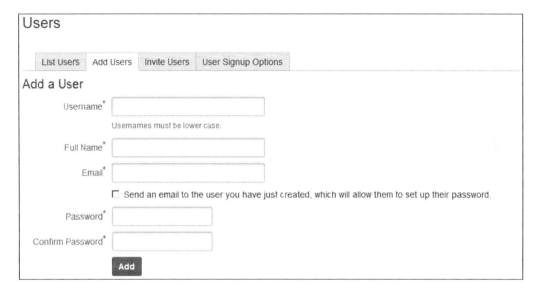

While filling out the form there are a few things you have to keep in mind:

- The username must be lowercase and unique to Confluence. If your company has a username policy, it's best to use this in Confluence too. If there is no username policy, I like to use `firstname.lastname` as a standard, that is, `arthur.dent` or `ford.prefect`.

- You can choose to send an e-mail to the user you have just created by selecting the corresponding checkbox. In this case, the password fields are ignored as the user will receive a link to set up their own password. If you choose to not send an e-mail, the password fields are required. Such an e-mail will look something like the following figure:

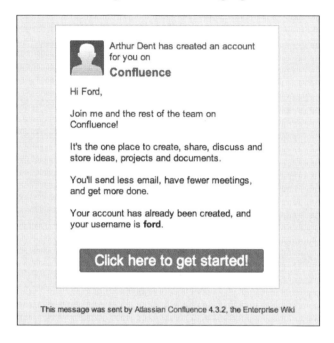

- After creating a user, Confluence will redirect you to the user details screen where we can change some of the user details. This will be discussed further on.

In the same way you can add more users.

Open registration

If your Confluence is a public installation or running on a local network, an open registration is available. The open registration allows all your users to register themselves with Confluence as shown in the following screenshot:

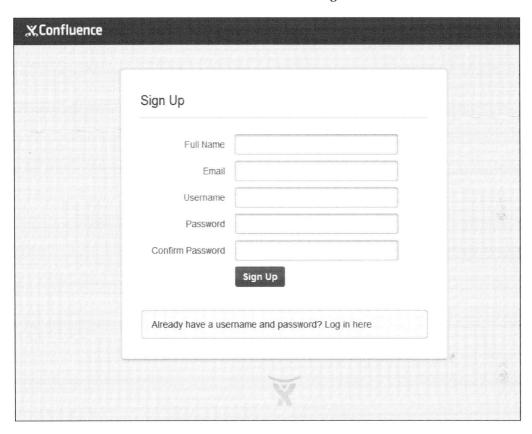

Your users can enter their own name, e-mail address, username, and password, but be aware, when users are allowed to register themselves, they can choose their own username, which may not comply with your company policy.

Users are directly added to the Confluence-users group and will get the permissions associated with that group.

Inviting users

Instead of adding all your users manually, it is also possible to send them a signup URL. This option is available in both public and private Confluence installations. When your users visit the URL in a browser, the Confluence signup screen will appear.

You can send invites from the Administration Console using the following steps:

1. Browse to the Administration Console (**Administration | Confluence Admin**).

2. Choose **Users** in the left-hand menu.

3. Click on the **Invite Users** tab. The following screen will be displayed:

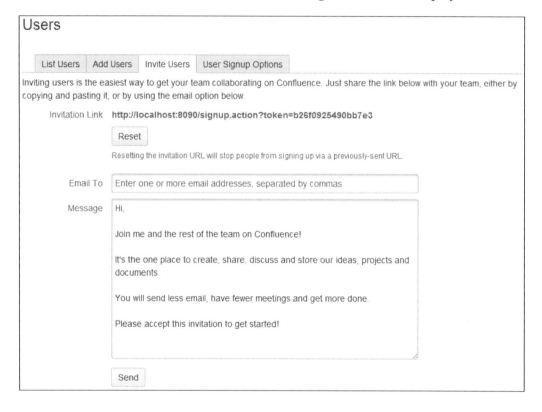

Add the e-mail addresses of the users you want to invite and, if needed, include a custom message for them to read. They will receive an e-mail with the message and an invite URL.

The invite URL has a security token as an argument. With this token, your users will be able to sign up themselves if your Confluence instance is set to be accessible privately. The security token can be reset on the **Invite Users** page; resetting it will make all the previously sent invites invalid, and they will be obsolete.

Managing groups

Groups are collections of users. A group can be used to successfully manage a large number of users. Administrators are allowed to create groups in Confluence and add users to these groups. Permissions are then assigned to groups instead of users to allow easier management.

There are two default groups already available in Confluence, and these are special groups:

- **confluence-administrators**: This group represents the "super users". The members of this group can access the Administration Console and perform side-wide administrative actions, such as installing plugins or changing the security of your site.
- **confluence-users**: This is the default group for all new users. Users in this group are allowed to log in to Confluence and add to your license user-limit.

> **The Confluence administrator permission and the confluence-administrators group are not related**
>
> Although the name suggests they are related, they are not. Granting a user or group the Confluence Administrator permission is not the same as adding the user to the confluence-administrators group. The Confluence Administrator permission gives the user access to only a subset of the administrator functions and not complete access.
>
> You can find more information on the differences between administrator roles in the *Global permissions* section in *Chapter 6, Securing Your Content*.

Creating groups

To add a group to Confluence, perform the following steps:

1. Browse to the Administration Console (**Administration | Confluence Admin**).
2. Choose **Groups** in the left-hand menu.
3. Select **Add Group** just below the table with the already existing groups.
4. Type the new group name.
5. Click on the **Save** button.

To prepare your Confluence installation for the future within your company, it is good practice to think of a naming convention before starting to create groups. A naming convention that worked for me looks like `<product>-<space>-<role>`. So all space administrators in Confluence, working on the project `MyExample` would be in the group `confluence-myexample-administrators` and all the users in `confluence-myexample-users`.

Adding users to groups

To assign users to groups, in order to determine their permissions, you have to be a Confluence administrator. There are two ways of editing group memberships in Confluence. They are as follows:

- From the user details screen
- From the group management screen

Editing group membership from the user details screen

One way of editing the group membership of a particular user is via the user details screen. This method only allows you to update one user at the time.

To edit a user's group membership, you have to go to the user details screen for that user. We will dive into finding users in the next section, for now we use the Administration Console.

1. Browse to the Administration Console (**Administration | Confluence Admin**).
2. Choose **Users** in the left-hand menu.
3. Select **Show all users** to get an overview with all the users in Confluence.
4. Click on the link on the username you want to edit.
5. Select the **Edit Groups** link below the user's details, then the following screen will be displayed:

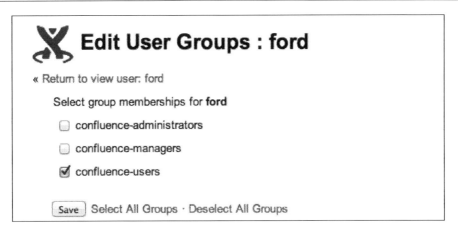

6. Check the boxes in front of the groups to which you want to add the user, or uncheck the box for any group to remove the user from it.

7. Submit the changes by clicking on the **Save** button.

Editing group membership via the group management screen

If you want to add multiple users to the same group at the same time, it is possible to use the group management screen, which allows you to do this.

1. Browse to the Administration Console (**Administration | Confluence Admin**).

2. Choose **Groups** in the left-hand menu.

3. Select the group to which you want to add users.

4. The **Group Members** screen appears, displaying all the users who are members of this group. Click on the link **Add Members**.

5. In the **Add Members** textbox, type in the usernames of the people you want to add to the group. You can also search for users by clicking on the search icon next to the box as shown in the following screenshot:

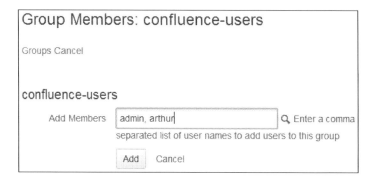

6. When you have added all the users you want to add to this group, click on the **Add** button to save your changes.

You can delete users from a group on the **Group Members** screen. By clicking on the icon on the same row as the user, the membership of that user will be removed.

Administrating users

We are now able to add users and groups to Confluence, and administer group memberships. There will be a point where we have to look up a user, change his or her details, or send a new password.

Searching for users

When we want to add users to certain groups, spaces, or do anything that has to do with permissions, we have the option to search for users. Whenever you are able to search for users within Confluence, a magnifying glass icon will be shown. When we click on this icon, a new pop up will be shown, giving us the following two options to search for users:

- Simple search
- Membership search

 Note that the search is not case sensitive; it doesn't make a difference if you type either upper- or lowercase text. Wildcards are supported but there is no need to use them, the search will return the same results.

Using the simple user search

To search via the simple user search:

1. Select the **User** tab on the **User Search** screen, as shown in the following screenshot.

2. Type some information about the user into the search box. You can use any part of the user's username, full name, or e-mail address.

3. Click on **Search**.

   Confluence will return a list of matching users. You can check the boxes in front of the usernames to select the users you where looking for.

Using the membership search

It is also possible to search for users who are members of a certain group with the membership search.

1. Select the **Membership** tab on the **User Search** screen.

2. Type all or a part of the group name in the search box.

3. Click on **Search**.

Confluence will return a list of users who are member of the groups matching your search. In the following example, I searched for "confluence". The results show all users belonging to the **confluence-administrators** group and all users belonging to the **confluence-users** group:

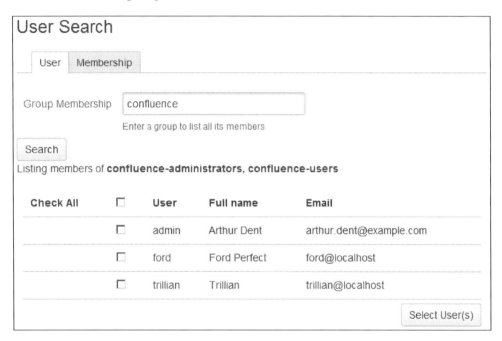

Editing user details

To change the details of a user, you need Confluence Administrator permissions. The user details include the user's name, password, e-mail address, group membership, and the ability to access Confluence. Users are allowed to change their own details, but not their group memberships.

Updating a user's details can be done via the user details screen as displayed in the upcoming screenshot. There are two ways to navigate to this screen.

- The first is via the Administration Console, using the following steps:

    1. Browse to the Administration Console (**Administration | Confluence Admin**).

    2. Choose **Users** in the left-hand menu.

    3. Search for the user, or use the **Show all users** link.

    4. Click on the link of the user you want to edit.

- The second way is via the user profile, using the following steps:

  1. If you are not in the Administration Console, you can quickly go to the user details screen via the user's profile.

  2. Click on a user's full name in Confluence to go to that user's profile page. A full name can be, for example, be found on any page in Confluence as displayed in the following screenshot:

- Click on the **Administrator User** link on the left.

  You should now see the user details screen and the links allowing you to edit the details.

The following is the explanation on the different links present on the user details page. Note that not all available options are displayed on the previous screenshot.

Link	Description
View Profile	View the user's profile.
Edit Groups	Add the user to or remove the user from a group.
Edit Details	Change the user details such as the user's name, e-mail address, contact details, and department information.
Set Password	Change the user's password.
Remove	Remove the user from Confluence, which is only possible when the user didn't add or edit any content on the site.
Disable	Disable access to Confluence for this user. You can use this option when a user has already added or changed any content on the site. Disabling a user will also remove the user from your license count.

Changing a username in Confluence is currently not supported via the interface and can only be done via the database. If you need to change a username, read `https://confluence.atlassian.com/x/nXUC` for more information.

Resetting the password

At some point in time, a user might lose their password and send you an e-mail with the question if you could reset it. Fortunately, Confluence has a **Forgot your password?** link on its login screen, which users can use themselves:

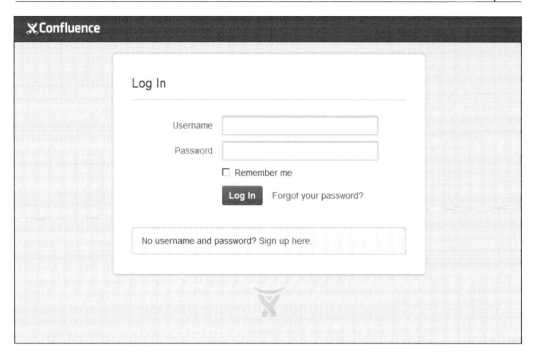

The **Forgot you password?** link allows a user to ask for a password reset. The user needs to fill in his/her username and will receive an e-mail with a reset link. The user's password isn't changed unless the link is used and a new password is saved.

If you don't have an e-mail server set up or an external user directory configured, this option is not available. In case of an external user directory, you will need to redirect your users to that system password recovery option.

If you haven't set up an e-mail server, you will have to reset the password manually via the **Set Password** option on the user's detail screen, as mentioned before. This password reset has to be done by an administrator.

Public signup

It is possible to enable a public signup for your Confluence site. People can then add their own usernames and log in to the site immediately.

If you want to restrict your site to a particular set of users, you may want to restrict the e-mail domains or disable public signup completely.

To enable or disable public signup:

1. Browse to the Administration Console (**Administration | Confluence Admin**).
2. Choose **Users** in the left-hand menu.
3. Select the **User Signup Options** tab.

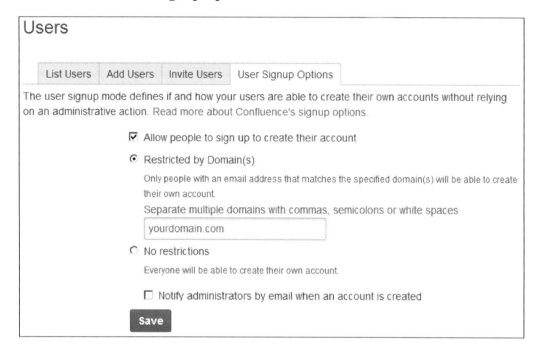

The preceding screenshot shows us a couple of options.

We can enable or disable the public signup with a single checkbox. Enabling public signup also gives us the possibility to restrict the users' e-mail addresses to one or more domains.

 You need to set up an e-mail server before you can configure domain-restricted signup. Confluence will send an e-mail to the person signing up, asking to click on a link to verify their e-mail address.

A very useful feature is to notify administrators by e-mail when an account is created. This way you can still detect if someone is signing up who shouldn't or grant extra permissions to users who need them.

External user directories

So far we have learned how to get users into our Confluence installation. This is very useful but what if your company has its own LDAP server or is already using some other Atlassian products, such as JIRA or Crowd?

Within Confluence we can configure one or more external user directories. A **user directory** is a place where you store information about users and groups, including some other user information. This information can be the person's full name, e-mail address, or department. When an external user directory is configured, Confluence will also use the directory to authenticate a user.

Confluence has support for the following external directories:

- Microsoft Active Directory
- Various LDAP directory servers including OpenLDAP, Apache Directory Server, and Novell eDirectory
- Atlassian Crowd
- Atlassian JIRA

You can add as many external directories as you need. Note that you can change the order of the directories, determining which directory will search first.

User Directories

User Directories ⑦

The table below shows the user directories currently configured for Confluence.

The order of the directories is the order in which they will be searched for users and groups. Changes to users and groups will be made in the first directory where Confluence has permission to make changes. It is recommended that each user exist only in a single directory.

Directory Name	Type	Order	Operations
Confluence Internal Directory	Internal	↑	
Crowd Server	Atlassian Crowd	↑	Disable Edit Test Synchronise

Add Directory

Additional Configuration & Troubleshooting

- LDAP Connection Pool Configuration
- Directory Configuration Summary

The effect of directory order

When you have more than one directory configured, the order of those directories is important and affects a couple of things within Confluence.

- **Login**: The directory order is significant during the authentication of the user, especially if the user exists in multiple directories. During login, the application will search the directories in the specified order, and will use the password of the *first occurrence of the user* to validate the login.

- **Permissions**: In the same way as the login mechanism, Confluence will look for group memberships only in the first directory where the username appears, based on the directory order.

  For example:

  - You have two directories: the employees directory and the customers directory
  - The employee directory is first in the directory order
  - A username `arthur.dent` exists in both directories
  - The user `arthur.dent` is a member of group G1 in the employees directory and group G2 in the customers directory
  - Based on directory order, the user `arthur.dent` only has permissions based on group G1, not G2

- **Updating users and groups**: If you update a user or group via Confluence's administration screen, the update will only be made in the first directory where Confluence has write permissions.

  For example:

  - You have two user directories: a read/write LDAP directory and the internal directory
  - The LDAP directory is the first directory
  - A username `arthur.dent` exists in both directories
  - You update the e-mail address of the user `arthur.dent` via Confluence's Administration Console
  - The e-mail address will only be updated in the LDAP directory, not in the internal directory

Limitations when using external directories

When using external directories, there are a couple of limitations you should be aware of.

Build-in user management

The first limitation you should be aware of depends on the read/write configuration of your external directory. If Confluence can't write to your external directory, or you don't want it to, you have to disable the built-in user management.

To disable management of users and groups within Confluence:

1. Browse to the Administration Console (**Administration** | **Confluence Admin**).
2. Choose **Security Configuration** in the left-hand menu.
3. Click on **Edit**.
4. Check the **External user management** checkbox.
5. Click on **Save**.

If the built-in user management is disabled, users won't be able to:

- Signup
- Reset their password
- Update their profile

Also, administrators won't be able to:

- Add new users and groups
- Assign users to groups from Confluence

All these features are now delegated to the administration of your external user management and they have to be performed there.

Editing directories

It's not possible to edit, disable, or remove the directory your user belongs to. This precaution is to prevent administrators from locking themselves out of the Confluence, by changing the directory configuration in a way that prevents them from logging in or removing their administration permissions.

In some cases, reordering the directories will change the directory that you're currently using, if your user exists in both directories. This behavior can be used to make changes to existing directories.

It's recommended to keep an administrator account in your internal directory (which can't be deleted) and use that internal user to make changes to the settings of other external directories.

Connecting to an LDAP directory

Connecting to an LDAP directory server is useful if your users and groups are stored in a corporate directory. When configuring the LDAP directory in Confluence, you can choose to make it Read Only, Read Only with Local Groups, or Read/Write. In the last case, any changes you make to your users and groups in Confluence will reflect in your LDAP directory.

Connecting to LDAP

To connect Confluence to an LDAP directory, perform the following steps:

1. Browse to the Administration Console (**Administration | Confluence Admin**).
2. Choose **User Directories** in the left-hand menu.
3. Click on **Add Directory**. Select one of these types and click on **Next**:
   - **Microsoft Active Directory**: This option provides a quick way to add an AD directory, as it is one of the popular choices.
   - **LDAP**: You will be able to choose a more specific LDAP directory type on the next screen.
4. Enter the values for the required settings as described in the following table.
5. Save the directory settings.

Server settings

The following are the different settings required for setting up an external user directory:

Setting	Description
Name	Enter a descriptive name that will help you identify the LDAP server. For example, `MyCompany Employee Directory` or `MyCompany Customer Directory`.
Directory Type	Select the type of LDAP server you will connect to. The value you select here will determine the default values for many options on the screen.
Hostname	The hostname of your directory server.

Setting	Description
Port	The port on which your directory server is listening. For example, **389** (default LDAP port), **10398**, or **636** (LDAP over SSL).
Use SSL	Check this checkbox if the connection to your LDAP server is an SSL connection.
Username	The distinguished name of the user that the application will use when connecting to the directory server. For example: • `cn=administrator,cn=users,dc=ad,dc=mycompany,dc=com` • `cn=user,dc=domain,dc=name` • `user@domain.name`
Password	The password of the user specified.

LDAP schema settings

Setting	Description
Base DN	The root **distinguished name** (**DN**) to use when running queries against the directory server. For example: • `o=myCompany,c=com` • `cn=users,dc=ad,dc=myCompany,dc=com`
Additional User DN	This value is used in addition to the base DN to limit the scope when searching and loading users. If no value is supplied, search will start from the base DN: • `ou=Users`
Additional Group DN	This value is used in addition to the base DN when searching and loading groups.

LDAP permissions

Setting	Description
Read Only	Users, groups, and memberships are retrieved from your LDAP server and cannot be modified in Confluence.
Read Only, with Local Groups	Users, groups, and memberships are retrieved from your LDAP server and cannot be modified in Confluence. However, users from LDAP can be added to groups maintained in Confluence's internal directory.

Setting	Description
Read/Write	Modifying users, groups, and memberships in Confluence will cause the changes to be applied directly to your LDAP server. Your configured LDAP user will need to have modification permissions on your LDAP server.
Default Group Memberships	This field only appears if you select the **Read Only, with Local Groups** permission. If you would like to automatically add users to a group or groups, enter those names here. The first time a user logs in, their group memberships will be checked and added accordingly. On subsequent logins, memberships will not be added automatically, allowing deleting a user from one of the default groups.

The **Read Only, with Local Groups** option is a very powerful configuration and is in many cases the best setup. Users and groups can still be managed in your company's centralized user management system. But you as an administrator still have the option to create new groups and change memberships of those groups, giving you the control you need in Confluence without cluttering your LDAP server. ines

Advanced settings

Setting	Description
Enable Nested Groups	Some directory services allow you to define a group as a member of another group, which is called **Nested Groups**. If you are using groups to manage permissions, check this box to enable the use of nested groups.
Use Paged results	Useful when querying large user directories, this option returns the results in specified pages instead of all the results at once.
Follow Referrals	Choose whether to allow the directory server to redirect requests to other servers. It is generally needed for Active Directory servers configured without proper DNS, to prevent a `javax.naming. PartialResultException: Unprocessed Continuation Reference(s)` error.
Naive DN Matching	If your directory server will always return a consistent string representation of a DN, you can enable naive DN matching. Using naive DN matching will result in a significant performance improvement, so it's recommended to use it wherever possible.

Setting	Description
Enable Incremental Synchronization	Enabling incremental synchronization causes only changes since the last synchronization to be queried when synchronizing a directory.
	Be aware that when using this option, the configured user account must have read access to:
	• The uSNChanged attribute of all users and groups that need to be synchronized
	• The objects and attributes in the Active Directory deleted objects container
	If these conditions are not met, it's possible that changes in your LDAP may not be synchronized correctly to Confluence.
Synchronization Interval (minutes)	Specify the interval in minutes between directory updates. The default value is 60 minutes.
Read Timeout (seconds)	This is the time to wait for a response to be received. If there is no response within the specified time period, the read attempt will be stopped. A value of 0 means there is no limit. The default value is 120 seconds.
Search Timeout (seconds)	This is the time to wait for a response from a search operation. A value of 0 means there is no limit. The default value is 60 seconds.
Connection Timeout (seconds)	This is the time to wait when opening new server connections, or getting a connection from the connection pool. A value of 0 means wait indefinitely for a pooled connection to become available, or to wait for the default TCP timeout to take effect when creating a new connection.

User schema settings

Setting	Description
User Object Class	This is the name of the class used for the LDAP user object. For example:
	• inetorgperson
	• user
User Object Filter	The filter to use when searching for user objects. For example:
	• (objectclass=inetorgperson)
	• (&(objectCategory=Person)(sAMAccountName=*))
User Name Attribute	The attribute field to use when loading the username. For example:
	• cn
	• sAMAccountName

Setting	Description
User Name RDN Attribute	The **relative distinguished name** (**RDN**) to use when loading the username. The RDN is the portion of your DN that is not related to the directory tree structure. For example: • `cn`
User First Name Attribute	The attribute field to use when loading the user's first name. For example: • `givenName`
User Last Name Attribute	The attribute field to use when loading the user's last name. For example: • `sn`
User Display Name Attribute	The attribute field to use when loading the user's full name. For example: • `displayName`
User Email Attribute	The attribute field to use when loading the user's e-mail address. For example: • `mail`
User Password Attribute	The attribute field to use when loading the user's password. For example: • `userPassword`
User Password Encryption	Choose the encryption algorithm used for passwords on your directory. For example: • SHA • MD5 • PLAINTEXT

Group schema settings

Setting	Description
Group Object Class	This is the name of the class used for the LDAP group object. For example: • `groupOfUniqueNames` • `group`
Group Object Filter	The filter to use when searching group objects. For example: • `(objectclass=groupOfUniqueNames)` • `(objectCategory=group)`

Setting	Description
Group Name Attribute	The attribute field to use when loading the group's name. For example: • `cn`
Group Description Attribute	The attribute field to use when loading the group's description. For example: • `description`

Membership schema settings

Setting	Description
Group members Attribute	The attribute field to use when loading the group's members. For example: • `uniqueMember` • `member`
User Membership Attribute	The attribute field to use when loading a user's group memberships. For example: • `memberOf`
Use the User Membership Attribute	Check this checkbox if your LDAP server supports the group membership attribute on the user. If the checkbox is checked, Confluence will use the group membership attribute on the user when retrieving the list of groups to which a user belongs. This will result in a more efficient retrieval. If the checkbox is not checked, Confluence will use the member attribute on the group for the search. Note that, if you use a nested group, this option is ignored and thus Confluence will use the members attribute on the group.

Connecting to a Crowd directory

Atlassian Crowd is an application security framework that can handle the authentication and authorization for your web-based applications, which is not just restricted to Confluence or JIRA. With Crowd, it's possible to integrate multiple user directories into one directory and add support for single sign-on and centralized identity management.

Crowd is a very useful option if you have multiple web-based applications and multiple user directories you want to configure, especially if you want to add SSO to those applications as well.

Connecting to Crowd

Use the following steps to connect to Crowd:

1. Go to your Crowd Administration Console and define Confluence as an application. More information about this step can be found at `https://confluence.atlassian.com/x/rQcD`.

2. Browse to the Administration Console (**Administration | Confluence Admin**).

3. Choose **User Directories** in the left-hand menu.

4. Click on **Add Directory** and select the **Atlassian Crowd** option.

5. Enter the value for the settings (explained in the following table).

6. Save the directory settings.

Server settings

Settings	Description
Name	A descriptive name of your Crowd server. For example: • `Crowd Server` • `MyCompany Crowd`
Server URL	The web address of your Crowd console server. For example: • `http://www.mycompany.com:8095/crowd` • `https://crowd.mycompany.com/`
Application Name	The name to authenticate Confluence with Crowd. This is the application name you created when setting up Crowd for Confluence.
Application Password	The password for the configured application name. This must be the same as the password you have registered in Crowd for Confluence.

Crowd permissions

Settings	Description
Read Only	The user, group, and membership information in this directory can only be modified via Crowd. It's not possible to change any information via the Confluence Administration Console.
Read/Write	If you modify a user, group, or membership via Confluence administration screens, these changes will be applied directly to Crowd. Please note, that Confluence needs modification permissions in Crowd.

Advanced settings

Settings	Description
Enable Nested Groups	Before enabling nested groups, be sure that the directories in Crowd support this feature. When nested groups are enabled, you can define a group as a member of another group, allowing inheritance of permissions from its parent group.
Enable Incremental Synchronization	If this is checked, only changes since the last synchronization will be retrieved when synchronizing a directory.
Synchronization Interval (minutes)	Specify the interval in minutes between directory updates. The default value is 60 minutes.

Connecting to JIRA for user management

If you are also running JIRA within your organization, it is possible to use JIRA as user management for Confluence. The advantage of this approach is that your user management system is not in multiple locations, but just in JIRA.

 Note that if you have more then 500 users, or over five applications connecting to JIRA, this integration is not recommended. LDAP or Crowd would be a better and a more stable option in such a case.

Connecting to JIRA

The method of connecting Confluence to JIRA changed in JIRA 4.3 and later. I will assume you will be using JIRA 4.3 or later for this exercise; if you are running an older version of JIRA, you will find more information online at https://confluence.atlassian.com/x/hg6zDQ.

To connect Confluence to JIRA 4.3 or later, perform the following steps:

1. Go to your JIRA administration screen and define the Confluence application to JIRA, using the following steps:

    1. For JIRA 4.3.x, select **Other Applications** from the **Users, Groups & Roles** section of the **Administration** menu.

    2. For JIRA 4.4 or later, select **Users | JIRA User Server** in the administration mode.

    3. Click on **Add Application**.

    4. Enter the application name and password that Confluence will use when accessing JIRA.

    5. Enter the IP address or addresses of your Confluence server, for example, 192.168.10.42.

    6. Save the new application.

2. Set up Confluence to use a JIRA user directory, using the following steps:

    1. Browse to the Administration Console (**Administration | Confluence Admin**).

    2. Choose **User Directories** in the left-hand menu.

    3. Click on **Add Directory** and select the **Atlassian JIRA** option.

    4. Enter the value for the settings (explained in the following table).

    5. Save the directory settings.

3. Make sure the Confluence groups are available in JIRA by performing the following steps:

    1. Add the **confluence-users** and **confluence-administrators** groups in JIRA.

    2. Add your own username as a member of both groups.

Server settings

Settings	Description
Name	A descriptive name of your JIRA server. For example: • `JIRA Server` • `MyCompany JIRA`
Server URL	The web address of your JIRA server. Examples: • `http://www.mycompany.com:8080/crowd` • `https://jira.mycompany.com/`
Application Name	The name to authenticate Confluence with JIRA. This is the application name you created when setting up JIRA for Confluence.
Application Password	The password for the configured application name. This must be the same as the password you have registered in JIRA for Confluence.

JIRA server permissions

Settings	Description
Read Only	The user, group, and membership information in this directory can only be modified via JIRA. It's not possible to change any information via the Confluence Administration Console.
Read/Write	If you modify a user, group, or membership via Confluence administration screens, these changes will be applied directly to JIRA.

Advanced settings

Settings	Description
Enable Nested Groups	Before enabling nested groups, be sure that nested groups are enabled on the JIRA server. When nested groups are enabled, you can define a group as a member of another group, allowing inheritance of permissions from its parent group.
Enable Incremental Synchronization	If this is checked, only changes since the last synchronization will be retrieved when synchronizing a directory.
Synchronization Interval (minutes)	Specify the interval in minutes between directory updates. The default value is 60 minutes.

Summary

In this chapter we have learned how we can add users to our Confluence installation. There are many options available, such as manually adding users, inviting users to sign up themselves, or having an open registration for users.

We have seen that if your company already has a user management system in place, Confluence can easily make use of that, either fully delegating authentication and authorization, or just partially.

Now that we have a running Confluence installation and have invited some users to use it, we are off to one of the most important parts of Confluence, creating content. In the next chapter we will go into how we can create engaging content with the Confluence editor.

3
Creating Content

In this chapter, we will dive into one of the most important things that we need to learn to use Confluence to its full potential: creating content. We will go over the concepts of spaces, pages, and blog posts, to explain how to add content to Confluence. Confluence's rich text editor has many features, and in this chapter we will learn to master a large part of those features by creating our first pages.

We will learn about the following things in this chapter:

- Confluence basic concepts
- Adding spaces and pages
- The Confluence editor
- Creating engaging content
- Importing and exporting content

The basic concepts

Before we start creating content in Confluence, we need to have a basic understanding of the concepts used within Confluence.

Spaces

To organize content in Confluence we use spaces, which come in two types. A space is an area within Confluence, containing your pages. Spaces can be thought of as a subsites or a containers, with their own page structure and home page.

Global spaces are areas that define your Confluence structure. For example, you may want to separate areas based on team, department, or topic.

Personal spaces belong to specific users. Personal spaces can be set to be kept private or open, for every user to see and edit. Personal spaces can be used for personal information such as blog posts, bookmarks, and attachments. Administrators can choose to disable personal spaces altogether.

Each space has space-specific content (pages, blog posts, and so on) and space-specific permissions. The space content can be exported individually.

There is no limit for the number of spaces in Confluence.

Pages

Pages are the core of Confluence and the way to store and share information. Pages are always contained within a space and, as opposed to spaces, can be nested.

If you were to organize the content of this book in a space in Confluence, you would organize it like this:

Blog posts

Blog posts are a special type of pages within Confluence and can be added to every space, provided you have the permissions to do so. Blog posts are generally used for announcements, journal entries, reports, or any other time sensitive information. Blog posts are sometimes also referred to as news.

Confluence lists blog posts chronologically and allows you to browse blog posts by navigating a calendar.

Blog posts differ from normal pages in the following ways:

- You cannot move a blog post to another space
- Blog posts have a publish date, which can't be changed after creation
- Blog posts don't have parents, and therefore, can only be structured based on their publish date

Comments

Comments are remarks, questions, or any other information you want to add to an existing page or blog post, but are not necessarily part of the content of the page. Comments can be used to interact with other users on a topic. Comments can be added to every page or blog post, provided the user has permission to do so.

Comments are displayed at the bottom of the page, below the content, ordered in such a manner that the newest comment is at the bottom. Comments are normally displayed as a thread, showing hierarchy and context in the responses. Administrators can change the settings and choose to display all comments in a single flat list, removing the hierarchy and context.

Adding global spaces

Before we can add any content to Confluence, we need to have a space to put it in. In this exercise we will create two spaces, which we will use for the rest of this book.

For setting up a new global space, the **Create Space** permission is required.

To add a new global space, perform the following steps:

1. Go to the Confluence dashboard and click on **Create Space** located at the top right of the dashboard. The **Create Space** dialog appears as shown in the following screenshot.

2. Enter the following information to create the first space:
    - **Space name**: The name for the space. This name doesn't need to be unique. Use the name **Project Documentation**.
    - **Space key**: A key to identify your space. The key can only contain characters and numbers, nothing else. This key is used when linking content between spaces, web URL, and for reports. For our **Project Documentation** space we use **DOC**. Space keys must be unique.

- ° **Make this space private**: Checking this box will make sure the space is only visible to the user who is creating it. If the space is not private, it will have the default space permissions. For now, we don't care about permissions and will create a public space.

3. Click on **Create**. You will be forwarded to the space's home page. This home page is automatically created, containing the default space content.

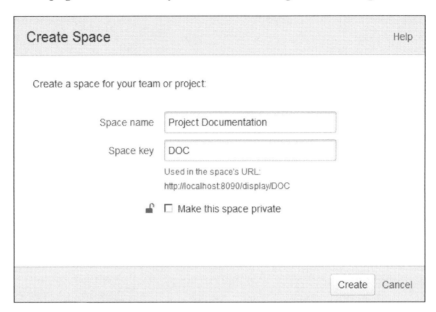

4. After creating the first space, create a second space with:

- ° **Space name** as **Management**
- ° **Space key** as **MGMT**
- ° The **Make this space private** box unchecked

Space permissions can be changed afterwards. More on permissions in *Chapter 6, Securing Your Content*.

Adding pages

There are several ways to create a page within Confluence, which I will explain here. Confluence also allows you to import existing Word documents, which is explained later in this chapter.

Adding a new page to Confluence

It is possible to create a page directly from the top navigation bar, without having to browse into a specific space.

1. Click on the **Create** button on the top navigation bar.

2. Use the **Select space** drop-down list to select the space where you want to add the page.

3. Then choose the type of content you want to create. It is possible to create a page based upon a certain template or just a blank page. Select **Blank page** for the time being.

4. Click on **Create**. Confluence will open the page in Edit mode.

5. Give the page the title **Introduction** and save the page.

The **Create content** dialog will look like the following screenshot:

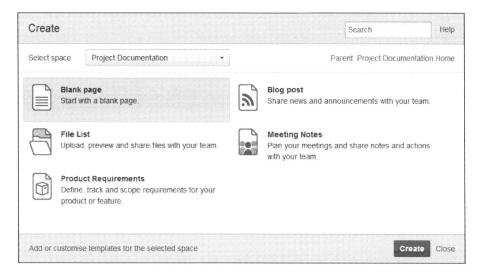

 Confluence will add the page to the root of the space. If this is not your intention, don't forget to set the location (explained in a later section) before saving.

Creating a page from another page

Another way to create a page in Confluence is directly from another page. By default this new page is added as a child of the current page.

1. Go to the **Introduction** page we have just created. If you didn't create it, go to any other page in your Confluence installation.

2. Choose **Create** from the top navigation bar, next to the **Select space** drop-down list. The parent of the new page is displayed.

3. Give this new page a title and click on **Save**.

Setting the location of a page

If you want to add a page in a different location than the default one, you can set the location before saving the page.

To set the location for a new page, perform the following steps:

1. While adding the page, click on **Location** at the bottom.

2. The **Set Page Location** dialog, as shown in the following screenshot, will appear. Use the tabs on the left to search for the parent page for your new page. The breadcrumbs at the bottom of the dialog will show you the current and new location.

3. If you want to define the position among the child pages, select **Reorder**. This will show you a list of sibling pages when you click on **Move**.

4. Click on **Move**.

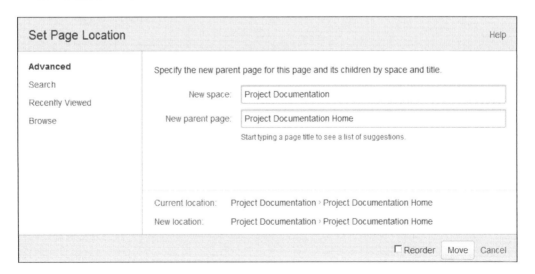

The Confluence editor

Confluence has a really powerful editor that allows you to create rich and engaging content. But before we go into creating content, we have to know a bit more about the editor and its options.

Let's go through the editor screen first, from top to bottom:

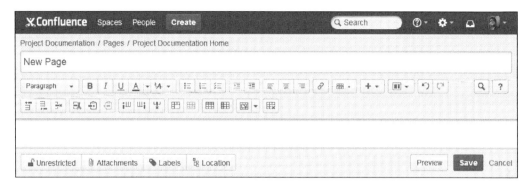

Item	Description
Confluence Navigation	The main Confluence navigation bar.
Page title	The title of the page; this is used in the URL and other links to the page. A page title is mandatory and should be unique within a space.
Editor toolbar	All the features to format your content, create tables and lists, change alignment, and add other content to the page. More about the editor toolbar in the next section.
Page content	Your content; words, images, and other media.
Restrictions	Control who can view or edit your page.
Attachments	View, manage, and insert attachments to your page.
Labels	Categorize your page by adding labels.
Location	Change the location of the page.
Change comment	Describe your changes to the page; only available when editing an existing page.
Notify watchers	Select this option to notify watchers of your changes to the page; deselect if the change was only minor. This is only available when editing an existing page.
Preview	See how your changes affect the page, without saving it first.
Save	Save your changes.
Cancel	Stop editing the page and reset all changes you've made.

During your edit session, Confluence will automatically save drafts of your page as you make your changes. If another user starts editing the same page, Confluence will notify the user, and if possible, will try to merge the changes.

The toolbar

If you are used to creating content online, or even in your office suite on your machine, most of the options on this toolbar should look familiar.

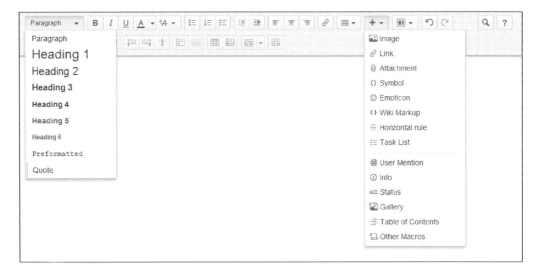

The toolbar can be used to (from left to right):

- Change paragraph and character formatting (such as headings, bold, italics)
- Color text, to emphasize or distinguish texts from each other
- Create bulleted, numbered, or task lists
- Select the indentation and alignment for text or images
- Insert links to other pages, attachments, and external websites
- Add tables, and add, remove, or merge rows and columns
- Insert other content into the page, such as images, videos, or symbols
- Add a layout to your page
- Search and replace content within the page you are editing

Formatting and autocomplete

Before Confluence Version 4, there was a concept called **wiki markup**, which was used to format the pages within Confluence. If you wanted to format your content or add a table, you had to be familiar with wiki markup. In the current editor, wiki markup isn't required anymore.

The current editor does allow wiki markup to be used for quick editing; wiki markup will automatically convert the pages to the associated format. With autocomplete and formatting, you can create and edit content faster, and all from your keyboard.

Autoformatting

With autoformatting, it's possible to type wiki markup directly into the editor. Some commonly used examples are listed in the following table. If you want to learn more, click on **?** on the editor toolbar and select the **Editor Autoformatting** tab.

Wiki Markup	Result
bold	Bold
italic	Italic
h1. Heading	Heading 1
h2. Heading	Heading 2
- item 1	Bullet list
- item 2	
| cell 1 | cell 2 |	a two-column table

Autocomplete

When editing in Confluence there are some "shortcut" characters that allow you to quickly add or attach images, files, macros, links, or user-mentions in the page.

Trigger character	Action	Description
[	Add a link	Shows a list of suggested (recently used) pages to link to
!	Display an image, video, audio file, or document	Shows a list with media attached to your page to embed in your page
{	Add a macro	Shows a list of macros as soon as you begin typing the macro name
@	Notify another user by mentioning them on your page	Shows a list of users to mention; type a username to get suggestions

Autocomplete can be canceled by pressing the *Esc* key on your keyboard, or by clicking somewhere else in the editor panel.

To autocomplete a link, perform the following steps:

1. Edit a page and click where you want to insert a link.
2. Type [and the first few characters of the page title and user's name of the file you want to link to.
3. Select the relevant link from the suggestions' list.

If the item you want to link to is not in the list, you can either:

- Choose **Search for 'over'** to continue looking for the page.
- Choose **Insert Web Link** to insert a link to an external page using the link browser.
- Choose **Insert Link to Create Page** to create a link to a yet-to-be-created page. The page will be created when the link is clicked for the first time.

Autoconverting

When you paste a URL into Confluence, the editor will check what you are pasting, and will automatically convert it to something to display in Confluence.

Confluence can recognize links from the services listed here, and the list is growing with every release:

- YouTube and Vimeo videos
- Single JIRA issues or complete JQL queries
- Google Maps
- Other Confluence URLs for pages and blog posts

Drag-and-drop

If you want to add files from your desktop to Confluence, it is possible to do so by dragging files from your desktop onto your browser. Depending on the Confluence view you are using, you will get different results:

- If you are viewing a page, the files are attached
- If you are browsing attachments, the files are attached
- If you are editing a page, the files are attached and embedded at the cursor position

Drag-and-drop requires a browser with the HTML5 drag-and-drop feature implemented. Most recent browsers meet this requirement. Older browser versions, such as Firefox 3.5, Safari 4, and Internet Explorer 8 and 9, only offer limited HTML5 support, and don't support drag-and-drop.

Adding content

Now that we have an understanding of the Confluence editor, we can look at using styling, layout, tables, and macros to create rich and engaging pages.

We start by creating a new page, which we call **Lorem Ipsum**, and use the generator located at `http://www.lipsum.com/feed/html` to generate some paragraphs of text for us to use. If you have another document you wish to use, you can.

Most formatting can be done using your mouse and the editor toolbar, or using a keyboard with shortcuts. The latter makes editing pages very easy, but needs some getting used to.

Styling

We use paragraph styling and character formatting to emphasize parts of content or to separate the content into logical pieces. For our **Lorem Ipsum** page we are going to add some headings and quotes, and emphasize a few lines.

- First we will add a header above each generated paragraph:
    1. Press **Enter** after the first two words of the paragraph.
    2. Select the two words, and then select **Heading 1** from the **Paragraph** drop-down list.
    3. Headings can easily be changed to a different styling. Change all headings to **Heading 2**, except the first heading.

- The second paragraph is actually a quote from somebody else:
  1. Select the complete second paragraph.
  2. Select **Quote** from the **Styling** drop-down list.

- Last we want to emphasize some sentences by making them bold:
  1. Select the sentence you want to make bold.
  2. Click on **B** on the toolbar to make the sentence bold. Or press *Ctrl + B* on your keyboard to make the sentence bold.

- Save the page. It should look something like this:

Pages / Project Documentation Home / Overview   🖉 Edit   📤 Share   ⚙ Tools ▾

Lorem Ipsum

Added by Arthur Dent, last edited by Arthur Dent on Apr 14, 2013

Lorem ipsum

dolor sit amet, consectetur adipiscing elit. **Nam eget diam vitae eros consequat pretium**. Phasellus vel nunc tempus urna vulputate accumsan. Mauris sed metus tortor, non congue nisi. Proin nec purus nec mauris luctus elementum eu in purus. Nulla facilisi. Vestibulum sed posuere dui. Aenean posuere bibendum odio, sit amet bibendum justo vestibulum eu. Proin egestas, diam sit amet dapibus luctus, lorem felis auctor ligula, porttitor fringilla diam quam in nunc.

Praesent vel ipsum

> non erat convallis sollicitudin vel ac mi. Proin luctus consequat pellentesque. Duis venenatis mattis nibh vitae lacinia. Proin eleifend orci vitae massa faucibus accumsan. Cras eu lorem ut metus imperdiet blandit et nec dolor. Nam commodo vehicula enim non malesuada. Praesent adipiscing, augue ut accumsan imperdiet, eros lectus hendrerit enim, vitae placerat tellus ligula eget risus. Nullam pellentesque ultrices hendrerit. Ut vel felis quis risus vestibulum tincidunt. Phasellus nibh libero, elementum ac sagittis eget, sollicitudin quis nulla. Nulla a lorem at ligula congue vehicula vel non sapien. Praesent bibendum urna in tellus rhoncus ornare.

Aenean malesuada

tellus non massa feugiat ultricies. Aliquam vel **eleifend lorem**. Nullam facilisis viverra orci. Etiam tincidunt odio eget lectus bibendum molestie. Nam lacinia libero id turpis molestie sit amet consequat felis bibendum. Aliquam gravida libero sit amet dui eleifend sed porta sapien rhoncus. Nunc eu lectus mi, eu placerat ante. Aliquam ultrices mi sed eros gravida ullamcorper. Phasellus cursus consequat leo vitae venenatis. Cras consectetur lacinia elementum. Vestibulum eget libero id nulla rutrum egestas. Nunc tempus aliquet sollicitudin. Cras commodo porta condimentum. Ut volutpat, augue ut mattis venenatis, leo metus vulputate mi, at facilisis lorem ante adipiscing sapien.

Praesent sodales

purus in quam aliquet vel faucibus nibh hendrerit. Duis varius, purus ut cursus iaculis, odio augue malesuada arcu, eget lobortis libero dui nec nunc. Integer facilisis, velit a placerat cursus, neque ante pretium felis, id facilisis quam massa dignissim ligula. Praesent nec massa sed justo auctor rutrum. Nullam mattis consectetur gravida. Nam eget tellus quis mauris molestie placerat id quis lorem.

Macros

With macros in Confluence, you can add extra functionality or include dynamic information to a page. For example, an attachment macro can be placed on a page listing all attachments; if you add a new attachment to this page, this list is automatically updated.

Let's add the Panel macro to our page we created earlier:

1. Open our **Lorem Ipsum** page and click on **edit**.

2. Select the third paragraph.

3. Click on **Insert** and choose **Other Macros**.

4. Confluence will display the macro browser.

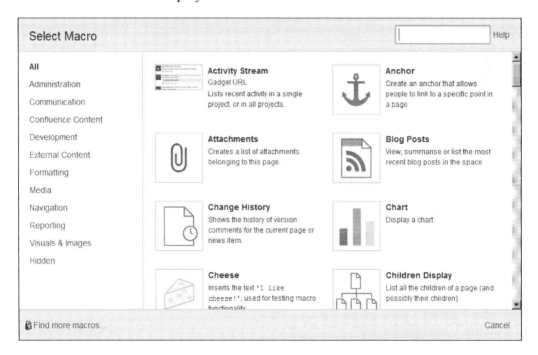

5. Use the search box and search for **Panel**, then click on the **Panel** macro.

6. In the next screen we can enter some details for this specific macro. Leave them empty and click on **Insert** located on the bottom-right corner.

7. Save the page.

The macro browser

In the previous section, we added a Panel macro to our page, which introduced the macro browser. The macro browser is a feature you will be using a lot to create your pages, and it is a great way to explore the different macros that are available to you.

Macros are grouped into one or more categories. The left panel of the macro browser is separated into categories. When a category is clicked, related macros are displayed in the right-hand section of the panel.

The macro browser search will use your query to filter by macro title and description.

Editing macros

After adding a macro to your page, Confluence will display a special box around your content. This is called the macro placeholder. This placeholder can be used to edit, remove, or copy/paste macros.

Left-click once on the placeholder to display the available options. These options can differ per macro. The options for a panel are displayed in the following screenshot:

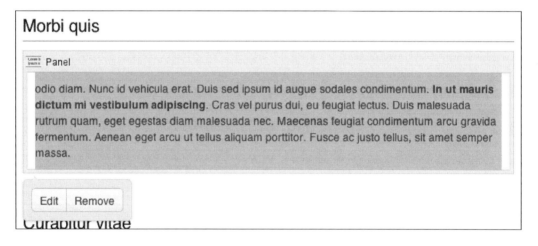

To edit a macro, select the **Edit** option or double-click on the placeholder. Confluence will display the **Edit 'Panel' Macro** screen:

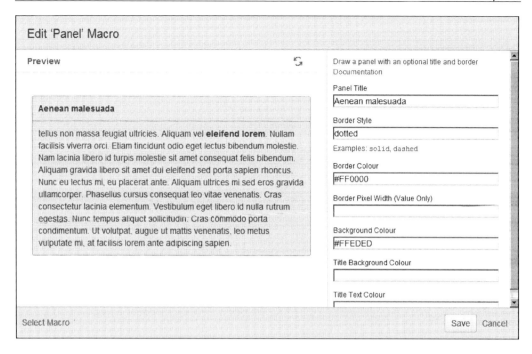

The large left section displays a preview of the content. On the right you can change the macro options, if those are available for your macro.

On the **Lorem Ipsum** page, we want to change the styling of the panel so that it looks like the previous screenshot. This can be achieved by performing the following steps:

1. Open the **Edit Macro** screen of the panel we just added.
2. Use the paragraph title as **Panel Title**.
3. Change the border style to **Dotted**.
4. If you want to give this panel a bit more attention, you can change the colors too. Colors should be added in hexadecimal notation:
   ○ Border color: #FF0000 (red)
   ○ Background color: #FFEDED (very light red)
5. Save the panel.

Almost every macro in Confluence can be updated using the context menu and **Edit Macro** dialog we just used.

Macro keyboard shortcut

When you are more familiar with the available macros in Confluence, you can also use the keyboard shortcut to add those macros to your page.

Type { to start the macro autocompletion. Continue to type the name of the macro you are looking for, and the suggestions will be updated. Select the macro you are looking for, and it will be added to your page.

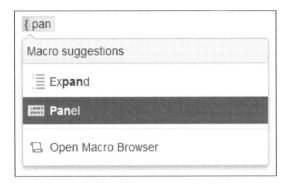

Panels

I already used the Panel macro to explain the macro browser, but it is worth mentioning again. The Panel macro is one of the macros I use the most. Panel macros are very useful for separating content, adding a bit of styling to your page, or to highlight a piece of content.

Page layouts and sections

When we want to add structure to our page, it's most common to split the information into columns. An example I often use is for adding event information in Confluence. On the left side I add the event information, and on the right I add an RSVP.

Confluence offers two ways to add structure to your page:

- **Page Layouts**, which are predefined columns and sections.
- The **Section** and **Column** macros that allow more flexibility but are more difficult to use than Page Layouts. You can set the width of the columns, and add as many sections and columns you need on your page.

Using page layouts

The Confluence editor comes with a predefined set of page layouts, each providing two or more columns. Some layouts also provide a horizontal header and footer to the page. The layout you select determines the position of the columns and the relative width of those columns on the page. If you use a page layout, the content of the page is confined within the border of that layout and it is not possible to add content before or after.

To choose a page layout, perform the following steps:

1. Open a page in Edit mode.
2. Click on the **Page Layout** icon (as shown in the following screenshot).
3. A drop-down list appears with the available layouts.
4. Select a layout.

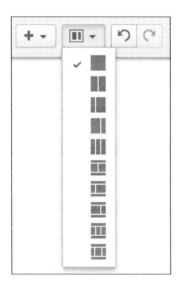

If your page already has content on it, Confluence will put the existing content into the upper-left column of the new layout. If the page was already using a different layout, Confluence will put the content into the appropriate column of the new layout.

For example: You have a three-column layout and want to switch to a two-column layout. Confluence will merge the second and third column to one column by placing the content of the third column underneath the content of the second.

Keep in mind that the width of each column is set to a percentage of the total page width. Confluence will adapt the width of the columns to fit the width of the page. If a column includes a large table or object, the content may not fit, and you will see a horizontal scroll bar when viewing the page.

Using Section and Column macros

If the predefined layouts are not what you are looking for, and you want a bit more flexibility, it is also possible to use the Section and Column macros provided by Confluence. The Section macro defines the area that will contain your columns. It's different from the page layouts, in that you can have as many sections as you like, and within a section you can add as many columns as you like.

To add Section and Column macros to a page, perform the following steps:

1. Open a page in Edit mode.
2. Find the **Section** macro by navigating to **Insert | Other Macros**, and insert it into the page.
3. Go to **Insert | Other Macros** again.
4. Find the **Column** macro and insert it into the Section macro.
5. Add your content to the column.
6. Insert as many sections and columns as you like.

In Edit mode, you would see the sections and columns represented as macro placeholders. This makes it a bit more difficult to see how your page would look in View mode.

In addition to the capability to add as many sections and columns as you like, the macros also have parameters that you can set.

The Section macro has the parameter `Show Border`, which will display a border around the section and columns, if set to `true`.

The Column macro has the parameter `Column Width`. It defaults to 100 percent, divided by the numbers of columns in the section. The column width can be set in pixels or as a percentage of the available width.

Tables

Tables are very powerful; you are able to do almost everything that you would expect from tables in an editor. Tables in Confluence can highlight cells, rows, or columns, and include a sort feature in View mode.

To create a table, perform the following steps:

1. Open a page in Edit mode and place your cursor at the point where you want to insert the table.
2. Select **Table** from the toolbar.
3. From the drop-down list that appears, select the number of rows and columns you want your table to have.
4. If you don't want a header on your table, press *Shift* while selecting your rows and columns.

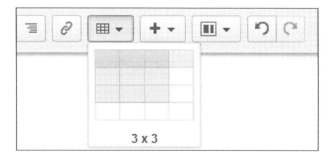

Editing a table

When you select the table in the editor, an extra toolbar will appear, with all the operations you can perform on a table. Let's go over the options available, from left to right.

Insert an empty row above the current selected row.

Insert an empty row below the current selected row.

Remove the current selected row.

Cut the current row and copy it to the clipboard.

Copy the current row to the clipboard.

Paste the row from the clipboard to the current row.

Insert an empty column to the left of the current one.

Insert an empty column to the right of the current one.

Remove the current column.

Merge the selected cells.

Split the selected merge cells.

Mark a row as a table header. The cells in the row will be highlighted in gray and the text will be displayed in bold.

Mark a column as a table header. The cells in the column will be highlighted in gray and the text will be displayed in bold.

Highlight the cells with a background color.

Remove the table.

Keyboard shortcuts

To speed up your work with tables, Confluence has keyboard shortcuts to perform most actions.

Windows	Mac OS X	Action
Ctrl + Shift + C	*Cmd + Shift + C*	Copy the current table or selected rows
Ctrl + Shift + I	*Cmd + Shift + I*	Insert a new table
Ctrl + Shift + V	*Cmd + Shift + V*	Paste the rows from your clipboard above the current row
Ctrl + Shift + X	*Cmd + Shift + X*	Cut the current table or selected rows

Windows	Mac OS X	Action
Alt + up arrow	*Alt* + up arrow	Add an empty row above the current row
Alt + down arrow	*Alt* + down arrow	Add an empty row below the current row

Sorting the table

In the View mode of a page, users can sort tables by clicking on the sort icons in the header row. This option is only available when viewing a page, and you can't configure the sorting. The initial display of the table (before sorting) will be the same as the order in the Edit mode.

Added by Arthur Dent, last edited by Arthur Dent on Apr 14, 2013 (view change)

Title	Auther	ISBN
JIRA Development Cookbook	Jobin Kuruvilla	1849681805
JIRA 4 Essentials	Patrick Li	1849681724
The Hitchhiker's Guide to the Galaxy	Douglas Adams	0345453743

Like   Be the first to like this

Attachments

Attachments are defined as any file that is included with your page. We already discussed images as attachments before, but there are other examples too, such as screenshots, Word or PDF documents, and videos. Attachments are useful when you want to share information in a different format than plain text.

When the page you are viewing contains attachments, a small paperclip icon appears next to the page byline, just below the page name. If you click on the paperclip icon, you will be taken to the Attachments view, where you will see all the attachments.

Attachments on a page inherit the permissions of the page so that if a user doesn't have view permissions on a page, he or she can't view or download the attachment.

Attaching files to a page

Attaching files to a page can be done using drag-and-drop, or by browsing for a file and uploading from your computer.

To attach a file using drag-and-drop, perform the following steps:

1. Browse to the page you want to attach files to.

2. Drag one, or more, files from your computer onto the page. The **Attach file** dialog will appear, showing you the upload progress of the file being attached to your page.

Files can also be dropped onto the Attachments or Editor view, and onto the **Insert Link** or **Insert Image** dialogs.

> Drag-and-drop requires a browser with the HTML5 drag-and-drop feature implemented. Most recent browsers meet this requirement.

To attach a file via the "classic" upload approach, perform the following steps:

1. Browse to the Attachments view of a page by going to **Tools | Attachments**.

2. Click on **Browse** and navigate to the file.

3. Select the file and click on **Open**.

4. Add a comment (optional) as description.

5. Choose **Attach more files** if you want to upload more files in one go.

6. Choose **Attach**.

Attachment version management

Confluence keeps track of the versions of an attachment uploaded to a page. By uploading an attachment with the same file name, a new version is added. Existing files will be kept with the name Version X, which is incremented with every upload.

To see all versions of an attachment, click on the arrow next to the attachment name.

Name	Size	Creator	Creation Date	Labels	Comment	
˅ 🖼 Arthur_Dent.png	178 kB	Arthur Dent	Apr 14, 2013 22:08	photo 🖉		Properties | Remove
Version 2 (current)	178 kB	Arthur Dent	Apr 14, 2013 22:08			Remove
Version 1	178 kB	Arthur Dent	Apr 14, 2013 20:22		Arthur Dent	Remove

Please keep in mind the following points:

- You cannot revert to a previous version of an attachment. Downloading and uploading the previous version would be a work-around.

- Confluence doesn't track changes within attachments.

- There is no limit to the number of attachments and versions, provided there is enough disk space on the server that Confluence is running on.

- Older versions of an attachment can be removed, given a user has the appropriate permissions.

Downloading attachments

Users can download all attachments in Confluence, provided the user has the permissions needed to view the page the attachment is attached to.

To download a single attachment, perform the following steps:

1. Browse to the Attachment view of a page by going to **Tools | Attachments**.
2. Right-click on the link on the attachment's name and select **Select Link as**, or a similar option in your browser.
3. Select the location where to download the file to.

To download all the attachments from a page, perform he following steps:

1. Browse to the Attachment view of a page by going to **Tools | Attachments**.
2. Click on the **Download All** button located at the end of the page, to download a ZIP file containing all the attachments (this link only appears if there are two or more files attached).

Downloading an attachment doesn't prevent somebody from uploading a new version of the attachment. This could potentially mean that, by uploading the attachment again, changes are overwritten. There are plugins available to enhance Confluence with a checkout mechanism, such as Lockpoint by Arsenale.

Embedding attachments

Once you have attached a file to a page, there are different methods for embedding the content of that file into your Confluence page.

Multimedia

You can embed many multimedia files with the Multimedia macro. This allows the user to directly watch or listen to your multimedia file without having to download it first. In some cases the user needs a separate plugin or decoder.

Supported multimedia files:

- Adobe Flash (.swf)
- Apple QuickTime (.mov)
- Windows Media (.wma, .wmv)
- Real Media (.rm, .ram)
- MP3 and MP4 files (.mp3, .mp4)
- MPEG files (.mpeg, .mpg)
- AVI files (.avi)

To insert the Multimedia macro, perform the following steps:

1. Open a page in Edit mode and place your cursor at the location where you want to add the macro.
2. Choose **Insert | Other Macros**, and search for the **Multimedia** macro.
3. Fill in the macro parameters (described in the following table).
4. Click on **Insert**.

The following table lists the macro parameters, and also provides a brief description for each:

Parameter	Default	Description
Page name	Current page	Name of the page to which your multimedia file is attached. Use autocomplete to find your page. If this field is left empty, the current page will be used.
Attachment	-	File name of the multimedia file.
Width	Based on the file type	Width of the movie window. Can be specified in pixels or as a percentage of the window's width.
Height	Based on the file type	Height of the movie window. Can be specified in pixels or as a percentage of the window's height.
Autoplay	Off	If checked, the video or audio file will start playing as soon as the page is loaded. If this option is not checked (the default), users will have to press the play button.

You can't embed multimedia files from remote servers, but Confluence allows this with the widget connector, which is available as a macro.

Office files and PDF

Confluence can display Office files that are attached to a page. This is useful for users who don't have Office suite installed on their desktop or don't want to download the complete file.

Supported Office files:

- Office Word (.doc, .docx)
- Office Excel (.xls, .xlsx)
- Office PowerPoint (.ppt, .pptx)
- PDF

To display an Office file in Confluence, perform the following steps:

1. Open a page in Edit mode and place your cursor at the location where you want to add the macro.
2. Choose **Insert | Other Macros**, and search for the macro. There is one for each Office file—these being the Office Word macro, Office Excel macro, Office Powerpoint macro, and the PDF macro.
3. Fill in the macro parameters (described in the following table)
4. Click on **Insert**.

Macro	Parameter	Default	Description
All	Page name	Current page	The Confluence page containing the attached file. If not specified, the current page is assumed.
	File name	None	The name of the attached file to be displayed.

Macro	Parameter	Default	Description
Excel	Show Grid?	Yes	Select to show grid lines around each cell. Deselect to hide these grid lines.
	Worksheet name	Last worksheet viewed	The name of the worksheet you want to display.
	Last row	Last row with content	The number of the last row you want to display, starting from 0 as the first row.
	Last column	Last column with content	The number of the last column you want to display, starting from 0 as the first column.
Powerpoint	Height		The height of the display in pixels or as percentage of the window's height.
	Slide Number	None	If specified, Confluence will display a single slide as image, instead of a slideshow. The first slide is numbered 0.
	Width		The width of the display in pixels or as an percentage of the window's width.

Text in PDF files may appear blurred when viewed using the PDF macro. This is by design, as Confluence converts the PDF to images and reduces their size to save bandwidth. This is not possible using the macro browser, so we have to use a trick which involves Wiki markup:

1. Open a page in Edit mode and place your cursor at the location where you want to add the PDF file.

2. Go to **Insert | Wiki Markup**, and paste the following line into the text editor:
   `{viewfile:my.pdf|width=800|height=1000}`.

3. Replace `my.pdf` with your file's name.

4. Click on **Insert**.

Drag-and-drop

Depending on your browser, you can also use drag-and-drop to embed multimedia and Office files into your page. Confluence will try to determine the correct macro and use it to display your attachment:

1. While in Edit mode, simply drag-and-drop the file from your desktop onto the editor.

   Confluence will attach the file to the page and insert the macro at your cursor position.

2. If needed, click on the macro and choose **Edit** to change the macro properties.

Images

Images can be displayed on a Confluence page if the image meets one of the following conditions:

- The image is attached to the current page
- The image is attached to another page of the same Confluence installation; this can even be in another space
- The image is on a remote web page that your server can connect to

Once an image is displayed on your page, you can:

- Change the appearance of the image
- Move the image to a new position
- Use the image as a link to another Confluence page or URL

Displaying an attached image

Once you have attached an image to a page, there are three different methods available for displaying the image:

- Using the **Insert Image** dialog:
  1. Open a page in Edit mode and place the cursor at the location where you want to display the image.
  2. Choose **Insert | Image** from the toolbar and select the **Attached images** tab in the dialog.
  3. Select the required image and click on **Insert**, or double-click on the image to select it.

- Using autocomplete:
  1. Open a page in Edit mode and place the cursor where you want to add the image.
  2. Type ! to trigger the autocomplete function.

3. Continue typing the image name and choose the image from the list that appears.

- Using drag-and-drop:

  This feature uses the drag-and-drop functionality of HTML5 and is, therefore, only available in browsers that support HTML5. Depending on your browser, you can attach and display an image with just one action. While editing a page, drag-and-drop an image from your desktop on to the page. The image is uploaded, attached, and displayed at the current cursor position.

Displaying an attached image on a different page

It is also possible to display an image that is attached to a different page within the same Confluence installation; the page doesn't have to be on the same space. All you need to know is the name of the image.

Displaying images from other pages can be used to manage your images easily. You could upload all your images to a single page and avoid them being uploaded more than once. Your users do need view permission to the page, so if you have images to which you want to restrict access, don't use this method.

To display an image attached to a different page, perform the following steps:

1. Open a page in Edit mode and place the cursor at the location you where want to display the image.
2. Go to **Insert | Image**, and select the **Search** tab.
3. Type in the name of the image you are looking for.
4. Choose if you want to search the current space or **All Spaces**, and click on **Search**.
5. Select the required image from the search results.

Displaying an image from a remote web page

You can display an image from a remote web page in your Confluence instance without needing to attach it to your page, if you know the URL of that image.

To display an image from an external web page, perform the following steps:

1. Open a page in Edit mode and place the cursor where you want to display the image.
2. Go to **Insert | Image** and select the **From the web** tab.
3. Type or paste the URL for the image.
4. Click on **Preview** to check that you used the correct URL.
5. Click on **Insert**.

Changing the image's appearance

Once you have added an image into a page, you often need to edit the image. Confluence provides ways to do this using the image properties panel.

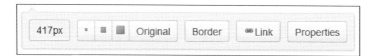

To change the size of an image, perform the following steps:

1. While editing a page, click on the image to show the image properties panel, as shown in the previous screenshot.
2. Change the image size manually within the text field at the left of the panel (the size can be between 16 px and 900 px). The image is resized proportionally to the original ratio. Or choose one of the size preset buttons next to the text field, to change the image size.

Images are displayed as thumbnails; clicking on the image in View mode will pop up a larger version of the image.

To add a border to the image, perform the following steps:

1. While editing a page, click on the image to show the properties panel.
2. Choose **Border** from the properties panel.

To use image effects, perform the following steps:

1. While editing a page, click on the image to show the properties panel.
2. Choose **Properties** from the properties panel.
3. Select **Effects** in the properties dialog.
4. Pick one of the five effects.

The **Instant Camera** effect only works with Latin character languages. This is due to the `handwriting style` font that is being used.

An example of an image with effects is shown in the next screenshot.

The only way to add a caption to an image is using the Instant Camera effect described earlier. Captions are very useful to add additional information about the image. Perform the following steps to add a caption to an image:

1. Select **Properties** from the image properties panel and choose the **Instant Camera** effect.

2. Save the page.

3. Go to **Tools | Attachments** to view the attachments of the page. If you are displaying an image from another page, go to the attachment view of that page.

4. Choose **Properties** located next to the image.

5. Add a comment to the attachments. This comment will be used as image caption.

 You will have to reapply the comment each time you upload a new version of the same image.

To add a link to your image, perform the following steps:

1. Select **Link** from the image properties panel.

2. Confluence will display the **Insert Link** dialog, which you can use to search for the page to link to.

Aligning your image

Aligning your image works the same way as aligning text. Select your image and choose from the paragraph alignment buttons on the editor toolbar.

If you choose to align your image left or right, the text will be wrapped around the image. Text does not wrap for center alignment.

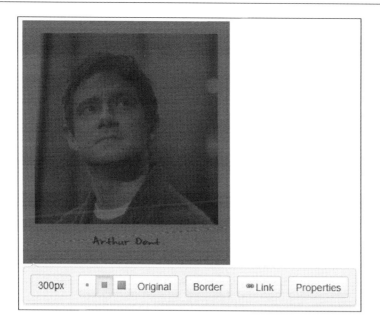

Displaying images in a gallery

When you have many images attached to a page, you might want to display them as a gallery. The gallery displays the page attachments as thumbnails. When a user clicks on the thumbnail, a larger version of the image is displayed.

To display the images attached to the page as a gallery, insert the Gallery macro using the steps described in the Macros section.

Features of the Gallery macro:

- The images in the gallery are taken from the attachments of that page. It is also possible to specify a different page to take the attachments from. A combination is not possible.

- Captions in the gallery are taken from the image comments.

- By default, the gallery will include all the images attached to a page. You can exclude or include images by name or label using the macro properties.

- The gallery can be sorted by name, date, and even size.

- The gallery width (columns) and title can easily be changed using the macro properties.

Links

Links are more important than you might think. Links enable you to connect to content from anywhere within Confluence, or from other websites or applications.

It is possible to link to the following content:

- Pages, from within or outside Confluence
- Blog posts
- Pages that don't exist yet, but that you want to create at a later stage
- Attachments, such as images and documents
- User profiles or personal spaces
- A section of a page, using an anchor

Linking to Confluence pages

Links to pages can be created using the following methods:

- **Autocomplete**: To link to Confluence pages
- **The Insert Link dialog**: To link to both Confluence and web pages
- **Cutting and pasting a link into the editor**: To link to both Confluence and web pages

Using Autocomplete

You can use Autocomplete to create a link to any page in Confluence, if you know the name of the page you want to link to.

Start your link by typing [to see a list of suggestions. Continue with the name of the page to search for the page you want to link to.

Using the Insert Link dialog

You can use the Insert Link dialog to create a link to a page. Perform the following steps:

1. Open a page in Edit mode and place your cursor at the location where you want to insert a link. You can also highlight the text you want linked.

2. Choose **Link** in the editor toolbar or press *Ctrl + K*. The **Insert Link** dialog will appear.

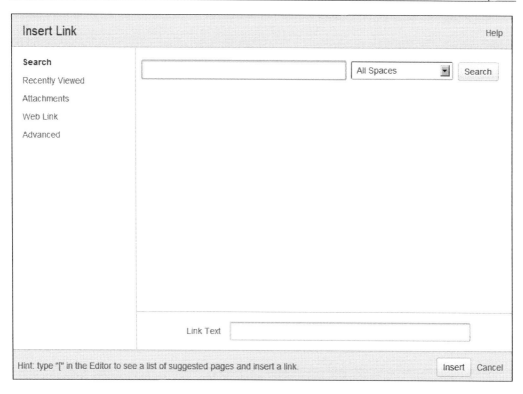

3. Use the tabs on the left to find the page you want to link to:
    ° **Search**: Use this tab to link to a page or file in Confluence
    ° **Recently Viewed**: This tab displays the pages you recently viewed (and created)
    ° **Attachments**: This displays the attachments on this page
    ° **Web Link**: This tab is used to link to web pages outside Confluence
    ° **Advanced**: This tab is used for linking to anchors and as-yet non-existent pages

4. Enter the link text that will be displayed on the page. If the link text is empty, the link will display either the target page name or the URL.

5. Click on **Insert**.

Using copy and paste

Links can also be created by cutting and pasting a link to an editor. Perform the following steps:

1. In your web browser, select and copy the title of a Confluence page.
2. Open a page in Edit mode and paste the title where you want the link.
3. Use **edit link** to change the link text, if needed.

Linking to web pages

To create a link to a web page, perform the following steps:

1. Open a page in Edit mode and place your cursor at the location where you want to create the link.
2. Click on **Link** in the toolbar, or press *Ctrl + K* to open the **Insert Link** dialog.
3. Choose **Web Link** from the left tabs, and paste the web address into the **Address** textbox.
4. Enter a link text.
5. Click on **Insert**.

You can also paste a link directly into the Confluence editor. The link text will be the complete URL, which can be changed afterwards using the image properties panel.

Linking to an anchor

It is also possible to link to a specific location within a page, by placing an Anchor macro at that location and then linking to the anchor.

To add an anchor to a page, perform the following steps:

1. Open a page in Edit mode and place your cursor at the location where you want to add an anchor.
2. Find the Anchor macro by:
   - Going to **Insert | Other Macros** and finding the Anchor macro
   - Typing {anchor to use autocompletion to insert the macro
3. Specify your anchor's name.

Choosing an anchor name

An anchor name should be descriptive of the section you want to link to. The anchor name can include spaces. Confluence will remove those spaces when building a URL to the anchor. Remember that the anchor name is case sensitive, when building your link.

To link to an anchor, perform the following steps:

1. Open a page in Edit mode and place your cursor at the location where you want to add the link.
2. Choose **Link** in the editor toolbar, or press *Ctrl + K*.
3. Choose **Advanced** and enter the anchor name into the link textbox.
4. Enter the link text that will be displayed on the page.
5. Click on **Insert**.

Use the following syntax when typing the anchor name:

Anchor Location	Link Syntax	Example
Same page	`#anchor`	`#footer` `#highlighted info`
Different page	`pagename#anchor`	`Overview#footer` `Overview#highlighted info`
Page in another space	`spacekey:pagename#anchor`	`DOC:Overview#footer` `DOC:Overview#highlighted info`

Don't use anchor links for a table of contents. There is another macro that can generate a table of contents for you; this macro can be inserted by using the macro browser to search for `Table of Content`.

Linking to a heading

You can directly link to a heading in Confluence without the need of an anchor. However, if somebody changes the heading, the link will be broken. Using an anchor will prevent this.

To link to a heading, perform the following steps:

1. Open a page in Edit mode and place your cursor at the location where you want to add the link.

2. Choose **Link** in the editor toolbar, or press *Ctrl + K.*

3. Choose **Advanced** and enter the heading into the **Link** textbox. The heading is case-sensitive and must be entered without spaces.

4. Enter the link text that will be displayed on the page.

5. Click on **Insert**.

Linking to an undefined page

In some case you want to insert a link pointing to a Confluence page that does not exist yet, but which you intend to create later. We call this type of link an **undefined link**.

To add an undefined link, perform the following steps:

1. Open a page in Edit mode and place your cursor at the location where you want to add the link.

2. Type [to trigger the autocomplete function, and type the name of the undefined page.

3. From the suggestion list, choose **Insert Link** to create a page.

Drafts

While you are working on your page, Confluence makes sure your work is saved. At regular intervals a draft is saved so that, in case of a network or server error, you can retrieve the last-saved draft and continue your work.

Drafts are created when you are adding or editing a page. By default, Confluence saves a draft every 30 seconds. A Confluence administrator can change this interval in the **General Configuration** setting. A draft is also created if you move to another site or page while editing a page.

When you edit the page again, Confluence will display a message stating there is an unsaved version of the page, and ask if you would like to discard it or continue with that version.

 Drafts are only available for unsaved pages. If you accidentally cancel your edit session, all changes are lost because the drafts are removed too.

Changing the draft interval

By default, Confluence saves a draft of a page that is being edited every 30 seconds. As Confluence Administrator, you can change this.

1. Browse to the Administration console (**Administration | Confluence Admin**).
2. Choose **General Configuration** in the left-hand menu.
3. Edit the settings and change the value in **Draft Save Interval**.

Resuming editing a draft

If you want to resume editing an unsaved page or blog post, you have two options:

- Using the draft view:
    1. Click on your avatar in the top-right corner of the navigation bar.
    2. Choose **Drafts** from the drop-down menu.
    3. You will see all the drafts Confluence saved for you.

4. Click on **Resume**, next to the relevant draft to continue editing.

- Resuming editing:

  If you created a new page but didn't save it, then the next time you create a new page in the same space, Confluence will ask you if you want to resume editing your previous page. If you choose **resume editing**, the draft is restored, and you can resume editing it.

Viewing unsaved changes

While you are editing your page or blog post, it is possible to review the changes you made, before saving them. As soon as there is a draft saved of your changes, you will see the line **Draft autosaved at ... (view change)** at the bottom right, just below the **Save** button.

If you click on **view change**, a dialog will appear with the changes you made during this edit.

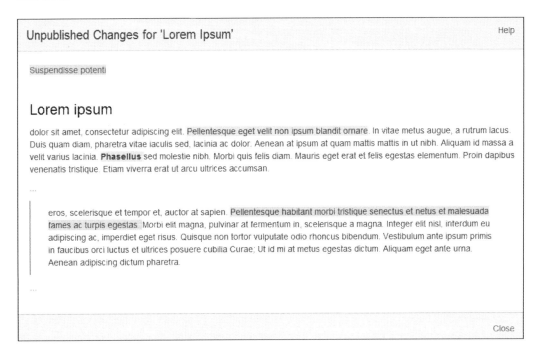

Working with content history

Confluence tracks all changes made to a page, by creating a new version each time the page is modified. You can view the changes between different versions of the page, and also rollback to a certain version of the page.

Viewing the page history

All previous versions of a page can be viewed.

To view the history of a page, perform the following steps:

1. Go to the page you want to view the history of.

2. Go to **Tools | Page History**.

3. In the **Page History** screen, as displayed in the following screenshot, click on a version number to view that specific version of the page.

	Version	Date	Changed By	Operations
☐	CURRENT (v. 4)	Apr 15, 2013 12:03	Arthur Dent	
☐	v. 3	Apr 15, 2013 09:38	Arthur Dent	Restore this version · Remove
☐	v. 2	Apr 14, 2013 17:36	Arthur Dent	Restore this version · Remove
☐	v. 1	Apr 14, 2013 15:49	Arthur Dent	Restore this version · Remove

Page History — Compare selected versions

To get an understanding of the changes, it is possible to compare two versions with each other. Confluence will display the newest version of the page and highlight the changes being made; an example of this is shown in the next screenshot.

To compare changes between versions, perform the following steps:

1. Go to the page you want to view the history of.

2. Go to **Tools | Page History**.

3. Use the checkbox in front of the versions to select up to two different versions.

4. Choose **Compare selected versions** to display the comparison.

Changes between versions are highlighted with colors:

- **Green**: Content added
- **Red**: Content deleted
- **Blue**: Formatting changed

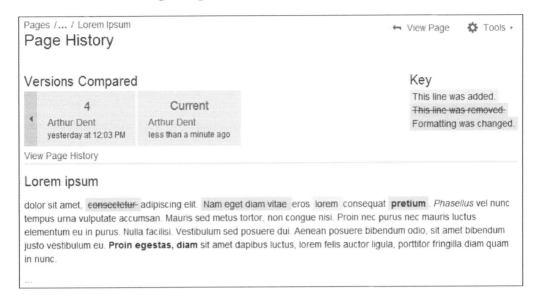

When a page comparison view is displayed, all unchanged text sections are hidden and reduced to an ellipsis, like this: . . . .

It is also possible to restore a previous version of a page. Confluence will then use the content of that version to create a new version. So if you are currently on Version 10 and want to restore Version 8, Confluence will create Version 11 with the content of 8. The advantage of this is that no changes are lost by reverting a version.

To restore a version, perform the following steps:

1. Go to the page you want to view the history of.
2. Go to **Tools | Page History**.
3. Click on **Restore this version**, next to version you want to restore.
4. On the next screen you can change the comment, if needed.
5. Click on **Ok** to restore the version.

Importing content

Confluence can import content from many different sources, including other Confluence sites. In most cases, people move from a document-based system to Confluence, and therefore, we will take a closer look at the Word document importer. If you are interested in importing content from other sources, such as another wiki, please take a look at `https://confluence.atlassian.com/display/ DOC/Importing+Content+Into+Confluence`.

Importing a Word document

If you import an Office Word document, it will be available as a Confluence page to your users, with all the advantages of a Confluence page. The Word document is no longer required.

The simplest way to import a Word document is to import the entire content of the document as a single Confluence page.

More advanced options allow you to import the content into a new page, split a single document into multiple pages based on headers, and resolve title conflicts.

Confluence can import valid Microsoft Word documents stored as 97-2007 (`.doc` and `.docx`) formatted documents.

 It is worthwhile to prepare your Word document before importing it into Confluence. Verify that all the headings are correct and that there is no Word Art (as Confluence doesn't support this) in your document. Make sure the images in your document are at 100 percent magnification; this will make sure Confluence imports the images in their full size.

Importing a Word document as a single page

Using this method will replace all the content on the current wiki page, so use it with caution:

1. Create a new page where you want to import the Word document, and save it.
2. Go to **Tools | Import Word Document**.
3. Click on **Browse** to find the Word document you want to import.
4. Click on **Next** to go to the **Import options** screen.

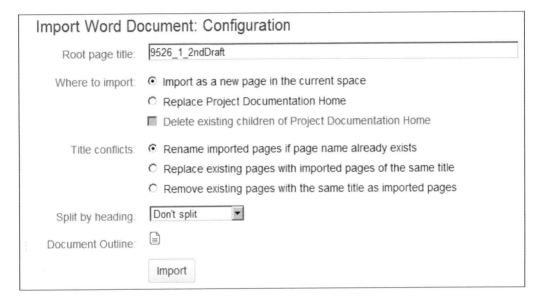

5. Specify the options and click on **Import**.

Option	Description
Root page title	The title of the new page that will contain the content of your Word document.
Import as a new page in the current space	Select if you want a new page to be created with the specified title.
Replace <current page>	Select if you want to replace the current page; the title will be renamed to the specified title.
Delete existing children of <current page>	The children of the current page will be removed.
Rename imported page if page name already exists	Rename the new page if there is already a page with the same title in the space.
Replace existing pages with imported pages of the same title	Replace the existing page when it has the same title as the imported document. Page history will be preserved.
Remove existing pages with the same title as imported pages	If an imported page has the same title as an existing page, then the existing page will be removed.
Split by heading	Create a new child page based on a heading.

 Please note that once imported, the page is no longer connected to the original Word document, and the new page and its content should be updated and edited directly in Confluence.

Importing a Word document into multiple pages

It is also possible to split a Word document based upon the headers in the document; Confluence will create child pages for those headers:

1. Import a Word document as described in the previous section.
    On the import screen, choose to split your document by heading.

2. Based on your selection, Confluence will show you a preview of
    the hierarchy after the import.

3. Click on **Import** to start the import.

Exporting content

You might need to export your content to a different format. For example, you might need to use documentation you've written in Confluence in an e-mail, or on another website. You can do this by exporting part of a space, all of a space, or individual pages to HTML, Word, or PDF. There are plugins available that help you to export content into other formats

Exporting a single page

You can easily export every page to PDF. This option is available to all users who have the export page permission in the space of the page:

1. Go to the page you want to export.
2. Go to **Tools | Export to PDF**.
3. Your browser will prompt you to download and save the PDF file.

Comments on the page are not exported to the PDF file.

Exporting a space

You can export a part, or all, of a space to HTML, PDF, or XML. For all three formats, the method of exporting is almost the same, with small differences in the options.

To export a space, perform the following steps:

1. Browse to a page in the space and choose **Space Tools** from the left sidebar.
2. Select **Content Tools**.
3. Open the **Export** tab. This option will only be available if you have the permissions to export a space.
4. Select the type of export and click on **Next**. The available exports are:
    - **HTML**: This will export the space as static HTML pages
    - **XML**: This creates an XML export, which can be used for backup, or to import the space into a different Confluence installation
    - **PDF**: This will export the space as a PDF file
5. Choose if you would like to have a **Normal** export or a **Custom** export.
6. Normal exports will contain all pages and blog posts in the space, including comments and attachments (images).

7. A custom export will be based upon the pages and options you select next.

8. If you have chosen **Custom**, be sure to select the pages you want to export.

9. Click on **Export**.

10. When the export process is complete, download the export and store it on your desktop.

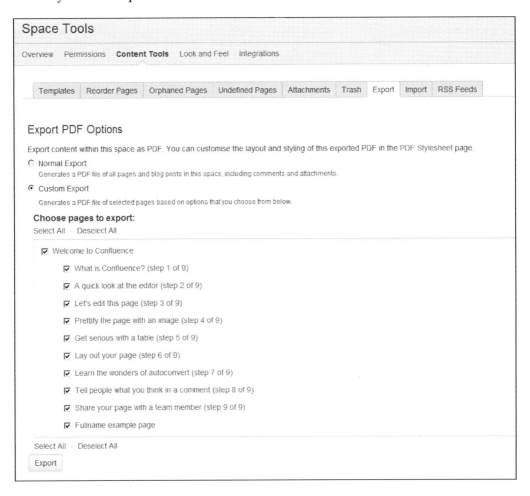

Summary

We had a detailed look at the art of creating engaging content, and at the rich text editor. Macros are at the core of the editor and provide many features we can use for creating our content.

We have seen that content in Confluence is not limited to text, and we can use images, audios, and movies too. Your current documentation, in the form of a Word document, can easily be imported into Confluence and taken to the next level there.

Creating content is really powerful, but what about finding it again? How do you make sure your users and colleagues can find your pages? Exactly the topic for the next chapter, *Managing Content*.

4
Managing Content

Finding content is as important as creating content. In this chapter we will learn how to organize content using labels, favorites, and use the watch feature to keep track of your content. With the use of the quick and advanced search features, we can find relevant content and documents.

The goal of this chapter it to learn how to organize your Confluence content, so that you and your users can easily find the up-to-date information they are looking for. By the end of this chapter we will have a good understanding of how to:

- Organize your spaces
- Use labels
- Track changes in Confluence
- Search within Confluence

Organizing your spaces

In *Chapter 3*, *Creating Content*, we learned how to create spaces and pages. Over time, your space will grow and pages might not be in the right order or location. Users might also start complaining that they can't find the page you are referring to. This is the moment your space could use a little organization and cleanup.

Changing the order of pages

Pages within Confluence have a hierarchical structure where other pages can be grouped under a parent page. We refer to this group as **page family**. Pages within a page family are, by default, ordered in alphabetical order. When you create a new page it will be inserted into the page family in alphabetical order. It is possible to move pages to a different position, automatically changing the order mode to manual. In manual mode, the new page will be placed at the bottom of a page family.

The easiest way to reorder the pages within a space is by using the **Reorder Pages** view, located in **Space Tools**. To get to this view:

1. Go to the space and choose **Space tools** on the left sidebar.

2. Select **Content Tools** followed by **Reorder Pages** as shown in the following screenshot:

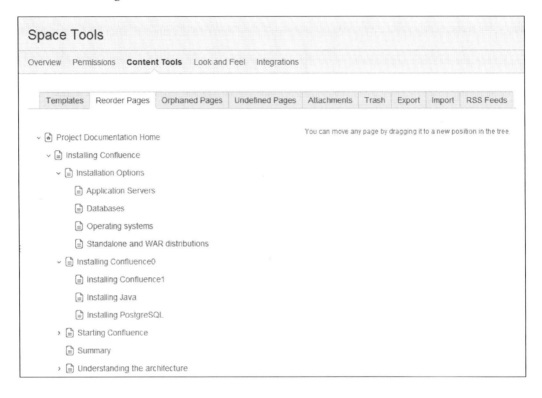

All pages can be reordered using drag-and-drop. While dragging the page you will see one of the following things happening:

- A thin line will appear between the existing pages. This indicates the potential new position for the page; releasing your mouse button will drop the page at that location.

- A highlighted section will appear over one of more existing pages. This indicates that you can drop the page into the page family. The dropped page will be added to the family according to the sorting order, alphabetical or manual.

Setting the page order to alphabetical

Once you have moved one or more pages in a page family, the order is set to manual. To restore this order to alphabetical, perform the following steps:

1. Go to the space and choose **Space tools** on the left sidebar.

2. Select **Content Tools** followed by **Reorder Pages**.

3. Expand the tree to find the page family you want to restore.

4. If the page family is manually ordered, there will be an **A/Z** icon shown next to the parent page.

5. Click on the **A/Z** icon to restore the alphabetical order to that page family.

6. Directly after clicking the icon, an undo icon will appear, allowing you to restore the manual order. This undo icon is only available while you are still on the tree view and don't change anything else.

Orphaned pages

An **orphaned page** is a page without a parent page or any incoming links. An orphaned page does not appear in any navigation, so users have to know of its existence to be able to search for it. This means that if you have content on an orphaned page, it is very unlikely that people will find it using the natural course of navigation. An orphaned page can be found using search.

Orphaned pages can arise when you are deleting a parent page. All child pages of the deleted parent page will be moved to the root of the space. From that moment the child page has become an orphaned page.

Especially in large spaces, it is difficult to keep track of orphaned pages. Confluence allows you to view all orphaned pages in a space so that you can reorganize or remove them.

To view the orphaned pages, perform the following steps:

1. Go to the space and choose **Space tools** on the left sidebar.

2. Select **Content Tools** followed by **Orphaned Pages**.

From the **Orphaned Pages** screen you can edit or delete the page. If you want to move the page and give it a parent page, it is easier to use the **Reorder Pages** feature discussed earlier. The alternative is to go to **Tools | Move** from the page in viewing mode, with the advantage that you are able to move the page to another space.

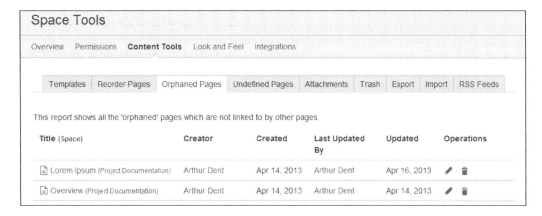

Orphaned pages aren't necessarily bad

It's not uncommon to have one or more orphaned pages being used as placeholders for attachments or information that is used on many other pages. With the "include" macro, these orphaned pages can be included in those pages. If then, the information changes, you only have to update one page.

Archiving a space

Some spaces might contain information that is not relevant anymore. For example, when you use Confluence to write a user documentation and have a space per product version, or a project is finished and the space is no longer needed.

Archiving a space will keep the content available in Confluence but it will be less visible than before. If a space is archived:

- The pages and other content do not appear in the suggestion list when using the Confluence search box.
- The pages and other content do not appear in any search results unless it is specified to also include archived spaces.
- The space isn't listed on the dashboard.
- Any updates to the space's content will not appear in the various activity streams.

- The space, pages, and other content will not appear in any of the drop-down menus in Confluence.
- The archived space will not appear in the general space list in the space directory. The space will be listed on the "archived spaces" tab and categories determined by the space labels.

While a space is archived the following functions will remain available:

- Users will be able to view the content as usual and any bookmarked URL will still work
- Users will be able to edit the content, provided they have the permissions to do so
- Any feeds, watches, or notifications will remain active

To archive a space, perform the following steps:

1. Go to the space and choose **Space Tools** on the left sidebar.
2. Select **Overview** to navigate to the space details page.
3. Select **Edit Space Details**.
4. Choose **Archived** from the status drop-down menu.
5. Click on **Save** as shown in the following screenshot:

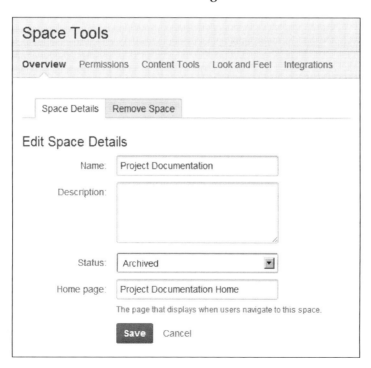

If your Confluence installation is open to the public, archived spaces will still be indexed and found via search engines such as Google.

Using Confluence labels

To categorize, identify, or bookmark content in Confluence we can use **labels**. Labels are keywords or tags that can be added to pages, blog posts, attachments, and spaces as metadata. Labels are user-defined so any word that identifies your content can be used.

For example, you can assign the label "requirement" to all pages with project requirements. It is then possible to browse, or list, all pages with that label in a single space or even across Confluence. It is also possible to search content based on that label.

The advantages of using labels are as follows:

- Labels are user-defined, so you can decide what information is relevant and how you want to label them, using words you and your users understand
- With labels you can group pages and spaces without having to restructure your site
- You can add as many labels as you like
- Labels are easily added without affecting the content to which you assign a label

Confluence doesn't support multiword labels. Which means that, to label a page with "needs review", the space has to be replaced with another character such as a dash or underscore.

Content labels

Any user with the permission to edit a page or blog post can also manage labels.

In order to add a label, you will have to perform the following steps:

1. Go to the page you want to label. At the bottom of the page, just below the content, there will be a list with labels (provided the page already has labels, otherwise, **No labels** will be displayed).
2. Click on the edit icon next to the list, or press *L* on your keyboard. This will display the labels dialog.

3. Type in a new label. Labels that are frequently used throughout your Confluence instance are suggested as you type.

4. Click on **Add** as shown in the following screenshot:

In order to remove a label, you will have to perform the following steps:

1. Open the label dialog (as described in the preceding steps for adding a label).

2. Next to each label there will be an **X** mark.

3. Click on the **X** mark to remove a label from a page.

Attachment labels

Attachments can also have labels, making it easier to find or filter them. Labels can be added or removed by any user who is allowed to edit the page that holds the attachment.

To add a label to an attachment, perform the following steps:

1. Go to the page that contains the attachment.

2. Choose **Tools | Attachments** to go to the attachment view.

3. On the attachment view you will see a list of attachments. If an attachment already has labels, these will be shown in the **Labels** column.

4. Click the edit icon to open the label dialog.

5. Type a new label; existing labels will be suggested as you type.

6. Click on **Add** as shown in the following screenshot:

Labels are deleted the same way as with pages. Click on the **X** mark next to a label to remove it from the attachment.

Using space categories

A **space category** is a special label that Confluence uses to group spaces in the space directory and in the recent activity area on the Dashboard. Let's assume that you have one or more spaces that contain information about the same project, **Project42**. We can categorize all those spaces as "Project42" to group them.

Grouping spaces with categories will reflect in the space browser and you can see the updated content in those spaces by choosing the **Project42** category under the **Space Categories** tab on your dashboard as shown in the following screenshot:

> You have to be space administrator or a Confluence (system) administrator to set up the space category for a space.

To add a category to a space, perform the following steps:

1. Go to the space and choose **Space tools** on the left sidebar.
2. Select **Overview** to navigate to the space details page.
3. Click on **Edit**, next to **Space Categories**.
4. Use the text field to add new categories to a space.
5. Click on **Done**.

Categories are removed the same way as labels. Click on the **X** mark next to the category to remove it.

 To completely remove a category or label, just remove the label everywhere it is being used. A category or label cannot exist if it isn't being used.

Viewing labels

When you click on a label on a page, blog post, or attachment, you will be forwarded to the labels view. Alternatively, if you are using the documentation theme, go to any page in a space and choose **Browse | Labels**.

The labels view in a space offers the following features:

- **Popular Labels**: Use this view to see a list of the most frequently used labels in that space. From this view you can also view the global popular labels. The bigger the label, the more popular it is.
- **All Labels**: This view will show all the labels in the space. Click on a label to see the associated content in that space. It will also display related labels if they exist. Related labels are labels that often appear on pages together.

- **See content from all spaces**: From both views it is easy to expand the list to include all labels content across your Confluence site.

Using labels to display content

Labels are very powerful when used in conjunction with macros to dynamically display content. Confluence comes with the following set of macros for labels:

- **Content by Label**: This lists pages tagged with one or more specific labels
- **Labels List**: This lists all labels of a space, grouped alphabetically
- **Navigation Map**: This creates a map of pages associated with a specified label
- **Popular Labels**: This generates a list or **heat map** of the most popular labels
- **Recently Used Labels**: This lists the most recently used labels in a predefined scope of spaces
- **Related Labels**: This lists labels used on other pages that have labels in common with the current page.

We will discuss the Content by Label macro as this is probably the most used macro of the set.

The Content by Label macro

The Content by Label macro will find and display a list of all pages, blog posts, and attachments in a space tagged with the specified labels. Imagine yourself with a space full of projects and customer information; with this macro you can easily create an overview of all customers provided you labeled them.

Using labels for reviews

We often use labels to indicate whether a page needs to be reviewed or is outdated. With the Content by Label macro we created an overview page showing those pages. When a page is reviewed, the label is removed and, therefore, doesn't show on the overview.

To add the Content by Label macro to a page, perform the following steps:

1. Open a page in the edit mode and place the cursor at the location where you want to add the macro.

2. Choose **Insert | Other Macros**.

3. Find and select the Content by Label macro.

4. Fill in the properties on the right-hand side of the screen; the label is required.

5. Click on **Insert** as shown in the following screenshot:

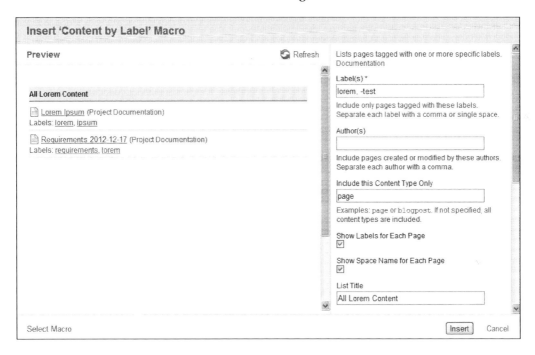

The following properties are available for the Content By Label macro:

Properties	Default	Description
Label(s)		The macro will only display content tagged with the labels specified here. You can specify multiple labels separated by a comma.
		Labels can be excluded by putting a minus (-) directly in front of the label. If you, for example, specify -lorum, you only get content that is *not* labeled with lorum.
Author(s)		This will filter by creator or last updated by.

Properties	Default	Description
Include this Content Type Only	All	Set the content type to **display**. The default will show **page**, **blogpost**, and **attachments** but you can specify one or more content types.
Show Labels for Each Page	Yes	This shows or hides the labels in the results.
Show Space Name for Each Page	Yes	This shows or hides the spaces in the results.
List Title		Here you can add a heading to the list.
Maximum Pages	15	This limits the maximum number of results to display. Note that the results are sorted first then limited.
Display Excerpts	No	Display the page excerpt (added by the excerpt macro).
Restrict to Spaces	@all	The macro will only display content in the specified spaces. You can specify multiple spaces separated by a comma. To exclude a space add a minus (-) in front of the space key. The special values include: • **@self**: The current space • **@personal**: All personal spaces • **@global**: All global spaces • **@favorite**: The spaces you have marked as favorite • **@all**: All spaces in your Confluence site
Operator	OR	This is the operator to apply when matching content against the specified labels: • **OR**: Displays content with any of the labels • **AND**: Displays content will all of the labels Labels prefix with a minus are not affected by this setting.
Sort By	Modified	This specifies how the results should be sorted.
Reverse Sort	no	Select **Reverse Sort** to change the sort from descending to ascending order. Use this parameter in conjunction with the **Sort By** parameter. **Reverse Sort** is ignored if **Sort By** is not specified.

Tracking content

When you come across some content that is relevant, you can choose to keep track of that content. Confluence offers features to allow you to quickly find your favorite pages again or get notified when a certain page or space content is modified.

We are going to take a closer look at how you can keep track of your favorite content without getting an information overload.

Watching content

You can "watch" a Confluence page, blog post, or space. Confluence will send you an e-mail notification whenever anyone updates the watched content.

You will receive a notification when:

- A page has been edited, unless the **Notify Watchers** checkbox is unchecked before saving the page
- Content is deleted
- Any changes are made to existing or new attachments
- A new comments is added
- A comment is updated or removed

Confluence will add you as watcher of any page or blog post that you create or edit. This behavior is called **autowatch** and is one of the settings you can change in your user profile.

Setting notification options

Before you start watching content, it is always a good idea to view your notification settings and change them if needed.

To edit your notification options, perform the following steps:

1. Click on your avatar in the top-right corner and choose **Settings** from the menu.
2. Select **Email** from the left-hand side menu.
3. Click on **Edit** and update the settings.

4. Click on **Submit** to save the changes.

Setting	Description	Frequency
Autowatch	The pages you create or edit will automatically be added to your watch list.	N/A
Subscribe to daily updates	This will allow you to received an e-mail report showing changes to content in all spaces for which you have permission to view. This does not include changes to attachments.	Daily
Subscribe to all blog posts	With this, you will receive a notification for changes to blogs in Confluence. This includes new blog posts.	Immediately
Subscribe to network	With this, you will receive a notification for changes made by users you follow.	Immediately
Subscribe to new follower notifications	With this, you will receive an e-mail message when anyone chooses to follow you.	Immediately
Notify on my actions	With this, you will receive a notification for your own changes.	N/A
Show changed content	Select this if you want to see the changes on the page in the notification.	N/A
Subscribe to recommended updates	With this, you will receive an update on the top content in the spaces you are allowed to view.	Daily (weekdays) or weekly.

Too many e-mails?

A common complaint is that Confluence sends too many e-mails. If this is the case, people tend to not read any e-mails anymore. You can cut down the number of e-mails by turning off the **Autowatch** and **Notify on my actions** features.

Also, be wary of what content you would like, or how much content you chose, to watch. Sometimes, the daily update is more than adequate to provide you with relevant information.

Watching a page or a blog post

To start watching a page or blog post, perform the following steps:

1. Go to the page or blog post.
2. Choose **Tools | Watch**.

You are now watching the page or blog post.

To stop watching a page or blog post:

1. Go to the page or blog post.
2. Choose **Tools | Stop Watching**.

Watching a space

When you start watching a space you will get notifications of updates to any content in the space, including new pages or blog posts.

To start watching a space:

1. Go to the space and choose **Pages** on the left sidebar.
2. Select **Watch this space** in the top-right corner.

To stop watching a space:

1. Go to the space and choose **Pages** on the left sidebar.
2. Select **Stop Watching this space** in the top-right corner.

In the case of a space, you can also choose to receive notifications only when a new blog post is added to the space. If you select this option, you will not receive any notifications of changes to or deletions of blog posts.

To start watching for new blog posts in a space:

1. Go to the space and choose **Blog** on the left sidebar.
2. Select **Watch this Blog** in the top-right corner.

 This option is only available if you are not watching the space.

To stop watching for new blog posts in a space:

1. Go to the space and choose **Blog** on the left sidebar.
2. Select **Stop Watching this Blog** in the top-right corner.

Managing your watches

All the pages or spaces you watch can be managed from a single view in your user profile. This view is especially useful if you want to stop watching many pages.

To manage your watches:

1. Click on your avatar in the top-right corner and choose **Watches**.
2. Click on **Stop Watching** next to a watch to turn it off.

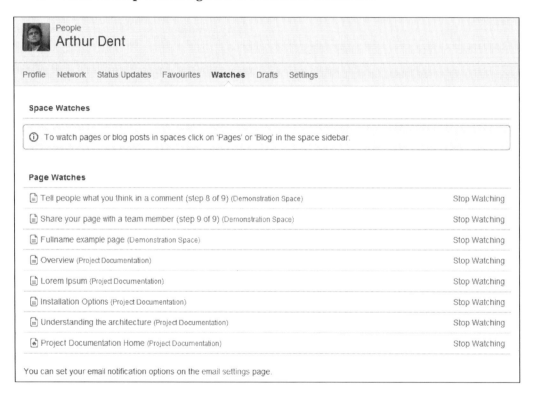

It is also possible to manage a particular watch directly from an e-mail notification you received. Depending on the content of the e-mail, the footer may vary, but in general you see one or more of the following links:

- **Stop watching page**: Click on this link to stop watching the page that triggered the notification

- **Stop watching space**: Click on this link to stop watching the space that triggered the notification

- **Stop following this user**: Click on this link to stop following the user whose update trigger the notification

- **Manage Notifications**: Click on this link to go directly to the e-mail settings page in your user profile

An example of the footer in a notification is shown in the following screenshot:

Favorites

The favorites feature can be thought of as a bookmark functionality, providing you with a way to quickly access specific pages or spaces you are interested in.

Adding favorites

To add a page as a favorite, perform the following steps:

1. Go to the page.
2. Choose **Tools | Favourite**. The menu item will change to **Remove Favourite**.

To add a space as a favorite, perform the following steps:

- Via the space directory:
    1. Choose **Spaces** from the top navigation.
    2. Tick the star icon next to each space to add the space as a favorite.

- Or, use the star icon next to a space on the dashboard.

To remove a page or space as favorite, repeat the preceding steps.

Viewing favorites

When you add pages or spaces as favorites, you can see them via your user profile or on the dashboard.

To view your favorites via your profile:

1. Click on your avatar in the top-right corner.
2. Choose **Favourites** from the drop-down menu.

To view your favorites via the dashboard:

- On the left-hand side of the dashboard you can see:
    ° Your favorite spaces, in the **Spaces** tab
    ° You most recent favorite pages, in the **Pages** tab

- On the **Favourite Spaces** tab on the right-hand side, you can see updated content in your favorite spaces.

Searching Confluence

While your Confluence installation is growing with content, it will become more difficult to find the information you are looking for using normal navigation. By now, you must have noticed the search box at the navigation bar of Confluence. This box is referred to as the **quick search**, or **quick navigation aid**, and that is the feature we are going to cover next.

Quick navigation aid

The quick navigation aid feature automatically offers you a drop-down list of pages, attachments, and user profiles, matched to the title of your search query. This list changes while you are typing your query. You can select one of the suggestions to directly browse to that item.

To use the quick navigation aid, perform the following steps:

1. Click on the **Search** box or use the keyboard shortcut /.
2. Start typing your query. Confluence will give you suggestions based on the title and your query.
3. Use the up and down arrows on your keyboard to navigate through the suggestions.
4. Press *Enter* to open the selected item.

5. If you don't find the item you are looking for, use the **Search for** link at the bottom to do a full site search. More about full searches will be discussed in the next section.

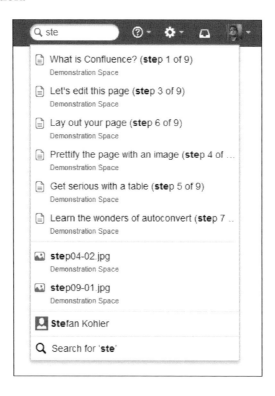

There are some things to know about the quick navigation aid:

- Confluence will truncate any titles that are too long to be displayed.
- Items are grouped by their content type. Confluence shows a maximum of six pages / blog posts, two attachments, three people, and two spaces. This way you can easily find the type you want.
- Items are ordered based on most recent updates.
- The matching part of the title is displayed in bold.
- A Confluence administrator can disable the quick navigation aid in the Confluence Administration Console.

Full and advanced search

A **full search** is a search in all contents in all spaces, global and personal, user profiles and attachments. Confluence will index the contents of your attachments too; the full search will therefore also search within your attachment's content.

To do a full search, perform the following steps:

1. Use the quick search to type in your query.
2. Press the *Enter* key. This means you will ignore any suggestions.
3. The search screen appears with the results, if any.
4. Click on an item's title to open the item.

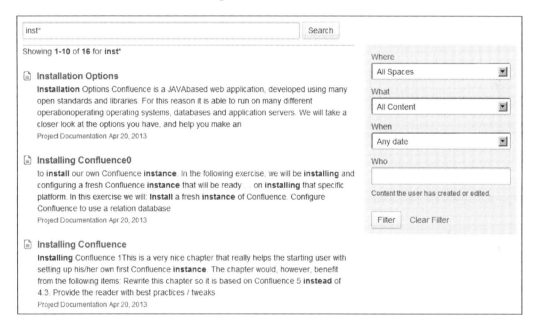

Each item will be represented by its title, a few lines of matching content, the containing space name, or the date the content was last updated. For attachments, there will be the size and a download link.

On the right-hand side of the screen, there are more options to filter your research; this is explained further on.

"Did you mean"

When you perform a full search, Confluence may offer you an alternative spelling of your search query. This alternative spelling will appear next to the words **Did you mean**. Click on the link to accept the suggestion. Some of the key features offered with this functionality are as follows:

- Confluence uses a bundled dictionary and words gathered from your own content. This means Confluence can make suggestions for your own jargon that may not appear in a standard dictionary.

- Confluence will favor words that appear more often in your content before words from the dictionary.

- Confluence may offer suggestions with incorrect spellings. This happens when the incorrect spelling occurs many times within your content. This is intentionally as the purpose of the "Did you mean" feature is to help find your content, not to correct your spelling.

- A Confluence administrator has to turn on the "Did you mean" index in the Administration Console.

Filtering results

The search screen, as shown on the previous page, appears when you do your first search. By default, Confluence will search all content in all spaces and attachments. You can filter this using the filter options on the right side of the screen.

Using the filter options, you can filter results based on the following categories:

- **Where**: This restricts your results to a particular space or a group of spaces (favorites, personal, or global)

- **What**: This restricts your results to a particular content type (pages, blog posts, comments, and so on)

- **When**: This restricts your results to the content modified within a given period of time (today, yesterday, last week, and so on)

- **Who**: This restricts your results to the content last modified by a particular user

Don't forget to click on the **Filter** button after specifying your filter. If you use more than one filter, Confluence will filter based on all those filters. Use the **Clear Filter** link to remove all filters and return the full result set.

Searching labels

You can also use the full search to search for labels. Use the `labelText:` prefix to search-specify for content with the specified label. The following are some examples how to use this prefix:

Searching for...	Returns content that...
`IpsumlabelText:lorem`	Contains the word "ipsum" or has the label "lorem"
`ipsum AND labelText:lorem`	Contains the word "ipsum" and has the label "lorem"
`labelText:ipsumlabelText:lorem`	Has the label "ipsum" or the label "lorem"
`labelText:ipsum AND labelText:lorem`	Has both labels "ipsum" and "lorem"

The `labelText:` prefix is an example of using search fields. Using search fields is a really powerful and advanced way of using the Apache Lucene search engine used in Confluence.

 Apache Lucene is a full-text search engine that Confluence uses for indexing all the content and providing the search functionalities discussed in this chapter.

There are more search fields available that can be used to find content in Confluence. They are as follows:

Search field	Description
`spaceKey`	You can search for content located in the space with the specified `spaceKey` field.
	For example, `spaceKey:doc`.
`creatorName`	You can search for content created by the user with the specified username.
	For example, `creatorName:arthur`.
`lastModifiers`	You can search for content where the last modifier is the user with the specified username.
	For example, `lastModifiers:ford`.
`macroName`	You can search for content where the given macro is used.
	For example, `macroName:table-plus*`.

Search field	Description
filename	You can search for attachments with the specified filename.
	For example, `filename:requirement*`.
created	You can search for content that is created within the range specified. The format is yyyymmdd.
	For example, `created:[20130524 TO 20130525]`.

More information on search fields is available online at `https://confluence.atlassian.com/display/DOC/Confluence+Search+Field`.

The search syntax

Confluence has a search syntax that will help you further refine your search queries. This search syntax is explained as follows:

Syntax	Example	Description
OR	lorem OR ipsum	You can search for content that contains one of the terms. Note that OR must be in capital letters.
AND	lorem AND ipsum	You can search for content that contains both terms. Note that AND must be in capital letters.
NOT	lorem NOT ipsum	In this example, you can search for content that contains lorem but not ipsum. Note that NOT must be in capital letters.
-	lorem -ipsum	This is similar to the NOT search.
( )	(lorem OR ipsum) AND dolor	In this example, the search *must* contain dolor but *can* contain either lorem or ipsum.
title:	title:lorem	In this example, you can search for content with lorem in the title.
?	l?rem	In this example, you can search for lorem or larem.
*	lo*	In this example, you can search for content with words starting with lo.
	i*m	In this example, you can search for ipsum or idem.
~n	"lorem ipsum"~1	The two words specified must be within a certain number of words of each other.

Syntax	Example	Description
[ ]	[ipsum TO lorem]	This searches for words that fall alphabetically within the specified range.
		Note that you can't use AND inside this statement and TO must be in capital letters.
~	octogan~	This searches for words spelled similarly. It is useful when you are not sure about the spelling. In this example, ~ will correctly return octagon.
macroName:	macroName:Panel	This searches for content where the macro "Panel" is being used.

Confluence will ignore common words such as "and" or "the". This is based on the default list of stop words used by Lucene.

Summary

In this chapter we have learned how we can better organize and restructure our spaces as our Confluence site starts to grow. We have also seen that, with the use of labels, content is easier to find and overviews are easily created. Labels, watches, and favorites can help us keeping track of interesting content to the point where we can receive notifications on new additions or changes to existing content.

The search engine behind Confluence is really powerful, yet there is an easy way of using it via the quick navigation aid. For power users, there is also an advanced search available. Confluence also indexes our attachments, so that we can search those documents and spreadsheets as well.

In the next chapter we will take a look at how to use Confluence in our day-to-day business, and learn how to collaborate and share information with colleagues using Confluence.

5
Collaborating in Confluence

By now, we have learned how to create engaging content and how we can track interesting content ourselves. Now, we will take a look at the Confluence workbox and how we can use Confluence features in our day-to-day job.

We will get familiar with sharing interesting content, tasks, and likes directly in your Confluence, and learn how to respond quickly without switching context. We will also learn how to engage other users with shares, likes, and mentions.

After this chapter, we will be able to:

- Share content and involve other people
- Manage in-app notifications
- Work with personal tasks
- Track content while you're on the road

Collaborating with other people

Confluence is a great tool for collaboration, but how do you use Confluence to collaborate with others? Imagine that you just wrote a great post, and you want somebody to review it before publishing it, or you just had a meeting and want some people to take actions based on that meeting.

The most important thing for collaboration is the availability of content, and in Confluence all the content is, by default, available for all the users. The next thing is to get people involved, and Confluence offers us several methods for doing exactly that.

Mentions

Mentions are a great way of getting people to participate in building useful and relevant content. You can mention a person in a special way that will trigger Confluence to send that person a notification. This is called an **@mention**. The @mention notifications work on pages, blog posts, and comments.

Confluence will send an e-mail message to users letting them know that they have been mentioned in that page. This message is sent when you save the page but only if the mentioned person has view permissions for that page.

Perform the following steps using autocomplete to mention someone:

1. Open a page in the edit mode and place your cursor at the location where you want to add a mention.
2. Type @ and then the first few characters of the user's full name.
3. Choose the user's name from the list of suggestions.

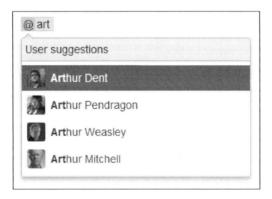

It is also possible to add a mention via the editor toolbar, as follows:

1. Open a page in the edit mode and place your cursor at the location where you want to add a mention.
2. Choose **Insert | User mention**. Confluence will add an @ sign to the page.
3. Start typing the person's full name.
4. Choose the user's name from the list.

Note that mentions work on a user's full name and not on usernames. It is currently not possible to mention groups.

The @mention notifications are a great way of involving people in your conversation or content. For example, if you want **Arthur Dent** to take a look at some requirement, just mention him in a comment to get him involved. Don't try to spam people you want to collaborate with; use the mentions sparingly. Another way to get people involved is by sharing your content.

Share content

Confluence provides a number of ways for you to share content with other users. The previously discussed Mentions are one of them, but you can also share a page link directly to one or more users, including a brief note about what you expect them to do with the link.

Sharing content via the **Share** button is only available if a Confluence administrator has configured a mail server.

To e-mail a link using the **Share** button, perform the following steps:

1. Go to the page or blog post you want to share.
2. Click on **Share** at the top right. Enter the name or username of a Confluence user or use a valid e-mail address. As you start typing, a suggestion list will appear.
3. Select the appropriate user or e-mail address from the list. You can add multiple recipients and combine both usernames and e-mail addresses.
4. Enter an optional message into the **Note** box.
5. Click on **Share** to send the link via e-mail.

Like

When you are reading a good blog post or page on Confluence, you can let other users know this by liking a page. Confluence has a like button on every page, blog post, and comment.

Likes are also being used for populating the **Popular Content** tab on the dashboard and the **Recommended Updates** e-mail.

Click on the **Like** button to let people know you agreed with or enjoyed the content or comment. Your name will be added to the list of other people who already liked the same content. Clicking on the **Unlike** button will remove you from the list.

When you like a page, blog post, or comment:

- The author of the content receives a notification
- People in your network receive a notification, unless they already know of the content, meaning:
  - Somebody else in their network already liked the content
  - The user himself already liked the content
  - The user already commented on the content or replied to a comment
- If enough people like the content, it will appear on the **Popular Content** tab on the dashboard
- If enough people like the content, it will be included in the **Recommended Updates** e-mail

The **Like** functionality is provided by a plugin called **Confluence Like Plugin** and can be disabled in the **Administration Console | Manage Add-ons**. This will disable the functionality on a site-wide basis. It isn't possible to disable on a space or page basis. You can find more information on managing add-ons in *Chapter 9, General Administration*.

Status updates

Status updates are short messages broadcasted to the different activity streams in Confluence. Such a short message could include:

- A description about what you are working on
- An interesting link or fact you want to share
- A question you may want to be answered quickly

The history of your status updates is available in a **Status updates** view, while the current status message is shown on your profile and profile hover.

Updating your status

To update your status:

1. Make sure you are logged in to Confluence.

2. Click on your avatar in the top-right corner and choose **Update Status...** from the drop-down menu.

3. Enter a short message (max 140 characters) that describes your current status or the content you want to share.

4. Click on **Update** to publish your new status.

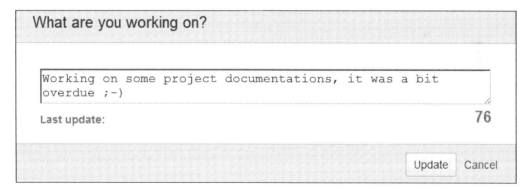

Managing status updates

Once you have updated your status, you can easily view, clear, or remove them if you have made a mistake. Editing a status update is not possible.

To view your status updates, perform the following steps:

1. Click on your avatar at the top-right corner.
2. Select **Status Updates** from the drop-down menu.

It is also possible to view another user's status by going to their profile.

To clear your current status, perform the following steps:

1. Go to the **Status Updates** view in your user profile.
2. Click on **Clear** below the top status update.

Clearing your status isn't the same as deleting it. If you clear your status, it doesn't show in your profile or profile hover, but it will still be visible on the **Status Updates** view.

To delete a status update, perform the following steps:

1. Go to the **Status Updates** view in your user profile.
2. Click on **Delete** below the status update.

Displaying status updates

Normally, status updates are only displayed on a user profile or in the recently updated content on the dashboard. A great way to make more use of status updates is to use the recently-updated macro to display the updates on a page.

To insert status updates in a page:

1. Open a page in the edit mode or create a new page.
2. Use the shortcut { (*Shift* + [) or **Insert** | **Other Macros** to select the recently Updated macro.
3. Open the macro's property panel by clicking on the macro container and selecting **Edit**.

4. In order to display only status updates, fill in the following properties:
    ◦ **Space(s)**: @all
    ◦ **Include these Content Types Only**: Status
    ◦ **Show User Profile Pictures**: Checked

5. Click on **Save** and save the page.

You can also place the macro inside a panel to make it stand out a bit from the other content. This is shown in the following screenshot:

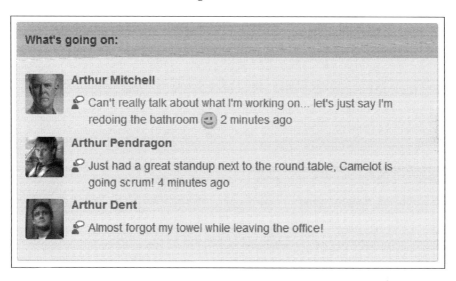

Working with notifications

One of the features of the Confluence workbox is getting all your notifications in one single location. The aim of the Workbox is to alleviate time-waste by context switching between e-mail, Confluence, and other tools. The workbox displays all notifications collected from Confluence page watches, shares, mentions, and tasks. If Confluence is linked to JIRA, Atlassian's issue tracking system, you will also see JIRA notifications in your workbox. The workbox also displays personal tasks, which are explained in the next section.

Managing your notifications

From the workbox you can use the inline actions to reply to comments, or like and watch comments and pages. Follow the link in a notification to open the related content.

You can't delete notifications yourself. Notifications that you have already read are automatically deleted after two weeks and unread notifications after four weeks.

 The workbox is not available in clustered Confluence environments. The feature will detect that a Confluence installation is running in clustered mode and not display the workbox.

To manage your notifications, perform the following steps:

1. Select the workbox icon in the Confluence navigation bar.

    1. You can also use the keyboard shortcut: Type g then n.

    2. The icon will also show the number of unread notifications.

2. Choose the notifications icon.

3. Select a notification from the list to see the notification details. Within the details you can do the following:

    1. Open the related page, blog post, or comment. The page will open in a new tab in your browser.

    2. **Like** or **Unlike** the content or comment.

    3. **Watch** or **Stop Watching** the relevant content to receive, or stop receiving notifications.

    4. **Comment** or **Reply** to respond to a comment directly from the workbox.

    5. Choose the add task icon to create a task based upon the notification.

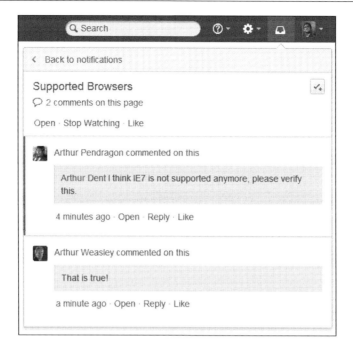

Included notifications

The workbox displays a notification when somebody performs one of the following actions in Confluence:

- Shares a page or blog post with you
- Comments on a page or blog post you are watching
- Mentions you in a page, blog post, or comment
- Likes a page or blog post that you are watching or created
- Assigns you a task by mentioning you in a tasklist

Notifications triggered, because you are watching a space, will *not* be shown in the workbox.

If your Confluence installation is linked to JIRA, you will also see the following notifications from JIRA in your workbox:

- Comments on issues you are watching

- Mentions in issues

- Shares of issues, filters, and searches

Configuring workbox notifications

The Confluence workbox is enabled by default; as a Confluence administrator you can disable it or change the configuration. A couple of configuration scenarios are possible:

- Your Confluence installation provides in-app notifications and displays them in its own workbox. There are two possibilities in this scenario:

    ° This Confluence installation is the only installation involved.

    ° Or, this Confluence installation displays its own notifications and also displays notifications from JIRA and/or another Confluence installation.

- Your Confluence installation sends in-app notifications to another Confluence installation.

- In-app notifications are completely disabled and unavailable.

The Confluence workbox includes both notifications and tasks, and when workbox notifications are enabled so are personal tasks. If you disable the notifications, personal tasks won't be available either.

Enabling workbox notifications

To use notifications and tasks, the Confluence workbox has to be enabled.

To enable the Confluence workbox, perform the following steps:

1. Browse to the Administration Console (**Administration | Confluence Admin**).

2. Select **In-app Notifications** from the left-hand side menu.

3. Select **displays in-app notifications** and click on **Save** to save the form. The workbox icon will now appear at the top-right of the navigation bar.

In-app Notifications

Configure how Confluence sends or receives notifications in-app (learn more). Select one of the options below.

This Confluence server:

⦿ displays in-app notifications

In-app notifications are displayed for this Confluence instance.

Active polling interval

| 30 | seconds

Time to wait before checking for new notifications on the page the user is currently viewing.

Inactive polling interval

| 300 | seconds

Time to wait before checking for new notifications when the user isn't focused on a page.

○ does not provide in-app notifications

In-app notifications are disabled on this server.

Save

- Active polling interval: This is the number of seconds that Confluence will wait before checking for new notifications relevant to the page that the user is currently viewing.

- Inactive polling interval: This is the number of seconds that Confluence will wait before checking for new notifications relevant to all pages currently not in focus. This can also be on other servers if configured.

Including notifications from JIRA

The Confluence workbox can include notifications from your JIRA issue tracker but this requires some extra setup.

To include notifications from JIRA, perform the following steps:

1. Make sure JIRA and Confluence are connected via application links.
   1. Browse to the Administration Console (**Administration | Confluence Admin**).
   2. Select **Application Links** from the left-hand side menu.
   3. Select **Add Application Link** and follow the wizard to create a new application link. (There is more about application links in *Chapter 8, Advanced Confluence*.)
   4. If your JIRA server is linked to multiple Confluence servers, make sure the primary application link is to the Confluence server that will display the in-app notifications.
2. Select **In-app Notifications** from the left-hand side menu from the Administration Console.
3. Select **display in-app notifications from other servers**.
   - Your JIRA server will appear in the list of linked applications.
   - Your users will see JIRA notifications in the Confluence workbox.

Note that this feature is only available for JIRA 5.2 or later. JIRA will send its notifications only to the Confluence server that is configured as the primary application link.

Sending notifications to another Confluence server

Confluence can send and receive notifications to or from another Confluence server. To demonstrate how to set this up, let's assume we have two Confluence servers ConfSend and ConfReceive, where ConfSend will send its notifications to ConfRecieve.

To send notifications to another Confluence server, perform the following steps:

1. Connect both Confluence installations via applications links.
   In ConfReceive:
   1. Browse to the Administration Console (**Administration | Confluence Admin**).
   2. Select **Application links** from the left-hand side menu.

     3. Set up an Application link as described in the *Including notifications from JIRA* section.

2. Configure `ConfReceive` to display in-app notifications.

     1. Select **In-app Notifications** from the left-hand side menu of the Administration Console.

     2. Select **displays in-app notifications from other servers**.

3. Configure the notification settings in `ConfSend`.

     1. Select **In-app Notifications** from the left-hand side menu of the Administration Console.

     2. Select **Sends in-app notifications to another server**.

     3. Select the Confluence installation to send the notifications to.

Working with tasks

Another important part of the Confluence workbox is tasks. With personal tasks, you create your own to-do list directly in Confluence, which is very useful for tasks related to content or comments in Confluence.

There are a couple of ways you and other people can assign a task to you:

- You can add a personal task via the workbox
- You can add a task via a notification in your workbox; this is useful if you don't want to forget something
- Someone can assign you a task from a tasklist on a Confluence page
- Other plugins could create tasks for you

Working with personal tasks

You can create your own personal tasks in Confluence using the workbox interface.

To create a new task, perform the following steps:

1. Open the workbox by selecting the workbox icon in the Confluence header.
2. Select the personal task icon.
3. Type the task summary in the textbox and click on **Add task** to add a personal task.

4. To add more details to the task, click on the newly created task. Enter any details and notes in the note textbox.

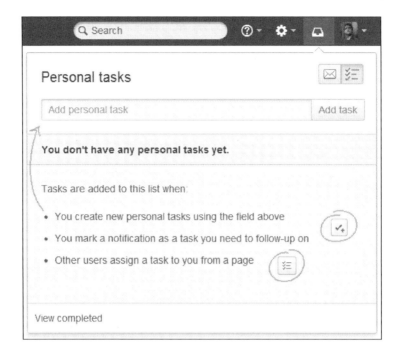

To change task priority, perform the following steps:

1. Open the workbox by selecting the workbox icon in the Confluence header.
2. Drag-and-drop the tasks to change their order. Click on a task and while holding down your mouse button, drag the task to its new position. Release the mouse button to save the change.

To complete a task, perform the following steps:

1. Open the workbox by selecting the workbox icon in the Confluence header.
2. Check the checkbox next to the task to complete it.
3. Completed tasks are hidden and can be displayed with the link at the bottom of the workbox called **View Completed**.

Working with tasklists

Tasklists can be placed on pages and are very useful to assign and manage tasks in a team. Tasklists will place the assigned tasks in the assignee's workbox and the progress is kept in sync, meaning completing a task in your workbox will also complete the task in the tasklist.

> Tasklists are very useful in meeting minutes where you want to assign and keep a track of the actions from that meeting.
>
> You can also use tasklists to track all the tasks needed when a new employee starts, for example user accounts, laptop, and internet access.

To add a task list on a page, perform the following steps:

1. Open a page in the edit mode.

2. From the editor toolbar, choose the tasklist icon or use the keyboard shortcut *[+]*.

3. Type the description of the task.

4. If you want to assign the task to someone, type @ and the person's full name in the task description (@mentions are explained elsewhere in this chapter.) The assignee will receive a notification and the task will appear in their personal tasklist. You can also mention yourself to assign a task to your own tasklist.

5. To finish the tasklist, press *Enter* twice.

Managing tasks on a page

Tasks can be marked as completed or incomplete when you, or others, are viewing the page. Updated tasks and their statuses will be synchronized with the workbox too.

- To be able to update a tasklist in the view mode:
    - You will need edit permissions
    - You need the Create page permission in the space

Confluence on your mobile device

With a collaboration tool like Confluence, it is important that you can access your information and keep up with discussions even when you are on the road. Confluence comes with a built-in mobile interface, which is easy to use on recent mobile devices with a web browser.

On your phone or other supported mobile devices, it is possible to:

- View the Confluence dashboard, pages, blog posts, and user profiles
- Add comments to a page or blog post
- Like content such as pages, blog posts, or comments
- Manage your personal tasks and notifications

With the mobile interface it is not possible to add or edit pages or blog posts, or edit the existing comments. Navigation in the mobile interface is also different as compared to navigation using a desktop. The space and tree view is not available in the mobile interface and navigation is done by searching the content using the Confluence search.

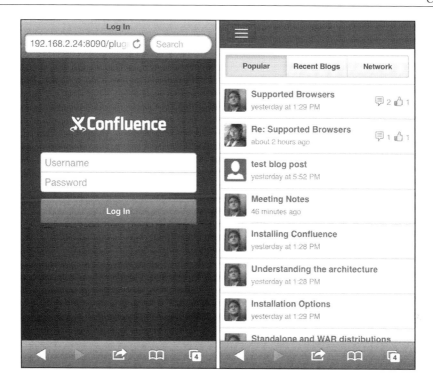

Viewing

The first thing you will see after logging in via the mobile interface is the dashboard, although not all updates are shown. The content that is available on the dashboard of the mobile interface is:

- Popular content – based upon comments and likes
- Recent blogs – recent blog posts in the space you can access
- Network – updates by people in your network

Tapping on the links will bring you to the full content of the page, blog post, or comment. While viewing the full content of a page or blog post you can:

- View the content. Tap on any link to move to another page within Confluence.

- Like or unlike a page, blog post, or comment.

- Add a comment. The mobile interface only supports plain text comments.

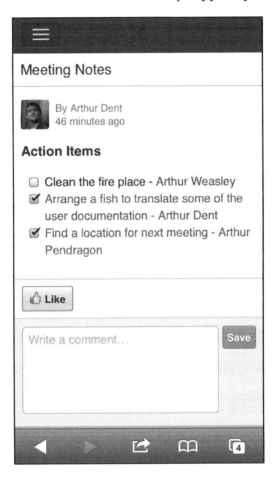

As suggested in the previous screenshot, it is possible to change the status of a task using the mobile interface.

User profiles

With the mobile interface you can search for users and then use your mobile to call, text, or e-mail that user directly, provided the user has entered their details in Confluence.

Company address book

With Confluence's mobile interface you can effortlessly create a company address book. Just make sure every employee keeps their details up-to-date.

Searching

Tap on the menu icon in the top-left corner to open the menu panel. Start typing the page title or person's name in the Search box. The search engine of the mobile interface is intended to be fast and offers only matches based upon page titles. For a full search, you have to switch to the desktop mode. Tap on the results to go to the full content.

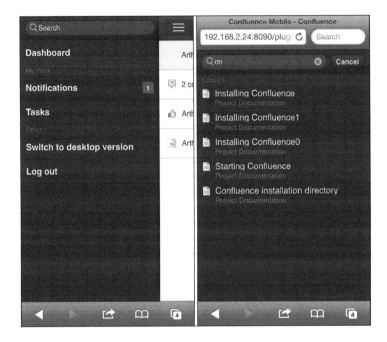

Notifications and tasks

You can view and respond to your notification directly from your mobile phone. Tap the menu icon to open the menu on the left. Choose **Notifications**, then tap on a notification to see its details. You can reply, like, or watch via the actions. Tap **Open** to open the page or blog post.

Choose **Tasks** to view and manage your personal tasks. Tap the plus sign (+) to add a new task. Tap on a task to see its details. Using your mobile you can add notes, complete a task, or browse to the related page.

Notes about the mobile interface

The mobile interface is a great way to keep up-to-date while you are not behind your normal desktop. However, not all features that the desktop version of Confluence offers can be transferred to a mobile interface.

- Some macros may not work.

  Confluence macros are not yet fully supported in the mobile interface. If you are viewing content with an unsupported macro, you will see a message inviting you to switch to the desktop version of the page.

- Swap between desktop and mobile interface.

  Using the left menu panel in your mobile interface, you can switch to the desktop version of Confluence. When you watch the desktop version on your mobile device, you will also see a link for switching back to the mobile interface.

- The mobile interface can be disabled.

  If you are running a public website on Confluence, you might want to turn off the mobile interface to preserve the look and feel. The mobile interface has a plugin called Confluence Mobile Plugin that can be disabled via the Administration Console.

Summary

We have learned about the Confluence workbox and its ability to work with in-app notifications and personal tasks. Both can be used to share content or get more people involved in your workflow, actions, and content.

Tasks are a great way to keep track of things to do after a meeting or when preparing for a new release. With the tasklist we can assign tasks to other people and track those tasks.

With the mobile interface, you can take Confluence with you while you are on the road (provided you have an Internet connection). The mobile interface can be used to search information, comments on pages, or blog posts, and manage your notifications and tasks. Searching for other users with the mobile interface allows you to call or message people directly from your mobile device.

With the ability to create, share, and track content within Confluence, it's time to dive into another aspect of Confluence, **content security**. Being able to control who can view or edit your content is something we will learn in the next chapter.

6
Securing Your Content

We now know how to create rich and engaging content and how to involve our colleagues in the content creating process. We have been using Confluence for a while now and more and more information has become available.

In this chapter we will learn how to keep our private content private. We will look at the different ways of securing content, but we will also take a look at how we can secure a complete Confluence installation.

The topics we will discuss in this chapter are as follows:

- Global permissions
- Space permissions and page restrictions
- Secure administrator sessions
- Some security best practices

Accessing the content

So far, all content we have created can be viewed and edited by anyone who has access to Confluence, and even without logging in if you're enabled an anonymous login. When your company's information and documentation is in Confluence, allowing anyone to view or edit them might not be the best security setting.

Confluence gives you all the tools to make your installation as open or as closed as you would like it to be. While we go over the options and how to enable them, please keep the following points in mind:

- Confluence is a tool for communication and collaboration; allowing your users to view and edit as much content as possible. This will help you getting the most out of the transparent knowledge exchange in your organization.

  So, restrict a space or page only if you have a good reason for doing so.

- Confluence keeps track of every change made to a page or blog post. This makes it easy to see who changed what and, if required, revert the content to a previously saved state.

In a situation where everybody works on documents on their own desktop, people aren't used to getting feedback and input. This can be a cultural shift that a company has to go through while starting to work with Confluence. Before restricting access to a space, page, or blog post, ask yourself, "Why should this document be private and what is the harm in making it more visible within my organization?"

Global permissions

Global permissions are site-wide permissions and can be assigned only by system administrators and Confluence administrators. Global permissions can be assigned to groups, individual users, and anonymous users.

Before we go into how to change the different global permissions, it's good to know the different administrator roles:

- **Super user**: Any user that belongs to the confluence-administrators group has full administrative access to Confluence. A super user can also view and edit all content even if it is restricted by permissions.

- **System Administrator**: Users with the System Administrator global permission have full administrative access to Confluence but cannot view or edit the content they don't have permissions to.

- **Confluence Administrator**: Users with the Confluence Administrator global permission have restricted access to the Confluence administrative functions. Confluence administrators cannot, for example, install new add-ons. More detail on which functions are restricted are in the *Comparing the administration roles* section.

The Confluence administrator permission and the confluence-administrators group are not related.

Although the name suggests they are related, they are not. Granting a user or group the Confluence Administrator permission is not the same as adding the user to the confluence-administrators group.

How the different roles are related to each other is illustrated in the following diagram:

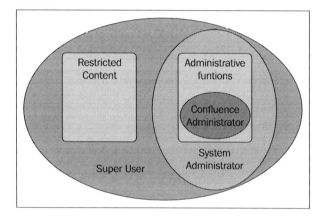

As a user within the confluence-administrators group is allowed to view and edit all content, it is recommended to use a different user account for day-to-day work. With the System Administrator permission, all administrative functions can be performed but your administrators aren't allowed to view all content.

A super user account would only be needed if restricted content can't be accessed by anyone anymore. The super user can still access the content and restore the restrictions.

Updating global permissions

If you are a Confluence administrator, you can add users and groups to the global permissions to determine their permissions.

To view the global permissions:

1. Browse to the Administration Console (**Administration | Confluence Admin**).

2. Choose **Global Permissions** in the left-hand side menu. The next screen would be as shown in the following screenshot:

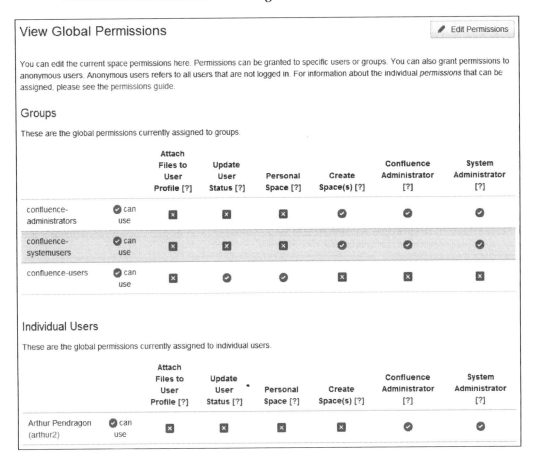

To add permissions for a group, perform the following steps:

1. Select **Edit Permissions**; this will show the **Edit Global Permissions** screen.

2. Type the group name in the **Grant browse permission to** box in the groups section. You can also search for the group name.

3. Click on **Add**.

4. The group will be added to the list and you can edit the permissions.

5. When all the relevant checkboxes are checked, click on the **Save All** button at the bottom of the page.

To add permissions for a user, perform the following steps:

 Before adding permissions to users, first consider the management overhead. Adding them to a group and assigning permissions to that group will result in less maintenance in the long run.

1. Select **Edit Permissions**; this will show the **Edit Global Permissions** screen.

2. Type the username in the **Grant browse permission to** box in the **Individual Users** section. You can also search for the username.

3. Click on **Add**. The user will then be added to the list and you can edit its permissions.

To add or edit the permissions of groups and users, perform the following steps:

1. Select or clear the checkbox under the relevant permissions for the relevant user or group. A selected box indicates that the permission is granted.

2. To allow anonymous access to your Confluence installation, select the **Use Confluence** option in the **Anonymous Access** section.

3. Choose **Save All** to save your changes.

Edit Global Permissions

You can edit the current space permissions here. Permissions can be granted to specific users or groups. You can also grant permissions to anonymous users. Anonymous users refers to all users that are not logged in. For information about the individual *permissions* that can be assigned, please see the permissions guide.

Groups

These are the global permissions currently assigned to groups.

		Attach Files to User Profile [?]	Update User Status [?]	Personal Space [?]	Create Space(s) [?]	Confluence Administrator [?]	System Administrator [?]
confluence-administrators	☑ can use	☐	☐	☐	☑	☑	☑
confluence-users	☑ can use	☐	☑	☑	☐	☐	☐

Grant browse permission to [_____] 🔍 Add

Individual Users

These are the global permissions currently assigned to individual users.

		Attach Files to User Profile [?]	Update User Status [?]	Personal Space [?]	Create Space(s) [?]	Confluence Administrator [?]	System Administrator [?]
Arthur Pendragon (arthur2)	☑ can use	☐	☐	☐	☐	☑	☑

Grant browse permission to [_____] 🔍 Add

Anonymous Access

When a user is using Confluence while not logged in, they are using it anonymously.
For example: Enabling anonymous 'USE' permission, allows non-logged-in users to browse pages and spaces in Confluence.

	Use Confluence [?]	View User Profiles [?]
Anonymous	☐ can use	☐

Save all   Cancel

Overview of the global permissions

In the previous steps we learned how to manage the different global permissions. In the following table those different global permissions are explained. These permissions are also displayed in the previous screenshot.

Permission	Description
can use	This allows a user to access your Confluence site.
	Users with this permission count towards the number of users on your license.
Attach Files to User Profile	This permission is no longer relevant since the introduction of personal spaces, and can be ignored.
Update User Status	This allows users to update their status messages.
Personal Space	This allows users to create and maintain a personal space.
Create Space(s)	This permission allows users to create new spaces within Confluence. When a space is created, the creator is automatically the Space admin for that space.
Confluence Administrator	This permission allows users to access the Administration Console that controls the site-wide administration. Users with this permission can perform a *subset of all* administrative functions.
System Administrator	This permission allows users to access the Administration Console that controls the site-wide administration. Users with this permission can perform *all* administrative functions.

Comparing the administration roles

We have already learned that a user with System Administrator permission is allowed to perform all administrative functions within Confluence. A user with Confluence Administrator permission is only allowed to administrate just a subset of those functions.

You can give the Confluence Administrator permission to users who should be able to perform most administrative functions, but should not be able to perform functions that can compromise the security of the Confluence system.

The following functions are granted to the System Administrator permission but excluded from the Confluence Administrator permission to ensure your Confluence instance integrity and security.

- General configuration – only the following options are excluded:
    - Change the server base URL
    - Enable/disable remote API
    - Enable/disable compress HTTP response
    - Change connection timeouts

- Backup administration
- External gadgets
- Mail servers
- User macros
- In-App notifications
- Attachment storage
- PDF export
- Office connector
- Add-ons – only the following options are excluded:
  - Upgrade add-ons
  - Install new add-ons
  - Confluence upgrade check

- Security configuration – only the following options are excluded:
  - External user management
  - Append wildcards to user and group searches.
  - Enable custom stylesheets for spaces.
  - Show system information on the 500 page.
  - Maximum RSS items
  - RSS timeout
  - XSRF protection
  - Anti XSS mode

- Change the global stylesheet
- Add custom HTML
- Backup and restore
- Mail queue
- Cache statistics
- Scheduled jobs
- Logging and profiling
- Atlassian support tools

Notes on global permissions

Some things to keep in mind while working with global permissions are that users with:

- The Confluence Administrators permission are able to access the global permissions page and change the permissions, excluding permissions for the confluence-administrators group

- The Confluence Administrators permission cannot grant themselves the System Administrator permission

- The Confluence Administrators permission cannot add themselves to the confluence-administrators group and become super users

- The System Administrators permission can change the permissions of the confluence-administrators group on the global permissions page

- The System Administrators permission are able to add themselves to the confluence-administrators group and become super users

Space permissions

Every space has its own set of permissions. These permissions determine the access to the space for specific users and groups. In order to assign these permissions, a user must be space administrator, that is, they should have the Admin permissions for that space.

Overview of the permissions

The following is the list of different permissions you can set on a space level:

Permission	Description
View	The user can view this space's content. This includes pages and blog posts. Without this permission the user cannot access the space at all.
Pages – Add	The user can add and edit pages in this space.
Pages – Restrict	The user is allowed to apply page-level restrictions.
Pages – Remove	The user is allowed to remove pages in this space.
Blog – Add	The user is allowed to create and edit blog posts.
Blog – Remove	The user is allowed to remove blog posts in this space.
Comments – Add	The user is allowed to make comments in this space.
Comments – Remove	The user is allowed to remove any comments in this space.
Attachments – Add	The user is allowed to add attachments to this space.

Permission	Description
Attachments – Remove	The user is allowed to remove any attachments in this space.
Mail – Remove	The user is allowed to delete mail items.
Space – Export	The user is allowed to export content from this space.
Space - Admin	The user has administrative permissions over this space.

If, by mistake, all administrative access to a space is removed, nobody has access to administer the space anymore. This could, for example, happen if somebody who was a space administrator leaves the company or a group with Space Administrator permissions is removed from Confluence. In such a case, somebody from the confluence-administrators group needs to help you to fix the permissions.

Managing space permissions

Permissions can be granted to groups or to individual users. You need to be a space administrator to assign space permissions. A Confluence administrator can also set the default permissions that will be applied when a space is created; this is explained in the following section.

To access the space permissions, you will need to perform the following steps:

1. Go to the space and choose **Space tools** on the left sidebar.
2. Select **Permissions** followed by **Permissions**.

Note that the permissions menu is only displayed if you are a space administrator or super user.

On the space permission screen you will notice the following three sections:

- **Groups**: A list of the groups that already have permission to access the space
- **Individual Users**: A list of users that already have permission to access the space
- **Anonymous Access**: Permissions that are granted to this space for anonymous users

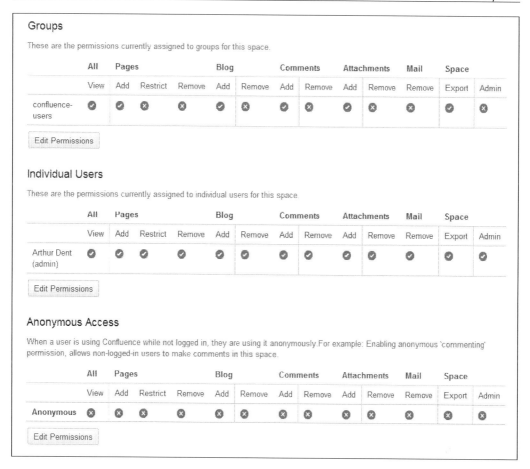

To assign permissions to groups, perform the following steps:

1. Click on the **Edit Permissions** button below the group section.

2. To assign a permission, check the relevant checkbox.

3. To remove a permission, uncheck the checkbox below the relevant permission.

4. To add a new group to the list, type the group name in the textbox in the group section and click on **Add**. You can also search for groups using the magnify icon next to the textbox.

For bulk actions:

Click on the cogwheel in the actions column.

Choose **Select All** or **Deselect All** to perform the bulk action.

5. Click on **Save All** to apply the changes.

To assign permissions to users:

1. Click on the **Edit Permissions** button below the **Individual User** section.
2. To assign a permission, check the relevant checkbox.
3. To remove a permission, uncheck the checkbox below the relevant permission.
4. To add a new user to the list, type the username in the textbox in the **Individual User** section and click on **Add**. You can also search for users by using the magnify icon next to the textbox.

For bulk actions:

Click the cogwheel in the actions column.

Choose **Select All** or **Deselect All** to perform the bulk action.

5. Click on **Save All** to apply the changes.

To assign permissions to anonymous users:

1. Click on the **Edit Permissions** button below the **Anonymous User** section.
2. To assign a permission, check the relevant checkbox.
3. To remove a permission, uncheck the checkbox below the relevant permission.
4. Click on **Save all** to apply the changes.

Anonymous users can't be granted space administration rights or the permission to restrict pages.

Setting default space permissions

Confluence administrators can set the default permissions that will be applied to every new space that is created. The default permissions are only configurable for groups, not for individual or anonymous users.

To set the default space permissions:

1. Browse to the Administration Console (**Administration | Confluence Admin**).

2. Choose **Space Permissions** in the left-hand menu.

3. Choose **Edit Permissions**.

4. Add groups and change permissions as described in how to assign permissions to groups in the previous section.

Page restrictions

Page restrictions are the lowest tier where you are able to control access to your content. With page restrictions you can control who can view or edit individual pages.

Page restriction hierarchy

Before we get to how to set and manage page restrictions, it good to know how Confluence handles permissions and restrictions. Permissions and page restrictions work in a hierarchical manner. This means that a user who can access and modify global permissions can define which users can access and modify space permissions. Space administrators can then define which users have access to create and modify pages. These users can then apply viewing and editing restrictions to a page. Child pages inherit the viewing and editing restrictions from their parent.

If you translate this into a diagram, it will look something like this:

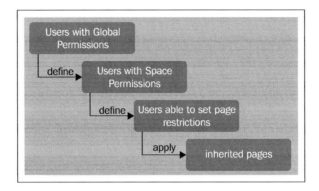

Inheritance

I already mentioned that child pages inherit the view restrictions set on the parent page. This is also true for child pages of those child pages and so on. If a view restriction is set to a page that already has inherited restrictions from its parent, users must satisfy both restrictions in order to see that page.

Edit restrictions are not inherited from the parent page, only from the space. Edit restrictions have to be reapplied to child pages.

Managing page restrictions

We will first talk about viewing page restrictions.

When you are viewing a page with page restrictions applied to it, you will notice a small padlock icon in the byline of the page, directly below the page title. If you click on that icon, the page restrictions dialog will appear, displaying the full details on the page restrictions.

When you are editing a page, you will notice a restrictions button at the bottom of the screen. Clicking on this button will also display the page restrictions dialog.

Next we will take a look at setting page restrictions. In order to set page restrictions, perform the following steps:

1. Browse to the relevant page.
2. Choose **Tools | Restrictions** to open the **Page Restrictions** dialog.
3. Select the restriction option you want to set (view or edit).

4. Choose the users and groups you want to be able to view or edit the page.

   ◦ To include yourself, click on **Me**.

   ◦ To select a particular user or group, type the user's username or the group name into the textbox. Click on **Restrict** to allow that user or group to view or edit the page.

   ◦ To search for a user or group click on the **Person...** or **Group...** button.

5. Click on **Save** to apply the new restrictions, as shown in the following screenshot:

To remove page restrictions, perform the following steps:

1. Open the **Page Restrictions** dialog by using the padlock icon or select **Tools | Restrictions**.

2. Click on the **Remove restriction** link next to a user or group to remove them from the restriction. Hereby, you will disallow them to view or edit the page, unless there are no restrictions.

3. Click on **Save**.

Next we will look at viewing restricted pages. As a space administrator you can view all pages that are restricted. From within this view, it is also possible to remove page restrictions. For example, you may need to do this when there is nobody who can access a certain page anymore.

1. Go to the space and choose **Space Tools** on the left sidebar.

2. Select **Permissions** followed by **Restricted Pages**.

 Note that the permissions menu is only displayed if you are a space administrator or super user.

3. Clicking on the unlock icon will remove the restriction.

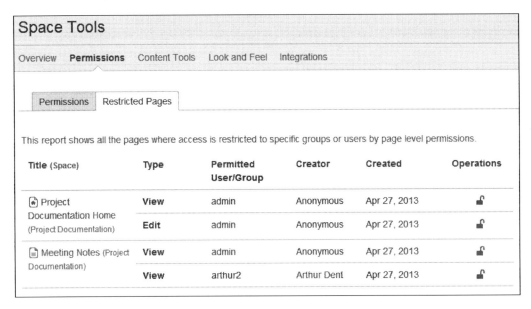

Confluence security

So far we have been talking about permissions and restrictions, which are of course a huge part of how to keep your data secure. But there are a few best practices and features in place to reduce the risk of your Confluence installation being corrupted and prevent the wrong people from getting access.

Secure administrator sessions

Confluence protects access to its administrative functions by a special administrator session. When a user attempts to access the Administration Console or space administration, they are prompted to log in again. This logs the administrator into a temporary secure session that grants access to those administration screens. In other parts of the documentation this feature is also referred to as **WebSudo**.

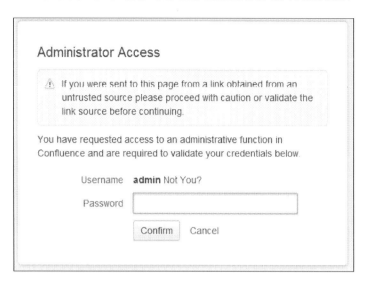

The administrator session has a rolling timeout of 10 minutes (default). This means that if there is no activity in the Confluence or space administration for 10 minutes, the user will be logged out of the administrator session. If the user does click on any administrative function, the timeout will be reset.

To configure the secure administrator sessions:

1. Browse to the Administration Console (**Administration | Confluence Admin**).
2. Choose **Security Configuration** in the left-hand menu.
3. Edit the settings:
    - To disable secure administrator sessions, uncheck the **Enable** checkbox next to **Secure administrator sessions**.
    - To change the timeout of the sessions, update the value next to **minutes before automatic invalidation**.
4. Click on **Save**.

If your Confluence instance uses a custom build authentication mechanism, the extra login might cause problems as it checks the authentication against Confluence instead your own custom authentication server. Disabling password confirmation would be a valid solution.

An administrator can always manually end the secure session by clicking on **Drop access** in the banner displayed at the top of their screen as shown in the following screenshot:

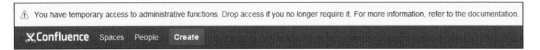

Atlassian security advisory

Software such as Confluence is not flawless and every now and then a vulnerability is discovered. When such a vulnerability is discovered, Atlassian will calculate its severity based on the industry-standard **Common Vulnerability Scoring System (CVSS)**.

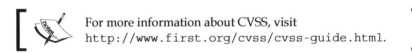

For more information about CVSS, visit
http://www.first.org/cvss/cvss-guide.html.

Based upon the CVSS scores, the severity will be mapped according to the following guidelines:

CVSS score range	Severity in advisory
0 – 2.9	Low
3 – 5.9	Medium
6 – 7.9	High
8 – 10	Critical

The following is a summary of the factors usually resulting in a specific severity. These ratings don't take your personal installation details into account, but are based upon an average installation.

- **Critical**: This means the information required in order to exploit the vulnerability is widely available to attackers.

The exploitation is usually straightforward, meaning that the attackers don't need any special credentials or knowledge about individuals in your installation.

The exploitation of the vulnerability results in root-level compromise of your servers or other infrastructure devices.

 For critical vulnerability, it is advised that you patch or upgrade as soon as possible, unless you have other measures in place. For example, if your Confluence installation is not accessed from the Internet.

- **High**: Here, the exploitation doesn't result in elevated privileges.

  The exploitation doesn't result in significant data loss or corruption.

  And, the vulnerability is difficult to exploit.

- **Medium**: The denial-of-service vulnerabilities are difficult to set up.

  These vulnerabilities affect only nonstandard configurations or obscure applications.

  This includes exploits that require an attacker to reside on the same local network as the victim.

  This includes vulnerabilities that require the attacker to manipulate individual victims via social engineering tactics.

  This includes vulnerabilities where exploitation provides only very limited access.

- **Low**: Vulnerabilities in the low range normally have very little impact on an organization's business. Exploitation of such vulnerabilities usually requires local or physical system access.

When a critical severity vulnerability is discovered, and resolved, Atlassian will inform their customers using the following channels:

- Atlassian will post a security advisory in the latest documentation of Confluence at the same time as a fix for the vulnerability is released. Check the following link:

  ```
  https://confluence.atlassian.com/display/DOC/Confluence+Securit
  y+Overview+and+Advisories
  ```

- Atlassian will send a copy of the security advisory to the "Technical Alerts" mailing list.

If you want to track noncritical vulnerabilities, you can monitor the issue trackers for Confluence at `https://jira.atlassian.com/browse/CONF`. Security issues will be marked with a "security" label.

Limiting access to Confluence administration

The Confluence Administration Console plays a vital role in keeping your Confluence installation running and making sure your users have the permissions they should have.

One way of further securing the Administration Console is limiting its access to certain machines on your network or on the Internet. If you are using an Apache web server in front of your Confluence installation, this would work as follows:

1. The first step is to create a file in a common location on your server. We will use this file to include the Apache configuration needed, making sure we only have one location to change instead of many. We can do that in the following manner:

    1. Create a file called `local_machines_only.conf` in your apache configuration directory.
    2. In this file add the following lines (only the bold part):
        ○ **Order Deny, Allow**: Look for the Deny rules first, then the Allow
        ○ **Deny from All**: Deny access for everybody
        ○ **Allow from 192.168.1.5 #Arthurs machine**: Allow access from Arthur's machine based upon IP

> More on access control with Apache at `http://httpd.apache.org/docs/2.2/howto/access.html`.

2. The next step is to add a long list of locations to your Apache Virtual Host configurations. The following configuration assumes you've installed Confluence under the context path `/confluence`, that is, `http://mycompany.com/confluence`. If this is not true for your installation, change the locations in the following configuration accordingly:

```
<Location /confluence/admin>
  Include local_machines_only.conf
</Location>
<Location /confluence/plugins/servlet/oauth/consumers/list>
```

```
        Include local_machines_only.conf
      </Location>
      <Location /confluence/plugins/servlet/oauth/view-consumer-info>
        Include local_machines_only.conf
      </Location>
      <Location /confluence/plugins/servlet/oauth/service-providers/
      list>
        Include local_machines_only.conf
      </Location>
      <Location /confluence/plugins/servlet/oauth/service-providers/add>
        Include local_machines_only.conf
      </Location>
      <Location /confluence/plugins/servlet/oauth/consumers/add>
        Include local_machines_only.conf
      </Location>
      <Location /confluence/plugins/servlet/oauth/consumers/add-
      manually>
        Include local_machines_only.conf
      </Location>
      <Location /confluence/plugins/servlet/oauth/update-consumer-info>
        Include local_machines_only.conf
      </Location>
      <Location /confluence/pages/templates/listpagetemplates.action>
        Include local_machines_only.conf
      </Location>
      <Location /confluence/pages/templates/createpagetemplate.action>
        Include local_machines_only.conf
      </Location>
      <Location /confluence/spaces/spacepermissions.action>
        Include local_machines_only.conf
      </Location>
      <Location /confluence/pages/listpermissionpages.action>
        Include local_machines_only.conf
      </Location>
      <Location /confluence/spaces/removespace.action>
        Include local_machines_only.conf
      </Location>
      <Location /confluence/spaces/importmbox.action>
        Include local_machines_only.conf
      </Location>
      <Location /confluence/spaces/viewmailaccounts.action>
        Include local_machines_only.conf
      </Location>
      <Location /confluence/spaces/addmailaccount.action?>
```

```
      Include local_machines_only.conf
  </Location>
  <Location /confluence/spaces/importpages.action>
      Include local_machines_only.conf
  </Location>
  <Location /confluence/spaces/flyingpdf/flyingpdf.action>
      Include local_machines_only.conf
  </Location>
  <Location /confluence/spaces/exportspacehtml.action>
      Include local_machines_only.conf
  </Location>
  <Location /confluence/spaces/exportspacexml.action>
      Include local_machines_only.conf
  </Location>
  <Location /confluence/plugins/servlet/embedded-crowd>
      Include local_machines_only.conf
  </Location>
  <Location /confluence/plugins/servlet/upm>
      Include local_machines_only.conf
  </Location>
```

This will make sure the administrative functions can only be accessed by the specified machines and IPs.

Best practices

How you set up your Confluence roles, permissions, and internal processes makes a big difference in keeping your Confluence installation secure. The following are some tips you could consider. None of these make your installation a full 100 percent secure, but they slow down or turn around any attacker.

In general you could say, "Don't put convenience go before security."

- Keep the number of Confluence administrators as low as possible, but having just one is also not without risks.
- Restrict the number of users with powerful roles or group memberships. If only one group of users should have access to some particular data, restrict access to the data to those users. Do not give all staff access to sensitive data when there is no need.
- Confluence administrators should have separate accounts for their administrative role and for their day-to-day work.

- Lock down administrative access as much as possible. If there is no reason to perform administrative tasks from outside the office, use the previously mentioned method to restrict access to a known IP address.

- Get documented procedures in place, for when people are leaving departments or the company, so that you can make sure those people cannot access you Confluence anymore.

- The Confluence database user should only have the permissions to read and write to the Confluence database, and should not be allowed to perform administrative database functions.

- Regularly monitor your security requirements as things change over time. Before you know it, you will have 10 administrators instead of three, or your Apache configuration will be modified when upgrading your systems.

Keep in mind that these tips may only be a small part of your entire infrastructure. Apply those that make sense to your company and security requirements.

Summary

We have learned more about how to keep our content private using space permissions and page restrictions. Confluence has a hierarchical permission structure starting with super users who are allowed to change all permissions and view all content. With regard to security, a good rule to follow is to limit the number of users with administrative access to an absolute minimum.

It's important to note that restricting permissions can help to limit access to content that you create, but this works against the intended use and benefits of the application. Confluence is a wiki and as such is intended to encourage collaboration and sharing. Keep this in mind when you limit access to areas of your Confluence instance to specific users and groups.

The next chapter will go into customizing the look and feel of Confluence, so that it incorporates your company's branding.

7
Customizing Confluence

If you are trying to introduce Confluence to your company, using your company branding and logo can go a long way. In this chapter, we are going to look at different ways to customize the look and feel of Confluence and methods to modify the user experience.

We will learn how relatively easy it is to customize Confluence to your needs. Even when those features aren't enough for your liking, Confluence gives you more advanced options to change the layout and style.

In this chapter, we will cover:

- Changing the landing page and altering the dashboard
- Selecting the theme for your instance or space
- Applying your company branding to Confluence
- Adding custom HTML and stylesheets
- Altering the default Confluence layouts

The Confluence dashboard

The first time you log in to Confluence you will see the dashboard. The Confluence dashboard will give the user a quick indication of the content that has changed recently. From the dashboard, users can navigate to spaces or sections within Confluence.

The Confluence home page

The default entry page of Confluence is the dashboard, but as a Confluence Administrator you can change this to any space home page you prefer. Keep in mind that the space must be accessible for all your users and if your Confluence installation allows anonymous access, the space should also be allowed to be viewed by anonymous users.

To change the default home page, perform the following steps:

1. Browse to the Administration Console (**Administration | Confluence Admin**).
2. Select **General Configuration** from the left-hand side menu.
3. Click on the **Edit** link at the top-left corner.
4. Select a space from the drop-down menu next to **Site Homepage**.
5. Click on **Save** to save the change.

Users can also change their personal default home page, which will override the global setting.

To change your personal default home page, perform the following steps:

1. Select your avatar in the top-right corner.
2. Select **Settings** from the drop-down menu.
3. Click on the **Edit** button.
4. Select a space from the drop-down menu next to **Site Homepage**.
5. Click on **Submit** to save the change.

The welcome message

The welcome message appears at the top-left corner of the Confluence dashboard, and can be used to display a common introduction to Confluence or some important company news.

Include a page as the welcome message

To change the content of the welcome message, a user has to be a Confluence Administrator. If you want to allow other users to change the welcome message, or just want to use the default Confluence editor, including a page is a perfect solution. We will learn how to set up this configuration in the later part of the chapter.

Perform the following steps to edit the welcome message:

1. Browse to the Administration Console (**Administration | Confluence Admin**).
2. Select **Global Templates** from the left-hand side menu.
3. Click on the **Edit** link to the right of **Default Welcome Message**.
4. Use the editor to create your own welcome message.
5. Click on **Save** to save the change.

> Keep in mind that the welcome message is just a small part of the Confluence dashboard. Try not to use page layouts and sections, as these may not get displayed correctly. If you insert images and other elements in your welcome message, try to keep those between 300 px and 400 px width.

Restoring the default welcome message

The default welcome message looks like the following screenshot. It is a common **Welcome to Confluence** and **Get started** text.

Welcome to Confluence

Confluence is where your team collaborates and shares knowledge — create, share and discuss your files, ideas, minutes, specs, mockups, diagrams, and projects.

Get started

Create a new space
and start creating content.

Invite your colleagues
to join you in Confluence.

Upload your picture
and edit your profile.

To restore the default welcome message, perform the following steps:

1. Browse to the Administration Console (**Administration | Confluence Admin**).
2. Select **Global Templates** from the left-hand side menu.
3. Click on the **Reset to Default** link to the right of **Default Welcome Message**.

Removing the Get Started text

By default, the Confluence dashboard displays a quick-start guide for administrators under the site welcome message. This guide is only visible to Confluence administrators and system administrators. A system administrator can update or remove it by editing the site layout as follows:

1. Browse to the Administration Console (**Administration | Confluence Admin**).
2. Select **Layouts** from the left-hand side menu.
3. Choose **Create custom** or **Edit** next to **Global Layout**. The **Edit** option will be available if the global layout has already been customized, otherwise you need to use the **Create Custom** link.
4. Locate the following section in the code and remove or edit it accordingly:

```
#if($permissionHelper.isConfluenceAdministrator($remoteUser))
  <div class="dashboard-item wiki-content">
    <h2>$i18n.getText("getstarted.heading")</h2>
    <ol id="dashboard-get-started">
      <li class="create-space">
        <h3><a href="$req.contextPath/spaces/createspace-start.
action">$i18n.getText("getstarted.add.space")</a></h3>
        <p>$i18n.getText("getstarted.add.space.desc")</p>
      </li>
      <li class="add-users">
        <h3><a href="$req.contextPath/admin/users/browseusers.
action">$i18n.getText("getstarted.add.users")</a></h3>
        <p>$i18n.getText("getstarted.add.users.desc")</p>
      </li>
      <li class="user-profile">
        <h3><a href="$req.contextPath/users/editmyprofilepicture.
action">$i18n.getText("getstarted.choose.profile.picture")</a></
h3>
        <p>$i18n.getText("getstarted.choose.profile.picture.
desc")</p>
      </li>
    </ol>
  </div>
#end
```

5. Select **Save**.

 These changes may need to be reapplied after upgrading your Confluence installation.

Including content from another page

In many cases, including another page as the welcome message gives you more flexibility, control, and allows you to regularly update the content. Using a normal Confluence page means that you can:

- Allow other people, who are not Confluence administrators, to edit the message
- Watch the included page, and get notified when something on the welcome message has changed

Make sure that the page you want to include is viewable by all the users, including anonymous users if your Confluence allows anonymous access.

If a user is not allowed to view a page, they will see the following message on their dashboard:

Unable to render {include} The included page could not be found.

To include content from another page, perform the following steps:

1. Create a page in Confluence as you normally would.
    1. Click on the **Create** button in the top navigation.
    2. Select the space you want to create the page in.
    3. Select the **Blank Page** template.
    4. Give the page a title like `Confluence Dashboard`.
    5. Enter some basic content on the page.
    6. Click on **Save** to save the page.
2. Change the page restrictions as you see fit. A commonly used setting is to restrict the editing of this page to a certain group of people.
3. Use the preceding steps to edit the site's welcome message.
    1. Select **Insert | Other Macros** and search the Include Page macro.
    2. In the macro property panel, search for the page you just created.
    3. Select **Insert**.

4. Click on **Save** to save the welcome message.

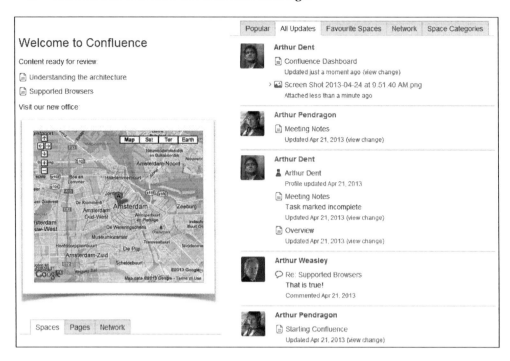

In the preceding example we added a Content by Label macro, which looks for content with a review label. We've also included an image with an effect that links to another page on Confluence.

Themes

Themes are sets of predefined styles and can be used to personalize the look and feel of Confluence. Themes can be applied to the entire site and individual spaces. Some themes add extra functionality to Confluence or change the layout significantly.

Confluence 5 comes with two themes installed, and an administrator can install new themes as add-ons via the Administration Console. We go into add-ons and the Atlassian Marketplace in *Chapter 9, General Administration*.

Atlassian is planning on merging the **Documentation Theme** with the **Default Theme**. As this is not the case in Confluence 5 yet, we will discuss them both as they have some different features. Keep in mind that, at some point, the **Documentation Theme** will be removed from Confluence.

To change the global Confluence theme, perform the following steps:

1. Browse to the Administration console (**Administration | Confluence Admin**).

2. Select **Themes** from the left-hand side menu.

3. All the installed themes will be present.

   Select the appropriate radio button to select a theme.

4. Choose **Confirm** to change the theme:

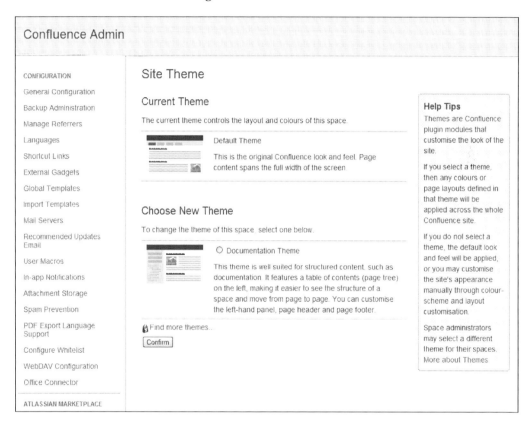

Space administrators can also decide on a different theme for their own spaces. Spaces with their own theme selections—and therefore not using the global look and feel—won't be affected if a Confluence Administrator changes the global default theme.

To change a space theme, perform the following steps:

1. Go to any page in the space.
2. Select **Space Tools** in the sidebar. (If you are not using the default theme, select **Browse | Space Admin**.)
3. Select **Look and Feel**, followed by **Theme**.
4. Select the theme you want to apply to the space.
5. Click on **Confirm**.

The Default Theme

As the name implies, this is the default theme shipped with Confluence. This Default Theme got a complete overhaul in Confluence 5 and looks as shown in the following screenshot:

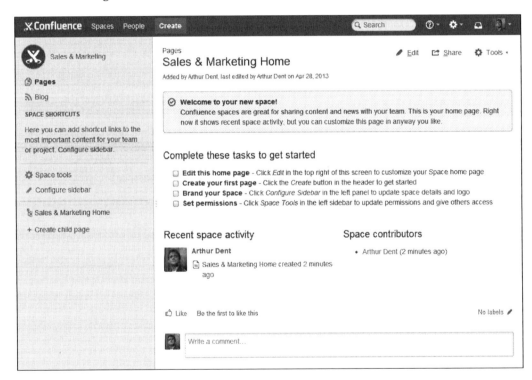

The Default Theme provides every space with a sidebar, containing useful links and navigation help throughout the current space. With the sidebar, you can quickly change from browsing pages to blog post or vice versa. The sidebar also allows important space content to be added as a link for quicker access, and displays the children of the current page for easy navigation.

> You can collapse or expand the sidebar. Click-and-drag the border, or use the keyboard shortcut: [. If the sidebar is collapsed, you can still access the sidebar options.

Configuring the theme

The default theme doesn't have any global configuration available, but a space administrator can make some space-specific changes to the theme's sidebar.

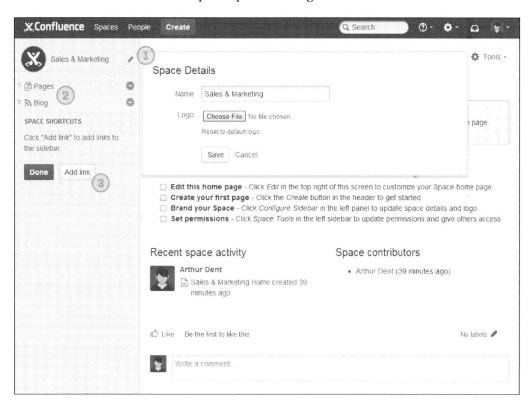

Perform the following steps to change the space details:

1. Go to any page in the relevant space.
2. Select **Configure sidebar** in the space sidebar.
3. Click on the edit icon next to the space title.
4. A pop up will show where you can change the space title and logo (as shown in the preceding screenshot, indicated as **1**).
5. Click on **Save** to save the changes
6. Click on the **Done** button to exit the configuration mode.

The main navigation items on the sidebar (pages and blog posts) can be hidden. This can come in handy, for example, when you don't allow users to add blog posts to the space.

To show or hide the main navigation items, perform the following steps:

1. Go to any page in the relevant space.
2. Select **Configure sidebar** in the space sidebar.
3. Select the - or + icon beside the link to either hide or show the link.
4. Click on the **Done** button to exit the configuration mode.

Space shortcuts are manually added links to the sidebar, linking to important content within the space. A space administrator can manage these links.

To add a space shortcut, perform the following steps:

1. Go to any page in the relevant space.
2. Select **Configure sidebar** in the space sidebar.
3. Click on the **Add Link** button, indicated as **3** in the preceding screenshot.
4. The **Insert Link** dialog will appear.
5. Search and select the page you want to link.
6. Click on **Insert** to add the link to the sidebar.
7. Click on the **Done** button to exit the configuration mode.

The Documentation Theme

The Documentation Theme is another bundled theme. It supplies a built-in table of content for your space, a configurable header and footer, and a space-restricted search.

The Documentation Theme's default look and feel is displayed in the following screenshot:

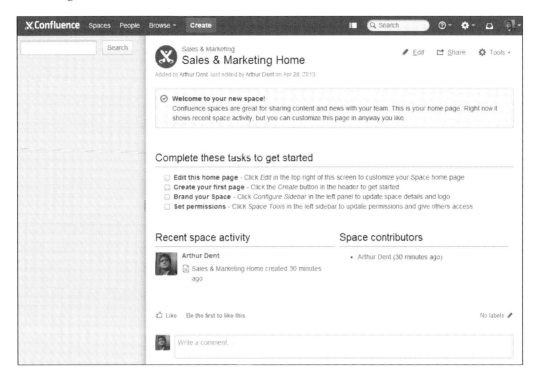

The sidebar of the Documentation Theme will show a tree with all the pages in your space. Clicking on the icon in front of a page title will expand the branch and show its children.

> The sidebar can be opened and closed using the / shortcut, or the icon on the left of the search box in the Confluence header.

Configuring the theme

The Documentation Theme allows configuration of the sidebar contents, page header and footer, and the possibility to restrict the search to only the current space.

A Confluence Administrator can configure the theme globally, but a Space Administrator can overwrite this configuration for his or her own space. To configure the Documentation Theme for a space, the Space Administrator should explicitly select the **Documentation Theme** as the space theme.

The theme configuration of the Documentation Theme allows you to change the properties displayed in the following screenshot. How to get to this screen and what the properties represent will be explained next.

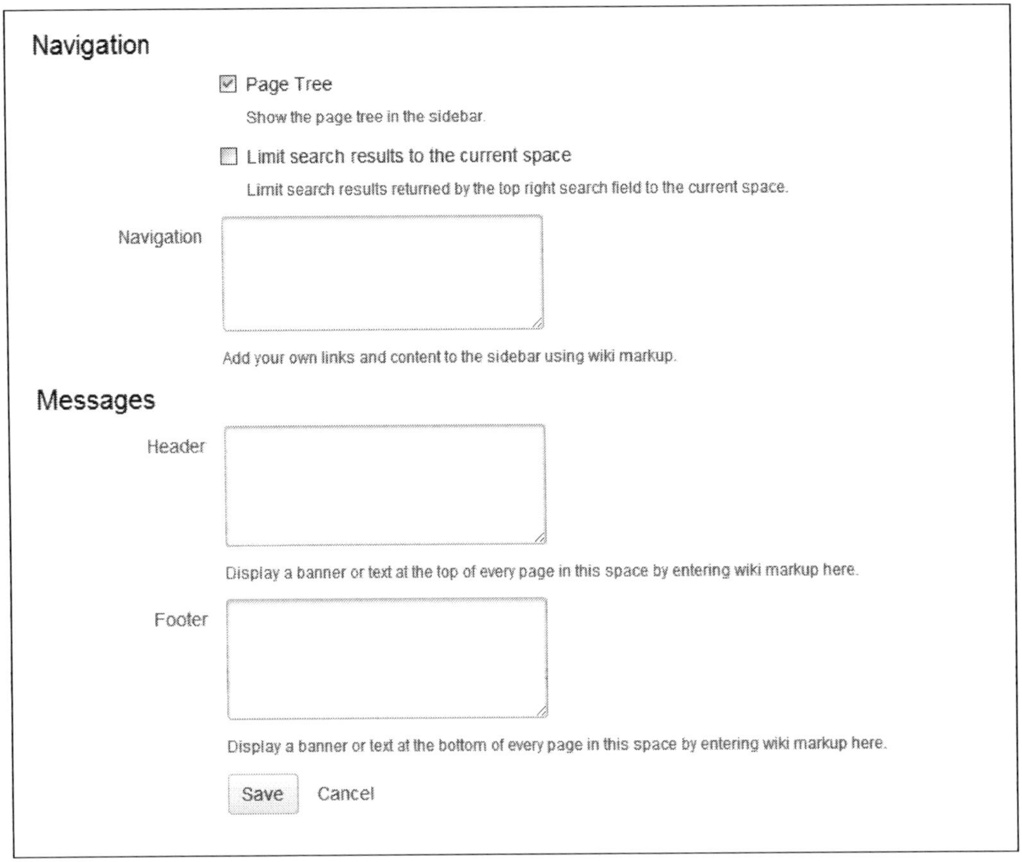

Navigation

☑ Page Tree

Show the page tree in the sidebar.

☐ Limit search results to the current space

Limit search results returned by the top right search field to the current space.

Navigation

Add your own links and content to the sidebar using wiki markup.

Messages

Header

Display a banner or text at the top of every page in this space by entering wiki markup here.

Footer

Display a banner or text at the bottom of every page in this space by entering wiki markup here.

Save   Cancel

To configure the Documentation theme, perform the following steps:

1. As a Confluence Administrator:

    1. Browse to the Administration Console (**Administration | Confluence Admin**).

    2. Select **Themes** from the left-hand side menu.

3. Choose the **Documentation Theme** as the current theme.

4. Click on the **Configure theme** link.

2. As a Space administrator:

   1. Go to any page in the space.

   2. Select **Browse | Space Admin**.

   3. Choose **Themes** from the left-hand side menu.

   4. Make sure that the **Documentation Theme** is the current theme.

   5. Click on the **Configure theme** link.

3. Select or deselect the **Page Tree** checkbox. This will determine if your space will display the default search box and page tree in the sidebar.

4. Select or deselect the **Limit search results to the current space** checkbox.

   ○ If you select the checkbox:

   The Confluence search in the top-left corner will only search in the current space.

   The sidebar will not contain a search box.

   ○ If you deselect the checkbox:

   The Confluence search in the top-left corner will search across the entire Confluence site.

   The sidebar will contain a search box, which is limited to searching in the current space.

5. In the three textboxes, you can enter any text or wiki markup you would like; for example, you could add some information to the sidebar or a notification to every page. The following screenshot will display these areas:

   ○ **Navigation**: This will be displayed in the space sidebar.

   ○ **Header**: This will be displayed above the title on all the pages in the space.

- ○ **Footer**: This will be displayed after the comments on all the pages in the space.

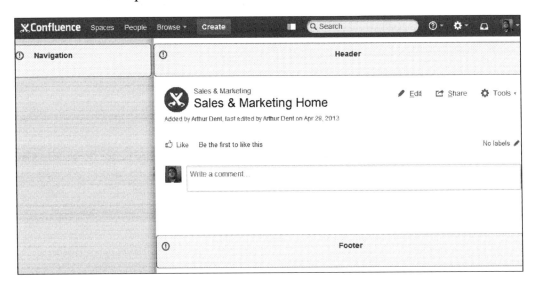

Look and feel

The look and feel of Confluence can be customized on both global level and space level. Any changes made on a global level will be applied as the default settings for all spaces.

A Space Administrator can choose to use a different theme than the global look and feel. When a Space Administrator selects a different theme, the default settings and theme are no longer applied to that space. This also means that settings in a space are not updated if the global settings are updated.

In this section, we will cover some basic look and feel changes, such as changing the logo and color-scheme of your Confluence instance. It is also possible to change some of the Confluence layouts; this is covered in the *Advanced customizing* section.

Confluence logo

The Confluence logo is the logo that is displayed on the navigation bar in Confluence. This can easily be changed to your company logo.

To change the global logo, perform the following steps:

1. Browse to the Administration Console (**Administration | Confluence Admin**).

2. Select **Site Logo** from the left-hand side menu

3. Click on **Choose File** to select the file from your computer.

4. Decide whether to show only your company logo, or also the title of your Confluence installation.

   ° If you choose to also show the title, you can change this in the text field next to **Site Title**.

5. Click on **Save**.

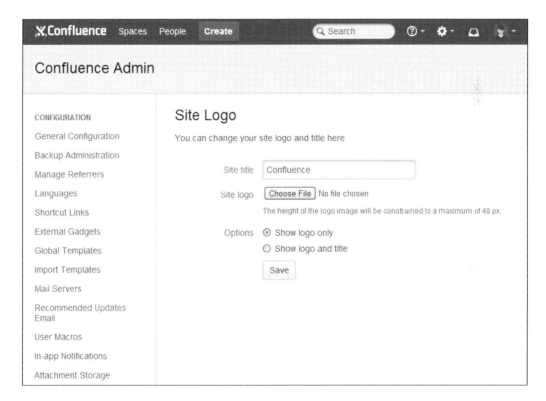

 As you might notice, Confluence also changed the color scheme of your installation. Confluence will suggest a color scheme based upon your logo. To revert this change, click on **Undo**, which is directly available after updating your logo.

Space logo

Every space can choose its own logo, making it easy to identify certain topics or spaces. A Confluence administrator can also set the default space logo, for newly created spaces or spaces without their own specified logo.

 The logo of a personal space cannot be changed; it will always use the user's avatar as logo.

To set the default space logo, perform the following steps:

1. Browse to the Administration Console (**Administration | Confluence Admin**).
2. Select **Default Space Logo** from the left-hand side menu.
3. Click on **Choose File** to select the file from your computer. For the best result, make sure the image is about 48 x 48 pixels.
4. Click on **Upload Logo** to upload the default space logo.

As a Space Administrator, you can replace the default logo for your space. How this is done depends on the theme you are using.

To change the space logo with the default theme, perform the following steps:

1. Go to any page in the relevant space.
2. Click on **Configure Sidebar** from the sidebar.
3. Select the edit icon next to the page title.
4. Click on **Choose File** next to the logo and select a file from your computer. Confluence will display an image editor to indicate how your logo should be displayed as shown in the next screenshot.
5. Drag and resize the circle in the editor to the right position.
6. Click on **Save** to save the changes.
7. Click on the **Done** button to exit the configuration mode.

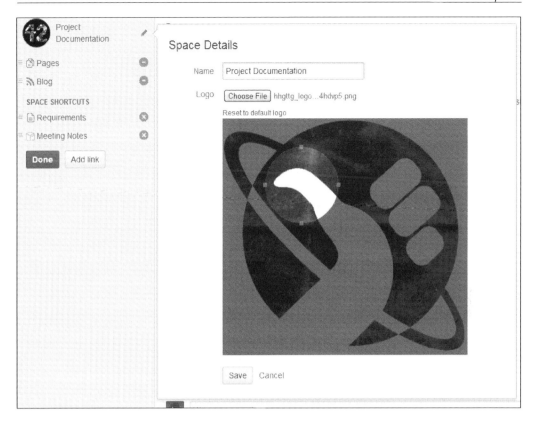

To change the space logo with the Documentation Theme, perform the following steps:

1. Go to any page in the relevant space.
2. Select **Browse | Space Admin**.
3. Select **Change Space Logo** from the left-hand side menu.
4. Select **Choose File** and select the logo from your computer.
5. Click on **Upload Logo** to save the new logo; Confluence will automatically resize and crop the logo for you.

Color schemes

Confluence and Space Administrators can configure new color schemes for Confluence and individual spaces. The global color scheme, configured by the Confluence Administrator, will also be the default space scheme. Space Administrators can configure different colors for their spaces. Changing the color schemes also applies to personal spaces.

To change the global color scheme, perform the following steps:

1. Browse to the Administration Console (**Administration | Confluence Admin**).
2. Select **Colour Scheme** from the left-hand side menu.
3. Click on **Edit** and the screen displayed in the next screenshot will be shown.
4. Use standard HTML/CSS color codes or the color-picker next to the text fields.
5. Click on **Save** to apply the changes to Confluence.

To change the color scheme of a space, perform the following steps:

1. Go to any page in the space.
2. Select **Space Tools** in the sidebar. (If you are not using the default theme, select **Browse | Space Admin**.)
3. Select **Look and Feel**, followed by **Colour Scheme**.
4. Select the color scheme below **Custom Colour Scheme**.
5. Click on the **Edit** link.
6. Use standard HTML/CSS color codes or the color-picker next to the text fields.
7. Click on **Save** to apply the changes to the space.

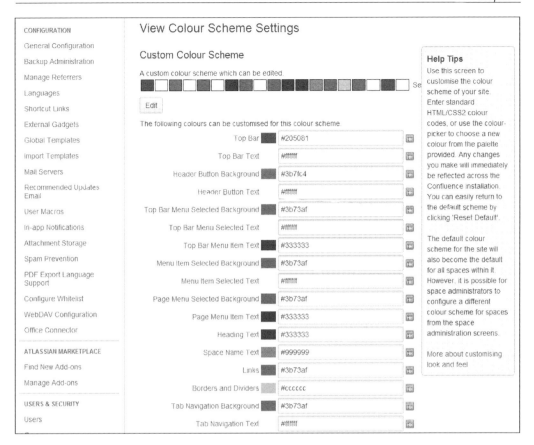

If you don't like the color scheme you selected, use the **Reset** button in the edit screen to return to Confluence's default settings.

Advanced customizing

Changing the look and feel of Confluence, using themes and color schemes isn't always enough. If you want to go a bit further by changing the appearance of Confluence, or you want to add some extra functionality to the layout, these more advanced topics might interest you.

The default space content

Whenever you create a new space, the first page of that space always has the same content. As a Confluence Administrator, you can change this default space content to contain any other content you like.

To change the default content of a global space, perform the following steps:

1. Browse to the Administration Console (**Administration | Confluence Admin**).

2. Select **Global Templates** from the left-hand side menu.

3. Under the section **System Templates,** click on the **Edit** link below the **Default Space Content** text.

4. Create the content you want to appear on the home page of new spaces. You can also use variables within the content.

   ° `$spacekey`: This will be replaced with the new space key.

   ° `$spacename`: This will be replaced with the new space name.

5. Click on `Save` to save the new default content.

To change the default content of a personal space, perform the following steps:

1. Browse to the Administration Console (**Administration | Confluence Admin**).

2. Select **Global Templates** from the left-hand side menu.

3. Under the section **System Templates,** click on the **Edit** link below the **Default Personal Space Content** text.

4. Create the content you want to appear on the home page of new spaces. You can also use variables within the content.

   ° `$userFullName`: This will be replaced with the space owner's full name.

   ° `$userEmail`: This will be replaced with the space owner's email address.

   ° `$userPersonalInfo`: This will be replaced with the space owner's **About me** text, entered in the user profile.

5. Click on **Save** to save the new default content.

Custom HTML

Confluence allows you to add some custom HTML to every page in Confluence. A very common use case for this is to add a Google Analytics tracker to Confluence.

There are three places where you can insert HTML, as shown in the next screenshot:

- **At end of the HEAD**
- **At beginning of the BODY**
- **At end of the BODY**

Before adding any custom HTML to your Confluence pages, make sure it is valid. Adding incomplete or broken HTML can result in not being able to use Confluence anymore.

Custom HTML

Insert Custom HTML

At end of the HEAD

At beginning of the BODY

```
<!-- INSERT GOOGLE CODE HERE -->
```

At end of the BODY

Save Cancel

To insert custom HTML, perform the following steps:

1. Browse to the Administration Console (**Administration | Confluence Admin**).
2. Select **Custom HTML** from the left-hand side menu.
3. Click on the **Edit** button.
4. Insert the HTML in the corresponding text area as shown in the preceding screenshot.
5. Click on **Save**.

Custom stylesheets

Confluence gives us the possibility to add custom CSS files to Confluence and potentially change the complete look and feel. In order to apply CSS, you need adequate knowledge on working with and writing in CSS. Beginner tutorials are widely available on the Internet, for instance at W3Schools (http://www.w3schools.com/css/default.asp).

Custom CSSs can be added on the global and space levels, although the last one is disabled by default and should be turned on by a Confluence Administrator. Spaces with their own custom CSSs will ignore the global custom CSS.

Keep in mind that Confluence HTML may change between versions and your CSS might stop working. Atlassian does not support custom CSS or any issues related to it. So, always check your custom CSS when moving to a newer version of Confluence and adjust the CSS as required.

To enable custom stylesheets for spaces, perform the following steps:

1. Browse to the Administration Console (**Administration | Confluence Admin**).
2. Select **Security Configuration** from the left-hand side menu.
3. Click on **Edit**.
4. Enable the checkbox in front of **Custom Style Sheets for Spaces**.
5. Click on **Save** to save your changes.

To add a custom style sheet to Confluence, perform the following steps:

1. Browse to the Administration Console (**Administration | Confluence Admin**).
2. Select **Style Sheet** from the left-hand side menu.
3. Click on **Edit**.
4. Add your CSS.

   To demonstrate the power of changing the stylesheet enter the next example.
5. Click on **Save** to save your changes.

Use the following example to get an understanding of what is possible with custom stylesheets:

```
body:not(.dashboard) #main { padding: 40px 80px 0px; font-size:120%; }
#title-heading { font-size: 200%; }

#breadcrumbs { display:none; }

.content-navigation {width: 300px; height: 30px; }
.content-navigation ul { display:none; }
.content-navigation:hover ul { display:block; }
```

The first block will change the padding of the main element so that there is more whitespace on the left and right of the content. It also resizes the text to 120 percent and the page title to 200 percent of its original size.

The second statement will remove the breadcrumbs above the page title.

The last section of the stylesheet will hide the page tools (**Edit**, **Share**, and **Tools**) unless someone hovers the location with their mouse.

This is how your page will look like with this custom stylesheet installed:

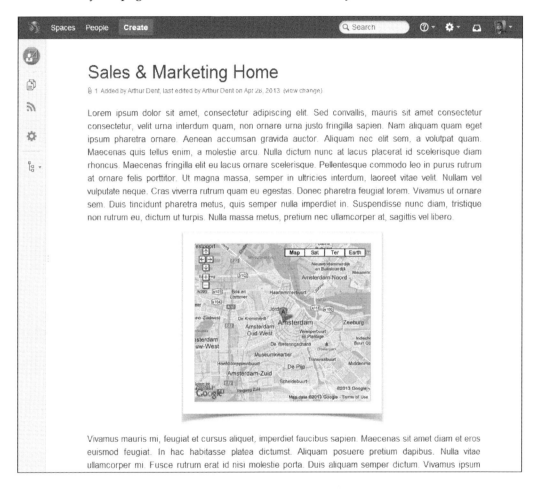

As the preceding example showed, changing the CSS is a powerful way to alter the appearance of your Confluence. It does require some basic CSS and HTML skills though.

There is a tutorial available online to get you started with changing the CSS at
`https://confluence.atlassian.com/display/DOC/Basic+Styling+Tutorial`.

Site layouts

Confluence is built on top of the open source library SiteMesh, a web page layout
system. To further change the look and feel of Confluence, you can modify these
decorator files. If you want to change the decorator files, you should familiarize
yourself with Velocity. The user guide is available online at `http://velocity.`
`apache.org/engine/releases/velocity-1.4/user-guide.html`.

The decorator files in Confluence are grouped in the following sections:

- **Site layouts**: These layouts are used to define the layout around the content
  such as the header and footer.

- **Content layouts**: These layouts control the appearance of content such as
  pages and blog posts. They do not change the way the pages themselves are
  displayed, but allow you to change the way the surrounding comments or
  attachments are displayed.

- **Export layouts**: These layouts control the appearance of spaces and pages
  when they are exported to HTML. If you are using Confluence to generate
  a static website, for example, you will need to modify these layouts.

To edit a decorator file, perform the following steps:

1. Browse to the Administration Console (**Administration | Confluence Admin**).
2. Select **Layouts** from the left-hand side menu.
3. Click on **Create Custom** to edit the default file.
4. Make any changes.
5. Click on **Save** to save the page.

Use **View Default** to view the default decorator file. If something goes wrong,
you can use **Reset Default** to return to the original layout.

While editing the decorator files, there are a couple of Velocity macros that you
can use to insert items like breadcrumbs or menus in your layout. The following
are some of these macros; more are available online at `https://confluence.`
`atlassian.com/display/DOC/Working+With+Decorator+Macros`.

Macro	Usage
`#includePage (pageTitle)`	Includes a confluence page with the specified title. If there are 2 or more pages with the same title across Confluence, this macro will use the page belonging to the space you are currently viewing.
`#searchbox ()`	Inserts a search box similar to the default search box in the top-right corner.
`#dashboardlink ()`	Inserts a link to the dashboard page.

These macros work reliably only when you're editing the main decorator. They may not work in other decorators; they will definitely not work in the normal Confluence editor.

If you have changed the layout so extensively that some features aren't visible anymore, you can reset the layout by directly browsing to the following URL. Substitute the base URL and the appropriate .vmd file.

```
http://<confluence_url>/admin/resetdecorator.
action?decoratorName=decorators/main.vmd
```

Summary

In this chapter, we went from some basic means to change the appearance of your Confluence installation to an advanced, change-it-completely, approach. Adding your company's branding to Confluence can be done by uploading your logo and changing the color scheme.

You can also change which page your users see when they login; this can be the Confluence dashboard or a space home page with your company news and other important information. Users can specify their own preferences as well.

We also learned that Confluence comes with some bundled themes with different looks, feels, and features. If those themes don't completely get you the user experience you're looking for, an option is to change the stylesheet and decorators yourself.

In the next chapter, we are going to take a look at more advanced options like creating and using templates to give your documentation more structure and to help your users get started quickly.

8
Advanced Confluence

So far we have been using Confluence out of the box, making use of all the features, templates, and macros that are bundled with the installation. Confluence also comes with the possibility to add your own features, templates, and macros to the product. This way you can tailor your Confluence installation to your company's needs.

In this chapter, we will learn about the more advanced features in Confluence, such as how to create and apply templates to give your content more structure. We will also take a look at creating our own macros, which can be used while creating content.

By the end of the chapter, you will have learned about:

- Creating and managing content templates
- Writing user macros
- Using the page properties macro
- Creating shortcut links

Templates

We have been adding a lot of pages by now and every time we started from scratch; but we don't have to. When you find yourself creating the same page structure over again, or you want your users to use the same structure for reasons of consistency, templates are the answer.

Templates are predefined pages that can be used as a scaffold when you are creating pages. Only new pages can be created from a template, and when a template is used the new page will contain the same content as the template. Templates are very useful when you want a uniform style or format for your pages.

Using templates

When there are templates available, you can start using them to create new pages. When you create a page based on a template, Confluence will copy the following content and information to the new page:

- Labels
- Text and styles
- Layouts and other formatting
- Macros
- Displayed media such as images or videos

The newly created page is not connected in any way to the original template; changes made to the template will not reflect on the created page. It is not possible to apply a template to an existing page; templates can only be used when creating a new page. The newly created page can be edited in any way a blank page can; content can be added, updated, and removed.

To create a page based on a template, perform the following steps:

1. Click on **Create** in the header.
2. Select a space to create the new page in.
3. Choose a template from the available templates.
4. If the template contains variables, you will see a form. Type the relevant information into the fields and click on **Next**.
5. You will see a new page based upon the template.
6. Give the page a title and add, update, or delete the content.
7. Click on **Save**.

The following screenshot displays the available templates that can be used to create a new page:

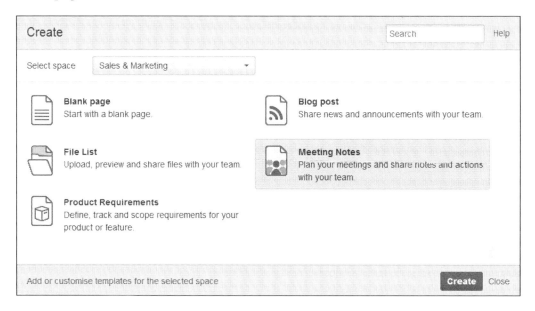

Creating templates

In Confluence, templates can be created on two levels of the Confluence hierarchy:

- **Space templates**: These templates are only available in the space you created them in. Space Administrators can define space templates via the space admin screen.

- **Global templates**: These templates are available in every space in Confluence. Confluence Administrators can define global templates via the Administration Console.

Space templates

Space templates can be created by Space Administrators and are only available in the space you create them in.

To add a template for a space, perform the following steps:

1. Go to any page in the space.
2. Click on **Space Tools** from the sidebar.
3. Select **Content Tools**, followed by **Templates** from the space admin menu.
4. Click on the **Create new Template** button.

If your space uses the documentation theme:

1. Select **Browse | Space Admin**.
2. Click on **Templates** from the left-hand navigation.
3. Click on the **Create new Template** button.

You will be redirected to the **Create Template** screen. How you can add content and create your template is explained in the *Adding content to your template* section.

Global templates

Global templates can be created by Confluence Administrators and are available in all spaces within Confluence.

To add a global template, perform the following steps:

1. Browse to the Administration Console (**Administration | Confluence Admin**).
2. Choose **Global Templates** in the left-hand side menu.
3. Click on the **Add New Global Template** button.

You will be redirected to the **Create Template** screen. How you can add content and create your template is explained in the *Adding content to your template* section.

Adding content to your template

The **Create Template** view is very similar to the regular editor in Confluence:

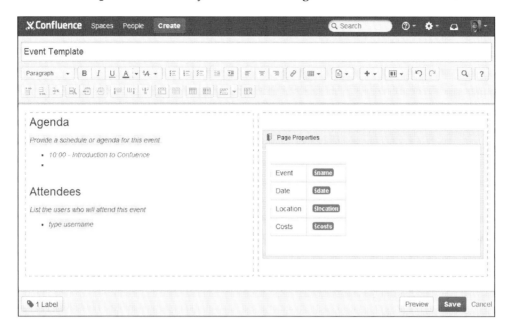

What normally is the page title will now be the template name. The template name will be displayed when you create a new page, so choose a descriptive name for your template.

The content of the template is just like a regular page; you can use styles, layouts, and other formatting. You can also add links and macros. In addition to the normal features, the template editor also allows you to add variables and instruction texts. Using variables in your template will create a form for collection of data when someone adds a page based on the template.

Some points to take into account when creating a template are:

- **Labels**: Select **Labels** from the bottom-left to add labels to the template. These labels will be included in all the pages created using this template.

- **Images and other attachments**: It is not possible to add any file or image to a template. If you want to use an image or attachment in your template, you need to attach this file to another page in Confluence.

Then insert the image by performing the following steps:

1. Select **Insert | Image**.
2. Use the media browser to find your image.
3. Click on **Insert** to insert your image.

- **Instructional text**: Instructional text allows you to add placeholder content to a template. This placeholder is only visible in the editor and disappears when the author of the page begins typing in that placeholder.

  These texts can provide instructions for users on how to use the template and which data is expected at certain locations.

  To insert an instructional text, perform the following steps:

  1. Place your cursor on the template where you want the instructional text to appear.
  2. Click on **Template** on the editor toolbar.
  3. Select **Instructional Text**.
  4. Start typing; the instructional text appears in italics with a shaded background to distinguish it from the normal paragraph text.

  The type of the placeholder can be changed from "text" to a "user mention", which starts the mention's autocomplete when the author starts typing. To change the placeholder type, click on the placeholder and select **User Mention**.

- **Variables**: With variables you can introduce data entry to your template, making sure not only the layout is organized but the content as well. Variables added to a template act as form fields. When somebody creates a page based on your template, Confluence will display an entry box for each variable as shown in the following screenshot. Users can enter data into each field and the data is then inserted onto the new page:

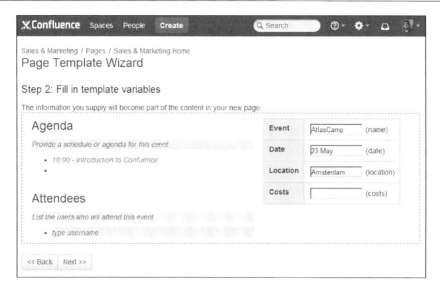

Each variable must have a unique name. If you add the same variable more than once in the same template, Confluence will provide both placeholders with the same value. This is useful when you need the same information in more than one position.

To insert a variable into a template, perform the following steps:

1. Place your cursor at the location you want to insert a variable

2. Select **Template** from the editor toolbar.

3. Select an existing variable or click on **New Variable**.

4. Enter the variable name.

5. Press *Enter*. This will create a single-line text input field.

6. To change the variable type, click on the placeholder. The property panel will appear where you can choose different types. See the next table for a description of those types.

Speed up variable entry by using the keyboard shortcut $ (*Shift* + 4) for autocomplete.

These are the types of variables available:

Variable type	Description
Text	Creates a single-line text input field as shown: 
Multi-line text	Creates a textbox that allows more than one line of text. By default, this textbox is of **5** rows with **100** characters wide. You can change the size in the property panel: 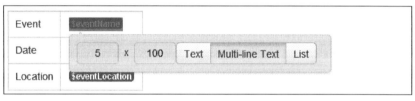
List	Creates a drop-down list. You must specify the values for the drop-down list. These values: • Must be separated by commas • Can include any letter, number, spaces, and other special characters except a comma, as these are used as separators 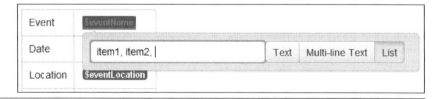

Importing templates

In addition to creating your own templates, you can download predefined templates from the Atlassian Marketplace in the form of a template bundle or Blueprints. Each bundle contains one or more templates, created by Atlassian or other parties.

An example of one of those bundles is available here:

```
https://marketplace.atlassian.com/20489
```

Downloading and installing add-ons, like template bundles, is described in more detail in *Chapter 9, General Administration.*

Checking installed template bundles

To check which bundles are available and can be imported, perform the following steps:

1. Browse to the Administration Console (**Administration | Confluence Admin**).

2. Select **Import Templates** from the left-hand side menu.

3. You will see a list of template bundles installed and all the templates included in each bundle:

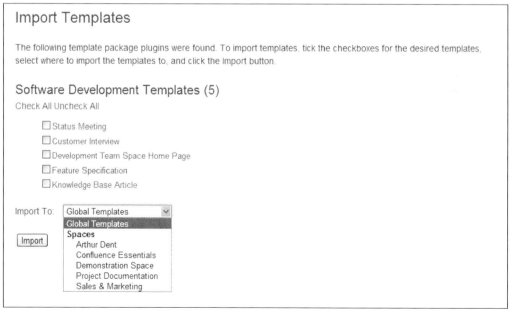

Display of template bundles available for import

Making templates available for usage

If you have one or more template bundles installed, you can import them to make those templates available for your users.

To import a template, perform the following steps:

1. Browse to the Administration Console (**Administration | Confluence Admin**).

2. Select **Import Templates** from the left-hand side menu.

3. You will see a list of template bundles installed and all the templates included in each bundle. If you click on the template name, a preview is shown.

4. Select the templates you want to import by checking the boxes next to the template names.

5. Choose the destination for the templates in the **Import To:** dropdown. If you want to import the templates to a specific space, select that space; otherwise select **Global Templates** to make the templates available for all spaces.

User Macros

Throughout the book, we have learned what macros are and how we can use them to make our content more engaging and alive. Most macros we have used so far are either bundled with Confluence, or part of an add-on we have installed. But there is another possibility to add macros: via user macros.

User macros are short pieces of code that make it easier to perform often-used functions or add custom formatting to your page. This could, for example, be a preconfigured panel macro with different styling than the defaults. We will create this example ourselves later in this chapter.

System Administrators can add user macros via the Confluence Administration Console.

Managing user macros

To manage user macros, you need to have System Administrator permissions. Be careful when installing user macros from an unknown source; macros could potentially affect the stability and security of your Confluence installation.

Perform the following steps for adding a user macro:

1. Browse to the Administration Console (**Administration | Confluence Admin**).

2. Select **User Macros** from the left-hand side menu.

3. Click on **Create a User Macro** at the bottom of the list of macros.

4. Enter the macro details as explained in the *Writing user macros* section.

5. Click on **Save**.

Perform the following steps for editing a user macro:

1. Browse to the Administration Console (**Administration | Confluence Admin**).

2. Select **User Macros** from the left-hand side menu.

3. Click on **Edit** next to the relevant macro.

4. Change the macro details as explained in the *Writing user macros* section.

5. Click on **Save**.

Perform the following steps for removing a user macro:

1. Browse to the Administration Console (**Administration | Confluence Admin**).

2. Select **User Macros** from the left-hand side menu.

3. Click on **Remove** next to the relevant macro.

If you remove a user macro that is being used on a Confluence page, you will need to remove the macro from the page manually.

 You can use the Confluence search to find pages that are using a user macro. More information on searching for macros can be found in the *Searching labels* section in *Chapter 4, Managing Content*.

Writing user macros

Writing a user macro is done via a form in the Administration Console. We'll go over the input fields to help you create your first user macro:

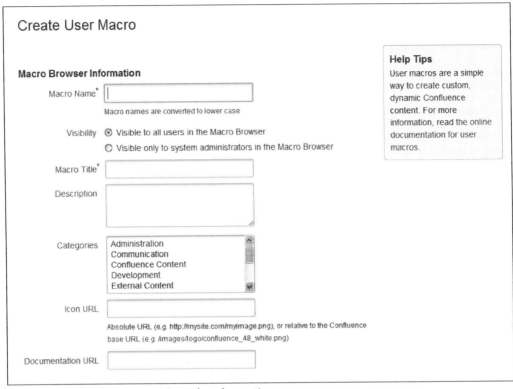

Input form for creating a new user macro

- **Macro Name**: This is the name of the macro and can only contain letters, numbers, and hyphens (-); for example: teaser-panel.

- **Visibility**: Here you can set the visibility in the macro browser; this can be all users or only system administrators. Hiding the macro for all users will still allow them to use the macro, but it avoids cluttering the Macro Browser and autocomplete.

Choosing **Visible only to system administrators in the Macro Browser** means that:

- ° Only system administrators will see this macro in the Macro Browser or autocomplete. For other users, the macro will not show up, even while searching the macro.

- ° The macro output will be visible to all users who have permissions to see the page.

- ° Any user with edit permissions will see the macro on the page if it is already on it. Your users are also allowed to edit or remove the macro.

- **Macro Title**: The macro title is the name that will appear in the Macro Browser and autocomplete. Choose a descriptive title to make it easier for your users to find the macro.

- **Description**: The description text shows next to the macro in the Macro Browser. The search in the Macro Browser will also use the description text to search in.

- **Categories**: Select one or more categories to place your user macro in. These categories relate to the categories a user sees in the Macro Browser. To select multiple categories, hold down the *Ctrl* key while selecting.

- **Icon URL**: The Macro Browser can display an icon for your macro if you provide a URL. This can either be an absolute URL, or a path relative to the Confluence's base URL; for example: `http://example.com/images/no-print-icon.png` or `/images/icons/macrobrowser/no-print-icon.png`.

- **Documentation URL**: If you have online documentation, enter the URL of this documentation here. The link will appear in the macro properties dialog. In some cases, a Confluence page documenting your user macro is very useful for your users.

- **Macro Body Processing**: You can specify that your macro can have a body, allowing your users to enter content in your macro. An example of a macro with a body is the panel macro.

If your macro has a body, this body will be available in your macro template with the $body variable. The content of your body depends on how the processing is done.

Processing option	Description
No macro body	Select this option if your macro doesn't need a body.
Escaped	If your macro has a body and you make use of the body in your template, Confluence will escape any HTML in the body.
	So, if the body is:
	`<b>Example HTML</b>`
	Then the value of $body is:
	`&lt;b&gt;ExampleHTML&lt;/b&gt;`
	This will be rendered as:
	`<b>Example HTML</b>`
Unrendered	Use this option if you want the $body variable to be exactly like the user entered it. You should process the body within the template to make sure HTML is output-ted by the template.
Rendered	The body will be rendered, so most HTML will be passed to the template unmodified; but Confluence-specific markup, such as macro definitions, will be processed and rendered.
	So, if the body is:
	`<b>Example HTML</b>`
	Then the value of $body is:
	`<b>Example HTML</b>`
	This will be rendered as:
	Example HTML

- **Template**: This is where the magic happens: the macro template. Here you should write the code that specifies what your macro will do. We will go into detail on how to write a user macro template soon, but here is a quick guide up front:

    ○ Use HTML and Confluence-specific XML elements in your macro template. Use the Storage Format tool to find the specific XML.

    ○ It is possible to use Apache Velocity in the template.

- If your macro has a body, the content is available in the `$body` variable.
- Each parameter for your macro should have matching metadata definitions. Use `@param` to define that metadata.
- Use `@noparams` if your macro does not access any parameters.

 Apache Velocity is a template engine that provides a template language to reference objects defined in the backend of Confluence. Velocity is the main template engine in Confluence and is used for displaying almost every page. Velocity can be used in your macro to add some logic (if-else) or to get information from the backend, that is, the current page title and other page properties.

Writing a user macro template

A user macro template is a piece of code that specifies what your macro does. It is written in a combination of HTML, XML, and Velocity. We will build a user macro together to give you some insight into what the possibilities are.

I assume you have filled in the other text fields of the macro based on the previous paragraph. Make sure that the **Macro Body Processing** option is set to **Rendered**.

A descriptive header

It is a good practice to have a descriptive header at the top of every template. The header tells what the macro does and what kind of parameters it expects.

Our header would look something like this:

```
## Macro title: Teaser Panel
## Macro has a body: Y
## Body processing: Rendered
##
## Developed by: Stefan Kohler
## Date created: 04/02/2013


## The Teaser panel is a predefined panel used as teaser
```

Parameters

It is possible to use parameters in your user macro, so that users can pass extra information for you to render. If you define your parameters, Confluence will display the corresponding fields in the **Macro properties** dialog and browser.

A parameter definition in the template consists of three parts:

- `@param` – to let Confluence know we are defining a parameter
- Name – to access the parameter's value in your template
- Extra attributes – to further describe your parameter

Parameters are generally defined at the top of the template, just below the header. The order in which you specify the parameters is also the order in which they are displayed in the parameter section (the right-hand side) in the Macro Browser.

```
## @paramTitle:title=Title|type=string|desc=What is the title for
the Teaser
```

As you may have noticed, there are quite a few extra attributes you can use to describe your parameter. The more you specify, the better Confluence can help your users with the Macro Browser and properties editor. Let's go over the available attributes:

Attribute name	Description	Required?
[unnamed first attribute]	The parameter name is the first attribute, and doesn't require a name. `## @param example` Will define the parameter `example`.	Required
`title`	The parameter title that will appear in the Macro Browser. If no title is specified, the parameter name is used.	Recommended
`type`	The field type of the parameters. Learn about types in the next pages.	Recommended
`desc`	The description of the parameter shown in the Macro Browser.	Optional
`required`	Specify if the parameter is required; default is **false**.	Optional
`multiple`	Specify if the parameters allows multiple values; default is **false**.	Optional
`default`	The default value of the parameter.	Optional

If you don't specify the type of the parameter, it will default to a string. But there are many more types available from which you can choose. Confluence will render the input field of your parameter based on the type you specify.

Type	Description
boolean	Displays a checkbox to the user and passes the value **true** or **false** to the macro as a string. `## @param hide:title=Should hide?|type=boolean`

enum	Offers a list of values for selection. You can specify the values to appear in the dropdown yourself. The variable will be passed on the to macro as it is, including capitalization.
	
	`## @param color:title=Color|type=enum|enumValues=Grey,`
	`Red,Green`

string	Shows a text field; this is the default if no other type is specified. `## @param title:title=Title|type=string`

confluence-content	Shows a quick search where the user can search for a page or blog post in Confluence.
	
	`## @param page:title=Page|type=confluence-`
	`content|required=true`

username	Shows a quick search for users. `## @param user:title=Username|type=username`
spacekey	Shows a list of spaces for selection; the space key is passed on to the macro. `## @param space:title=Space|type=spacekey`
date	Currently threated as a normal string. Users can type a date in any format; be sure to check the date in your template. `## @paramfromDate:title=From Date|type=date`
int	Type is accepted, but currently treated as a normal string. `## @param numItems:title=Number of items|type=int`
percentage	Type is accepted, but currently treated as a normal string. `## @param pcent:title=Percentage|type=percentage`

The parameters are available in your template as, for example, `$paramtitle` and `$paramcolor` for parameters called title and color respectively.

Normally, if a parameter like `$paramtitle` is missing, it will appear as `$paramtitle` in the output. To output nothing when a parameter is not set, use an exclamation mark after the dollar sign: `$!paramtitle`.

When your macro doesn't have any parameters, you should use @noparams in your template. This will let Confluence know that it doesn't need to display a parameter input field. If your macro doesn't contain parameters and does not specify @noparams, the macro browser will display a free-format textbox allowing users to enter undefined parameters. You should use @noparams in your template as follows:

```
## @noparams
```

Template code

Now that we have a good descriptive header and parameter declarations for our macro, it is time to write to the macro template code.

When writing your macro, the following objects are available to you to use:

Variable	Description
$body	The body of the macro, if your macro has one.
$param<name>	Named parameters as described in your macro template.
$renderContext	The PageContext object, useful for (among other things) checking $renderContext.baseUrl or $renderContext.spaceKey. More information on the PageContext object is located at http://docs.atlassian.com/atlassian-confluence/latest/com/atlassian/confluence/renderer/PageContext.html.
$space	The space object where this page or blog post is located. This object can be used to retrieve information as the space name, description, and URL. More information is available at http://docs.atlassian.com/atlassian-confluence/latest/com/atlassian/confluence/spaces/Space.html.
$content	The current ContentEntity object in which this macro is included. This can for example be used to retrieve attachments, labels, or comments. More information is available at http://docs.atlassian.com/atlassian-confluence/latest/com/atlassian/confluence/core/ContentEntityObject.html.

Using these objects it is possible to get access to certain extra information that is otherwise not available on a Confluence page; this makes user macros really powerful.

Including another macro

For our user macro we want to include a predefined version of the panel macro, bundled with Confluence. This means we need to find out what the Confluence-specific XML is that defines the panel.

The easiest way to do this is consulting the Storage Format tool. To get the storage format for the panel macro:

1. Create and save a new page containing the panel macro, including all the parameters we want to have predefined.

2. Select **Tools | View Storage format**. This option is only available for Confluence Administrators, and shows the XML source for the page, exactly what we need.

   ° A Confluence macro starts with `<ac:macroac:name`....

   ° A macro parameter starts with `<ac parameter ac:name`....

For our panel, the XML we want to use in our template looks like this:

```
<ac:macro ac:name="panel">
<ac:parameter ac:name="titleBGColor">#00a8e1</ac:parameter>
<ac:parameter ac:name="title">$!paramTitle</ac:parameter>
<ac:parameter ac:name="borderStyle">dashed</ac:parameter>
<ac:parameter ac:name="borderColor">#00a8e1</ac:parameter>
<ac:parameter ac:name="titleColor">#ffffff</ac:parameter>
<ac:rich-text-body>$body</ac:rich-text-body>
</ac:macro>
```

As you might have noticed, I have already included the `title` parameter and `@body` in the XML. I did this by using the value in the `panel` attribute I created on the page, so that I know I put the variables on the right spot.

If we put all the pieces of code together, we have our own teaser macro.

```
## Macro title: Teaser Panel
## Macro has a body: Y
## Body processing: Rendered
##
## Developed by: Stefan Kohler
## Date created: 04/02/2013

## The Teaser panel is a predefined panel used as teaser

## @param Title:title=Title|type=string|desc=What is the title for the
Teaser

<ac:macro ac:name="panel">
<ac:parameter ac:name="titleBGColor">#00a8e1</ac:parameter>
<ac:parameter ac:name="title">$!paramTitle</ac:parameter>
<ac:parameter ac:name="borderStyle">dashed</ac:parameter>
```

```
<ac:parameter ac:name="borderColor">#00a8e1</ac:parameter>
<ac:parameter ac:name="titleColor">#ffffff</ac:parameter>
<ac:rich-text-body>$body</ac:rich-text-body>
</ac:macro>
```

If you want to read more about writing user macros, take a look at some online examples at `https://confluence.atlassian.com/x/V4lYDQ`.

The end result of our user macro looks like this:

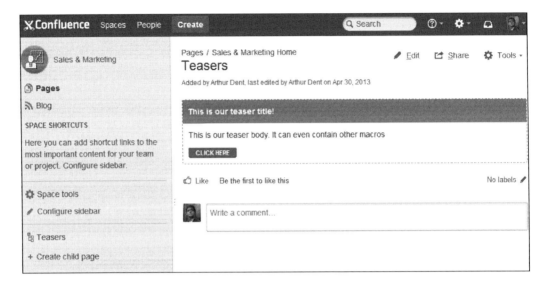

The Page Properties macro

There is one macro I want to emphasize a bit more. The **Page Properties macro**, also known as the **metadata details macro**, is a little beauty.

The Page Properties macro enables you to embed data on a page and then display that information in a tabular form on another page. The Page Properties macro can be placed upon as many pages as you like, and you can use the Page Properties Report macro to display all the data.

An example, which we will implement, is customer contact information where every customer has a page with contact details, using the Page Properties macro. Then on an overview page, we will display all the customers contact information in a table.

To create customer details pages, perform the following steps:

1. Create a `Sales & Marketing` space for this exercise, or use a test/sandbox space if you have one available.

2. In the new space, create a page called `Customers Overview`.

   1. In the body, add the macro Page Properties Report.

   2. In the macro properties, use the label `customer-contact-details`.

   3. Click on **Save** to save the page.

3. Create a new page as the child of the Customers Overview page.

   1. Use your customer name as title.

   2. Insert the Page Properties macro.

   3. In the body of the macro, create a table with two columns and four rows.

   4. Enter some contact details in the table:

      Name – `Ford Prefect`.

      Position – `Managing Directory`.

      Email – `ford.prefect@example.com`.

      Phone – `317-822-2752`.

   5. Give the page a label `customer-contact-details`.

   6. Click on **Save** to save the page.

4. Repeat this step for a couple of customers. (This is a great example on where to use a template.)

So now we have a couple of pages with customer information, looking similar to the following screenshot:

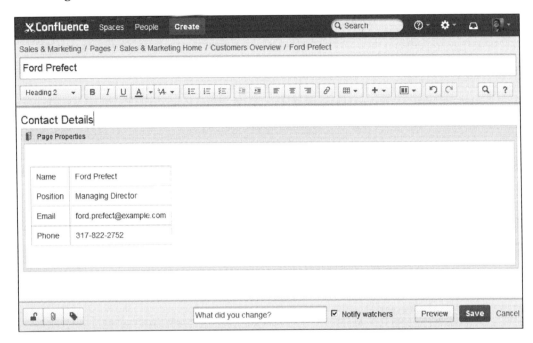

If we now browse back to our **Customer Overview** page we created earlier, we should see a table with our customers. As with all tables in Confluence, you can sort the table by the columns.

 The columns are ordered alphabetically and not as you specified in the Page Properties macro. If you want to reorder the columns, adding a number to them is a good trick.

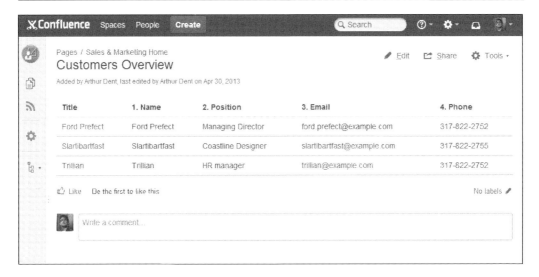

 The table generated by the Page Properties Report macro can also be used as input for other macros like the Charting macro.

Shortcut links

Shortcut links provide a quick way of linking to resources that you use often, for example, a link to a Google search. Shortcut links need to be configured by a Confluence Administrator before users can use them.

Creating a shortcut link

If you search for a book on the Packt Publishing website, the URL will look like `http://www.packtpub.com/books?keys=`. If you create a shortcut for this search with the key `packt`, every time a user needs to visit the website they can just type `[terms@packt]` and Confluence will link to `http://www.packtpub.com/books?keys=terms`.

1. Browse to the Administration Console (**Administration | Confluence Admin**).
2. Select **Shortcut Link** from the left-hand side menu.
3. Enter a key for you shortcut value. In our case, we will use `packt`.
4. Enter the **Expanded Value**: `http://www.packtpub.com/books?keys=`. You can use `%s` in the URL to specify where the term needs to be inserted. If there is no `%s` in the URL, the term is put at the end.

5. Enter a **Default Alias**. This is the text of the link that will be displayed in Confluence. %s can also be used within the text. If no value is entered, Confluence will use term@key as the link text.

6. Click on **Submit**.

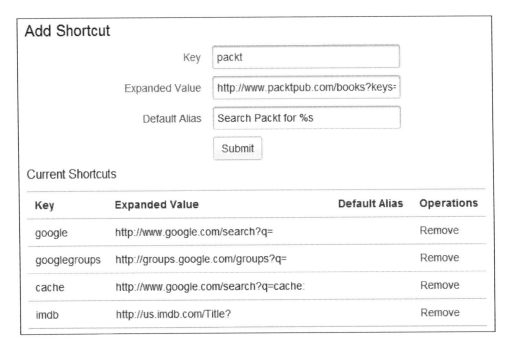

Using shortcut links

Your users can use the shortcut links you created earlier just like any other link.

1. Open a page in the edit mode and place your cursor at the location where you want to add the link.

2. Click on **Link** in the toolbar, or press *Ctrl + K*.

3. Click on **Advanced** and enter the shortcut link confluence@packt into the link textbox.

4. Enter a link text that will be displayed.

5. Click on **Insert**.

You can also use the *[* keyboard shortcut and type the link, enclosed with ' '; for example '[confluence@packt]'.

Users need to be told which shortcuts are available. The best way of doing this is to create a separate page listing the shortcuts. Confluence doesn't provide a way to list them automatically.

Summary

If you want to create uniformity or just want to give your users a head start creating content, templates are there for you. Templates are preformatted pages that can be used when you add a new page. We have learned how to create those templates and that templates can be added on a space or global level.

Another mechanism to automate things you find yourself doing often is user macros. User macros allow you to code some functionality or formatting, which your users can reuse. User macros can easily be added via the Confluence user interface, but they do require a bit of knowledge about HTML and XML. With the example in this chapter, you should have a solid base to start building your own macros.

That macros can be really powerful is demonstrated by the Page Properties macro that you can use to get metadata from pages and show this in an overview table.

There are many add-ons available that add templates, macros, and other functionalities to Confluence. These add-ons can be installed via the Atlassian Marketplace, which we will learn about in the next chapter.

9
General Administration

Confluence is a very powerful and flexible application. We have seen how we can customize the look and feel of Confluence, add a structure, create content, and how we can involve other people. Apart from the areas we have already covered, there are some other useful features worth learning.

In this chapter we will take a look on how to manage add-ons, to add new features to Confluence, how Confluence can be integrated with different applications using application links and how we can troubleshoot Confluence and get in contact with Atlassian Support.

By the end of this chapter we will have learned:

- Working with add-ons
- Integrating Confluence with other applications
- Content indexing
- Getting support

Working with add-ons

Throughout the book we have been using a plain vanilla Confluence installation without any added features or functionalities. Add-ons are separately installed components that supplement or enhance functionality in Confluence. This can vary from a single feature such as a macro to something that could be a product on its own, such as the add-on "Team Calendars".

There are over 500 add-ons for Confluence available via the Atlassian Marketplace and more are being added. These add-ons can be downloaded, evaluated, and purchased via the Marketplace. The Marketplace can be access directly via the Internet or by making use of the Universal Plugin Manager, from within the Confluence Administration Console.

 The term "add-on" and "plugin" are both being used to indicate extra functionality. While both terms are sometimes used interchangeably, they are not the same. A plugin is a type of add-on that can be added to Confluence and is developed using the Atlassian Plugin SDK. Not all add-ons are plugins. A native app for you mobile device would be considered an add-on, while the "content formatting macros" are plugins.

The Marketplace

The Atlassian Marketplace, located at `https://marketplace.atlassian.com`, is the resource for finding, evaluating, and purchasing add-ons for Confluence.

Finding add-ons using the normal search functionality of the Marketplace is usually very easy and will find you the right add-on. Sometimes you want to narrow down the search parameters and search for an add-on specific to a certain version. This can be done via the advanced search.

To find an add-on using Advanced Search, perform the following steps:

1. Browse to `https://marketplace.atlassian.com`.
2. Select **Advanced Search** from the top navigation to browse to the advanced search as displayed in the next image.
3. Select **Confluence** as **Application** and choose your version from the values of the **Version** field.
4. Fill in other options to specify the add-on you're looking for.

5. Click on **Advanced Search**.

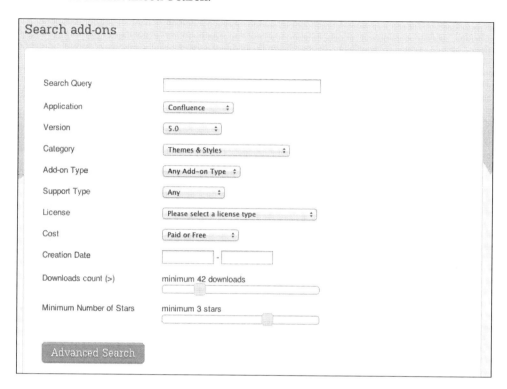

When you have found a plugin that you like, there are two possibilities:

*   The add-on is *free*, and can be used without a license.
*   The add-on is one that you have to *pay for*; then you have to buy a license if you want to use the add-on. The add-on can be evaluated for 30 days, which can be extended to 90 days.

In either case, you have to download the add-on and install it in your Confluence installation. The Marketplace offers a download link, but there is an easier way to install new add-ons to your application, the Universal Plugin Manager.

The Universal Plugin Manager

The **Universal Plugin Manager (UPM)**, which is an add-on itself, can be used to administer add-ons from within Confluence. The UPM is called universal, because it works across other Atlassian products.

With the more recent versions of Confluence, the Universal Plugin Manager comes preinstalled, so you don't have to install it yourself. However, as the UPM is a plugin, it gets updated regularly, so you'll need to update it from time to time.

Online and offline modes

The Universal Plugin Manages relies on an available Internet connection to perform the following tasks:

- Searching and installing new add-ons

- Checking for and installing updates for the add-ons

- Performing application upgrade checks

If your Confluence server is not connected to the Internet, it is possible to switch the UPM to offline mode. In offline mode, the UPM does not connect to the Internet, and the features using Internet are disabled. In offline mode, you will still be able to use the UPM for:

- Managing installed add-ons

- Uploading a new add-on from a local server

- Checking the UPM audit log

Another option is to protect your server with a firewall, and allow the UPM to connect only to the required services. To allow the UPM to perform online functions from behind a firewall, make sure Confluence can connect to port 443 (HTTPS) on the following servers:

- ***.atlassian.com**: The UPM connects to several servers in the `atlassian.com` domain. These include `marketplace.atlassian.com` and `id.atlassian.com`.

- **dq1dnt4af4eyy.cloudfront.net**: The Marketplace uses Amazon CloudFront as the CDN. This is where your add-ons are downloaded from.

 These links are subject to change, check `https://confluence.atlassian.com/x/Y4tCEg` if the previously mentioned settings don't work for you.

Information transmitted by the UPM

If the Universal Plugin Manager is in online mode (default), information is transmitted every time a Confluence administrator visits the "manage add-ons" page in the Administration Console. In addition, a background task will send the same information every 24 hours to the Marketplace to check for new versions.

The information transmitted to Atlassian includes:

- The type and version of the application (for example, Confluence 5.1.2)
- The add-on key and version of the installed add-ons (for example, `com. atlassian.calendar 1.2`)
- The current UPM version

When analytic information collection is enabled, the following information is also transmitted to Atlassian:

- **Support Entitlement Number (SEN)** and server ID
- License statistics, such as maximum number of users
- License type (Commercial, Evaluation)
- Certain usage events, for example, uninstallation of an add-on

If you want to disable transmitting license information to Atlassian, you can disable this function by setting a Java system property. The property is `atlassian.upm. server.data.disable=true`.

To set a Java system property:

1. Open the `setenv.bat` file that is located at `CONF_INSTALL/bin`.
2. Find the `set JAVA_OPTS=%JAVA_OPTS%` section.
3. Add `-Datlassian.upm.server.data.disable=true` to the section; the list is space separated.

> If you are running Confluence as a Windows Service, the system property has to be set elsewhere; refer to `https://confluence. atlassian.com/x/JoUDCg` for more information.

Switching to offline mode

If you want to set the Universal Plugin Manager in offline mode, no data will be transmitted to Atlassian. You cannot download any add-ons directly via the UPM though.

To turn on offline mode:

1. Browse to the Administration Console (**Administration | Confluence Admin**).

2. Choose **Manage Add-ons** in the left-hand menu.

3. Click on the **Settings** link at the bottom of the page; a dialog will appear as shown in the following screenshot:

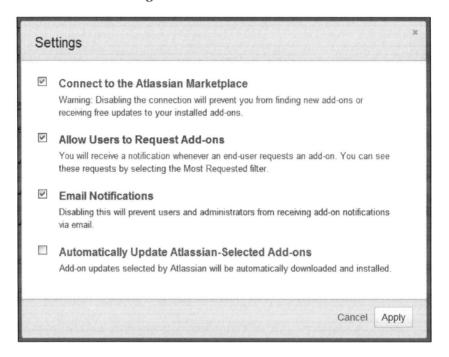

4. Uncheck the checkbox in front of **Connect to the Atlassian Marketplace**. This is enabled by default.

5. Click on **Apply** for the settings to take effect.

Features that are disabled in offline mode, such as **Find new add-ons** are hidden from the user interface.

Finding new add-ons

Any user, administrator or nonadministrator, can browse the Atlassian
Marketplace from within Confluence. System administrators can use this
page to install add-ons, while other users can use this to request add-ons for
installation (more about requests in the *User request for add-ons* section).

To find an add-on, perform the following steps:

1. Click on your avatar in the top-left corner.
2. Select **Atlassian Marketplace** from the drop-down menu. The in-product
   view of the Marketplace appears as shown in the following screenshot:

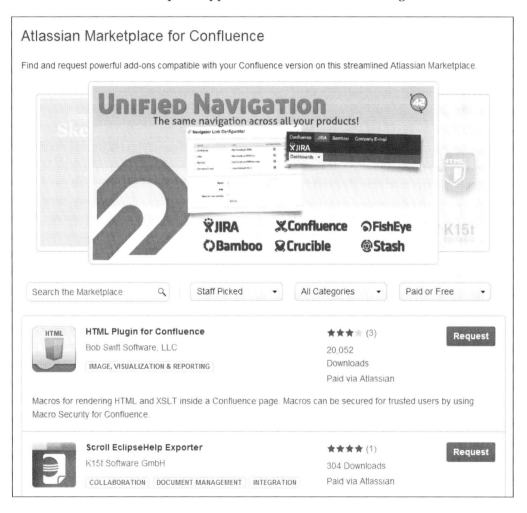

3. Search for add-ons by browsing the suggestions or by:

  ○ Typing a search string in the **Search the Marketplace** box. This will filter the results based upon add-on names.

  ○ Use the pull-down menus to filter the add-ons based on:

    ○ Attributes such as **Recently Added** or **Staff Picked**

    ○ Category, such as **Themes & Styles** or **Blueprints**

    ○ Based on pricing such as **Free**, **Paid via Atlassian**, or **All Paid**

There is a difference between **Paid via Atlassian** and **All Paid**. Add-on vendors may choose to let Atlassian handle all the purchases for their add-on. This is a great advantage for users, who can now purchase add-ons via Atlassian, making use of their standardized process and my.atlassian.com. The **All Paid** option also displays add-ons by vendors who choose their own purchasing system.

Installing add-ons

The Universal Plugin Manager makes it very easy to install new add-ons in your Confluence installation. With a few clicks, you can browse through all add-ons and install the ones you like.

Alternatively, you can use the file upload to install an add-on manually by uploading a JAR or OBR file to Confluence. The archive file should contain plugin code and resources. You can use this method if other operations will not work because you're behind a firewall.

Add-ons are really powerful and can change the behavior of many aspects of Confluence. However, it is very important to verify the add-on vendor and test the add-on before adding it to your production environment.

Installing directly via the Marketplace

If you are a system administrator and the UPM is connected to the Internet, you can install add-ons by clicking on the **Install** button from the **Find New Add-ons** page. This single-click installation is the quickest way to install add-ons.

To install a plugin directly:

1. Click on your avatar in the top-left corner.

2. Select **Atlassian Marketplace** from the drop-down menu. The in-product view of the Marketplace appears.

3. Find the relevant add-on.

4. Click on the **Install** button to install the add-on.

If the add-on is a paid add-on, there will be buttons **Buy Now** and **Free Trail**. Clicking on either one of these buttons will download and install the add-on, and ask you to get a valid license via `https://my.atlassian.com`.

Installing by file upload

When the single-click installation method is not available to you, you can use the manual file upload to install your add-ons. Add-ons are normally distributed as JAR or OBR files, containing the add-on code and resources. These are the only two file types that the UPM accepts for installation.

Before uploading your add-on manually, be sure to have the distribution file on your desktop or a local server, for example, downloaded from the Marketplace to your desktop.

To upload an add-on:

1. Browse to the Administration Console (**Administration | Confluence Admin**).

2. Choose **Manage Add-ons** in the left-hand menu.

3. Click on the **Upload Add-on** link at the top-right side of the page. The following upload dialog appears:

4. Choose a JAR or OBR file from your computer, or enter a URL that the server can access.

5. Click on the **Upload** button. A confirmation message will appear when the add-on is installed successfully.

Updating add-ons

Add-on providers periodically release new versions of their add-ons to incorporate bug fixes and new features. These updates can be release at any moment, independent of the releases of Confluence. It is generally recommended to keep add-ons up-to-date, but do validate an update before applying it to your production environment.

If the Universal Plugin Manager is connected to the Marketplace, the **Manage Add-ons** page will help you to keep your installed add-ons up-to-date. If the UPM is not connected, keeping the add-ons up-to-date needs a manual check via `https://marketplace.atlassian.com`.

To update an add-on, perform the following steps:

1. Browse to the Administration Console (**Administration | Confluence Admin**).

2. Choose **Manage Add-ons** in the left-hand menu.

3. Add-ons that have an update available will be displayed in the **Add-ons Requiring Action** list, as shown in the following screenshot:

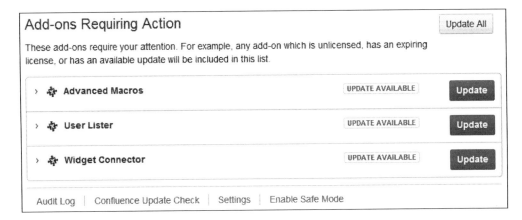

4. Click on the **Update** button next to the add-on. The UPM will then download and install the latest available version. A success message will appear when it is finished.

Alternatively, the updated add-on can be manually uploaded. The update procedure is identical to the single-click option. Generally, it is not needed to remove the "old" add-on before updating it, provided the add-on developer incremented the version number.

> Updating add-ons can fail in some cases, for example, when a plugin developer did not anticipate a new version of the UPM such that updating the add-on on a newer version of the UPM fails. Other reasons exist too. It is then helpful to stop the Confluence instance, remove the cache folders (`https://confluence.atlassian.com/x/TgG_EQ`), restart the instance, and re-try updating or uploading the previous add-on version.

Removing installed add-ons

You can remove an installed add-on from Confluence in the **Manage Add-ons** page. Uninstalling an add-on permanently removes it from Confluence and the file is removed from the home directory. If you only want to temporarily remove it, you may choose to disable your add-on instead.

To uninstall an add-on, perform the following steps:

1. Browse to the Administration Console (**Administration | Confluence Admin**).
2. Choose **Manage Add-ons** in the left-hand menu.
3. Find the add-on you want to uninstall in the add-on list.
4. Click on the add-on to open the details view.
5. Click on the **Uninstall** button.
6. Confirm by clicking on the **Continue** button in the dialog.

7. When finished, a notice appears in the add-on details view.

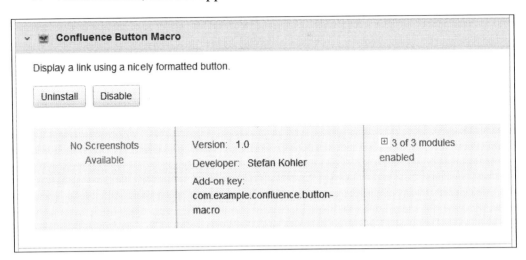

If you want to have the add-on features temporarily removed, you can also disable the add-on. Disabling an add-on will make its features unavailable.

To disable an add-on, perform the following steps:

1. Browse to the Administration Console (**Administration | Confluence Admin**).
2. Choose **Manage Add-ons** in the left-hand menu.
3. Find the add-on you want to disable in the add-on list.
4. Click on the add-on to open the details view.
5. Click on the **Disable** button.

 Some add-ons are part of Confluence and can't be disabled.

User requests for add-ons

When enabled, all users in Confluence can view the in-product Marketplace to search for add-ons. Instead of installing or trying add-ons, they can choose to request the add-on.

When the **Request** button is clicked on, a pop up appears where an additional message for the system administrator can be given, as in the following screenshot:

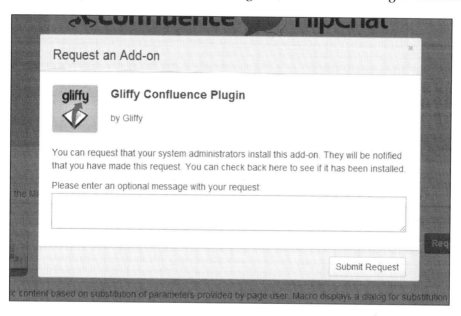

If a user requests an add-on, the system administrators will receive an e-mail notification.

Viewing user requests

Via the **Find New Add-ons** page, administrators can easily see the most requested add-ons and by whom were they requested.

To watch the most requested add-ons:

1. Browse to the Administration Console (**Administration | Confluence Admin**).
2. Choose **Manage Add-ons** in the left-hand menu.

3. From the add-on filters, choose **Most Requested** as displayed in the following screenshot:

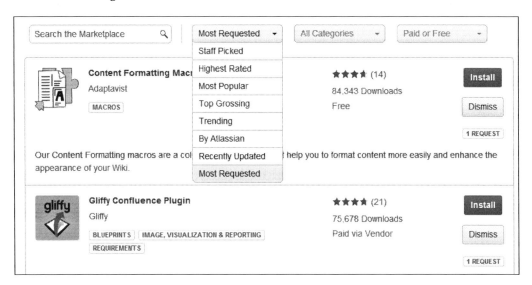

The requested add-ons will appear, with the most requested at the top.

4. Click on an add-on to view more details about the request. The users, dates of request, and additional messages are displayed here.

5. From this view, you can install, buy, or dismiss the request, removing the request count from the add-on.

Disabling user requests

The user add-on request feature is enabled by default, but can be disabled by a system administrator. This will remove the in-product Marketplace link for users and the **Most Requested** add-on filter.

Disabling user requests will not remove request counts. If the feature is enabled again, previously requested add-ons would appear.

To disable user add-on requests:

1. Browse to the Administration Console (**Administration | Confluence Admin**).
2. Choose **Manage Add-ons** in the left-hand menu.
3. Click on the **Settings** link at the bottom of the page; a dialog will appear.
4. Clear the **Allow Users to Request Add-ons** checkbox.
5. Click on **Apply** to save the setting.

Content indexing

Everything stored within Confluence is considered to be content. To be able to search this content, it needs to be indexed first. Confluence Administrators can adjust the behavior of the indexes and Confluence search.

Content is not directly added to the index. New and modified content is placed in a queue and the queue is processed once every minute.

Rebuilding the indexes

Normally the content indexes are maintained automatically, but you may need to rebuild the indexes manually under the following circumstances:

- Created content doesn't appear in "Recently Updated" or the search results
- The **Did You Mean** feature is not working
- After a Confluence upgrade, if mentioned in the upgrade release notes
- If you changed the indexing language

To rebuild a content index, perform the following steps:

1. Browse to the Administration Console (**Administration | Confluence Admin**).

2. Choose **Content Indexing** in the left-hand side menu.

   This will display both **Search Indexes** and the current status:

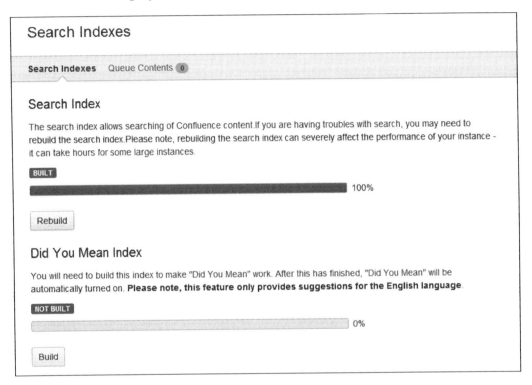

3. Click on the **Rebuild** button below the index you wish the rebuild. The button is called **Build** if the index has never been built before.

Building the Confluence content index can take a long time to complete, this depends on:

- The number of pages in your installation
- The number, type, and size of the attachments
- The amount of memory available to Confluence

Changing the indexing language

If the majority of your content is in a different language than English, changing the indexing language in Confluence may improve the accuracy of the Confluence search results. Confluence supports content indexing in English, German, Russian, Chinese, Japanese, French, Brazilian Portuguese, Czech, and Greek.

To change the indexing language:

1. Browse to the Administration Console (**Administration | Confluence Admin**).
2. Choose **General Configuration** in the left-hand menu.
3. Choose **Edit**.
4. Select the indexing language from the drop-down list in the **Formatting and International Settings** section.
5. Click on **Save** to apply the settings.

 Even in an unsupported language (for example, Dutch), the content indexing function works rather well, as it does not only rely on an idiom but it will also look into the available content (pages and attachments) to build the search index.

Application links

Confluence can be integrated with other Atlassian tools using **application links**. An application link is a trusted relation between two applications. These applications are allowed to share information and work with each other.

To explain the possibilities, we will be connecting our Confluence installation to a JIRA installation. Using the same technique, Confluence can be connected to Bamboo, FishEye, Crucible, Stash, or another Confluence installation.

Integration of Confluence with JIRA allows you to, among others, display a list of JIRA issues in your Confluence page as shown in the following screenshot:

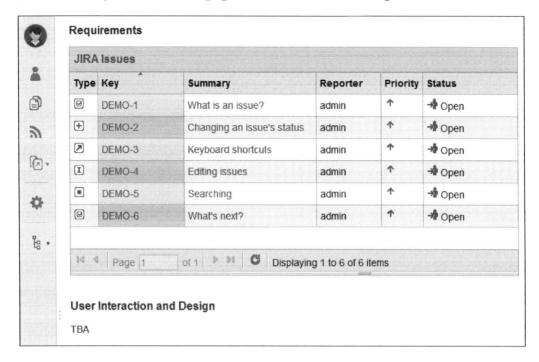

Adding an application link

Make sure that the base URL is set correctly (in **General Configuration**) for both applications before adding an application link.

To connect Confluence to JIRA, perform the following steps:

1. Browse to the Administration Console (**Administration | Confluence Admin**).
2. Choose **Application Links** in the left-hand side menu.
3. Click on **Add Application Link**. **Step 1** of the link wizard will appear.

4. Enter the server URL of JIRA and click on **Next**.

5. In **Step 2** of the wizard, enter the following information:

    ○ **Also create a link from 'Your Company JIRA' back to this server**:
      Select this option if you want to create a two-way link between
      Confluence and JIRA. If so, provide an administrator account for
      JIRA to create the link.

    ○ The provided credentials are not stored.

    ○ The credentials need to be a user account with administration access.

        ° **Reciprocal link URL**: This URL will override the base URL. Application links will use this URL to connect to JIRA.

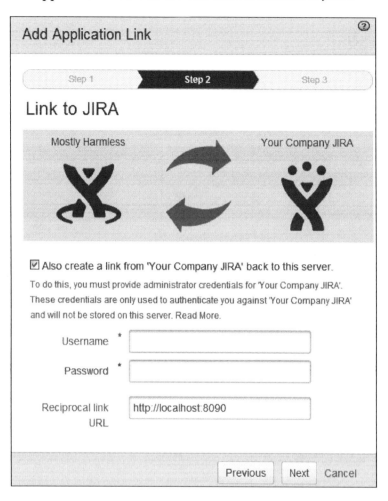

6. Click on the **Next** button; **Step 3** will appear.

7. Enter the information required to configure the authentication:

        ° **The servers have the same set of users and usernames** or **The servers have different sets of users or usernames**: Select either one of these options, depending on how the users are managed in Confluence and JIRA.

        ° **These servers fully trust each other**: Selecting this option will allow to Confluence and JIRA connect to each other as any user. This is the most useful connection.

Editing an application link

A Confluence system administrator can change the application name and display URL for any existing application link.

To edit an application link, perform the following steps:

1. Browse to the Administration Console (**Administration | Confluence Admin**).
2. Choose **Application Links** in the left-hand menu.
3. Click on the **Configure** link, next to the application link you want to edit.
4. The application link details will be displayed:

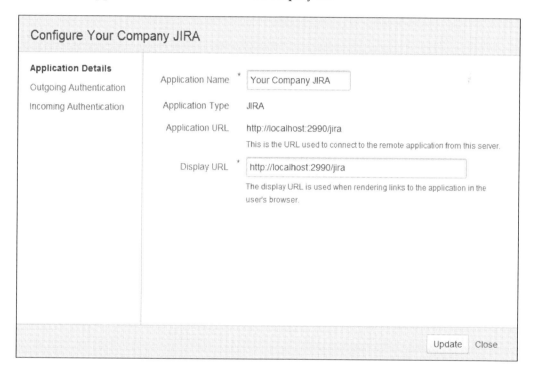

5. Update the details as you like; the **Application Type** and **Application URL** fields cannot be changed after creating the link.
    ○ The **Display URL** field is used when displaying links to the application. When you created the application link, you may have used an internal URL or IP, which your users can't access. This URL overrides that URL when displaying a link.

6. Click on **Update** to save your changes.

Space project links

Application links are, as the name suggests, application-wide. Once an application link is set up between applications, it is possible to create a more specific links, called **project links**. With project links, you can connect a specific Confluence space to a specific JIRA project, Bamboo project, or FishEye repository. Doing this makes it easier to gather your information in one place.

To link a space to a JIRA project:

1. Go to the space you want to connect to JIRA.
2. Select **Space Tools** in the sidebar. (If you are not using the default theme, select **Browse | Space Admin**.)
3. Select the **Integrations** tab.
4. Click on the **Add Link** link. A drop-down with the configured application links appears; select the application you want to link to.
5. Select one of the options on the **Authorization Required** screen.
    ° **Authorize**: Select this option if you want to grant your space access to the target project. You will be prompted for JIRA credentials.
    ° **Skip – Your access is anonymous**: Select this option if you want anonymous access to JIRA.
6. In the **Name or Key** field, enter the name/key of the JIRA project you want to connect to.
7. Select **Yes** or **No**, to create a link in JIRA back to the Confluence space too.
8. Click on the **Create** button to create the project link.

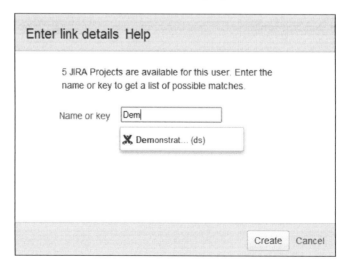

Configuring authentication

On every application link, you can configure which authentication method should be used for incoming and outgoing connections. Incoming authentication is used for all requests from JIRA to Confluence and outgoing authentication goes the other way around.

The authentication for an application link is basically defining the level of trust between Confluence and the other application. The level of authentication that you should configure depends on a number of factors:

- **Do both applications trust each other?**: In case of an Atlassian application, it would be safe to answer "yes". If you are connecting Confluence to another application, make sure that application is secure.

- **Do both applications share the same user base?**

- **Do you have administrative access to the other application?**

Common scenarios are as follows:

- Both Confluence and JIRA are internal and use the same user base. In this case, **trusted applications** is the best authentication for both incoming and outgoing authentications.

- If Confluence and JIRA don't share the same user base, use **OAuth** (explained in the next section) for authentication (both ways). This could be your internal Confluence and external (customer-facing) JIRA instance.

- In the case where you don't have administrative rights on the JIRA server, you can configure a one-way outgoing authentication using **basic HTTP authentication**.

Trusted applications authentication

Trusted applications authentication allows one application to access functions on another application on behalf of any user, without the user having to log in to the other application. So in our situation, every Confluence user will see the exact same list of JIRA issues when they use the "JIRA Issues" macro as they would when they use the JIRA issue navigator.

To configure trusted applications authentication:

1. Browse to the Administration Console (**Administration |
   Confluence Admin**).

2. Choose **Application Links** in the left-hand menu.

3. Click on the **Configure** link, next to the application link you want to edit.

4. Select the **Incoming Authentication** tab; all incoming authentications will
   be displayed with the **Trusted Applications** tab selected.

5. The tab will display if the authentication is currently enabled or not.
   The trusted applications configuration has the following properties:

   - **IP Patterns**: Enter the IP addresses (IPv4) from which Confluence
     should accept requests. You can specify a wildcard by using an
     asterisk, for example, `192.168.2.*`.

   - **URL Patterns**: Enter the URLs that JIRA is allowed to access.
     For Confluence this should at least be the following:

     `/plugins/servlet/streams`

     `/plugins/servlet/applinks/whoami`

   - **Certificate Timeout (ms)**: Enter the certificate timeout. The default
     time is 10 seconds. The timeout is used to prevent replay attacks.
     If the second request is 10 seconds after the initial (authorization)
     request, it will be rejected. Note that the timeout relies on the clocks
     on both servers being synced.

6. Click on **Apply** to save your changes.

The settings for outgoing authentication have the same properties. The outgoing authentication can also be set up from Confluence, but you might be prompted for the JIRA credentials.

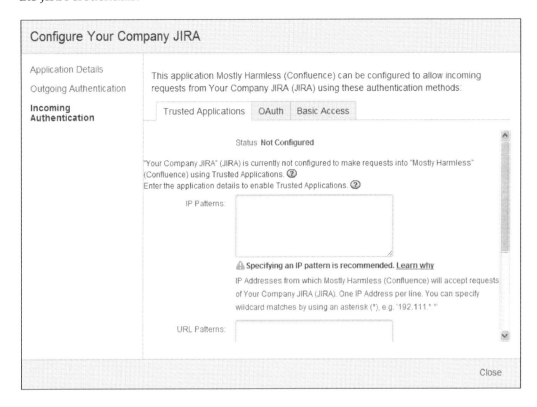

OAuth authentication

OAuth is a protocol that allows web applications to share data with other external applications. This could be another web application (such as JIRA) or a desktop or mobile application.

OAuth is typically used when two applications trust each other, but don't share the same set of users and do have the option to connect via application links.

 Use SSL
It is recommended that your applications use SSL (HTTPS) instead of basic HTTP, as sensitive information is transmitted via the Internet.

To configure OAuth Authentication, perform the following steps:

1. Browse to the Administration Console (**Administration | Confluence Admin**).
2. Choose **Application Links** in the left-hand menu.
3. Click on the **Configure** link, next to the application link you want to edit.
4. Select **Incoming Authentication** and select the **OAuth** tab.
5. Click on the **Enable** button to enable OAuth authentication for the incoming link. The remote application will be automatically set up to be the "consumer" and your local application a "service provider".

For outgoing authentication a login dialog will display if you are not currently logged in to the remote application. Log in with your credentials for the other (JIRA) server. Selecting the **Enable** button will set up OAuth for outgoing authentication.

Basic HTTP authentication

Using basic HTTP authentication relies on the connection between Confluence and JIRA being secure. It is recommend to use a different authentication method, provided you are able to do so.

Basic HTTP authentication allows you to provide Confluence with user credentials for JIRA, and visa versa. Once authenticated, Confluence can access JIRA functions and resources on behalf of that user. This also means that if you provide user credentials of a user with administrative functions, your application link would be able to access those functions as well.

To configure basic HTTP authentication:

1. Browse to the Administration Console (**Administration |
   Confluence Admin**).
2. Choose **Application Links** in the left-hand menu.
3. Click on the **Configure** link, next to the application link you want to edit.
4. Select **Incoming Authentication** and select the **Basic Access** tab.
5. Enter the **User Credentials**.
6. Click on **Enable** to store the credentials and enable basic
   HTTP authentication.

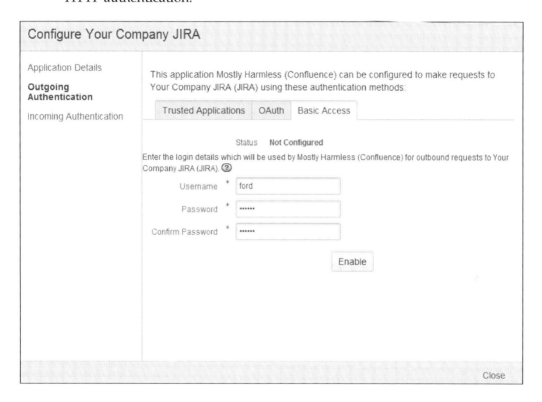

Using Application Navigator

Application Navigator appears in the top-left corner of Confluence, as soon as there is more then one link configured. Application Navigator can be used to quickly navigate between different applications.

Not all Atlassian applications currently have this navigator, but they will in the future.

Adding a new link

A Confluence administrator can add new links to the navigator. By default application links are also added to the navigator; it is not possible to remove them.

To add a new link:

1. Browse to the Administration Console (**Administration | Confluence Admin**).

2. Choose **Application Navigator** in the left-hand menu.

3. Fill in the details for the new link:

    ○ **Name**: The name which will be displayed in the navigator drop-down list

    ○ **URL**: The link to the application or website

    ○ **Hide**: Select this checkbox if you don't want to show the link in the navigator drop-down list

    ○ **Restricted to Groups**: Links can be restricted to certain groups; select the groups that are allowed to see this link

4. Click on **Add**, to save the link.

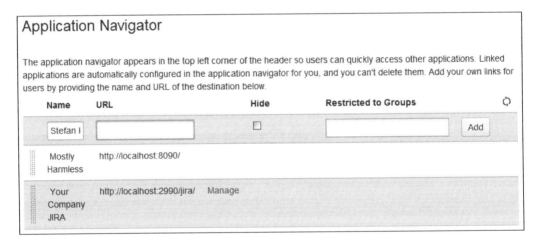

Managing links

Existing links can easily be altered, ordered, or removed, with the exception of configured application links, those are a bit limited.

To change an existing link:

1. Browse to the Administration Console (**Administration | Confluence Admin**).
2. Choose **Application Navigator** in the left-hand side menu.
3. Hover over the link you want to change and watch the background turn yellow (if the background doesn't change, you can't change the value).
4. Click on the value to change to edit mode.
5. Update the values you wish to change.
6. Press *Enter*, or click on **Update** to save the changes.

Changing the order in which the links appear in the navigator is done by dragging-and-dropping the links.

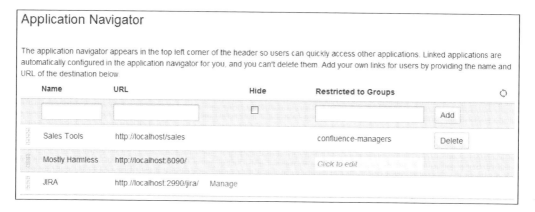

To remove a link:

1. Browse to the Administration Console (**Administration | Confluence Admin**).
2. Choose **Application Navigator** in the left-hand side menu.
3. Click on the **Delete** button.

Getting support

Sometimes you run into a situation where you need help to continue. Atlassian provides a couple of channels to which you can resort in this case.

In many cases the online documentation (`https://confluence.atlassian.com/display/DOC/`) has detailed information to get you sorted out. If you cannot find what you need in the documentation, you could ask your question online via Atlassian Answers. Of course it is always possible to create a support ticket with Atlassian or turn to an Atlassian Expert to help you.

Atlassian Answers

Atlassian Answers is the community-driven Q&A site that is available for everybody. In case you need help, you can log in to `https://answers.atlassian.com` with your Atlassian ID (the same account you use for maintaining your licenses).

Answers is a reputation system that uses **Karma** to incentivize users to participate and give correct answers to the questions that are posted. With enough Karma points, you will receive a T-shirt from Atlassian.

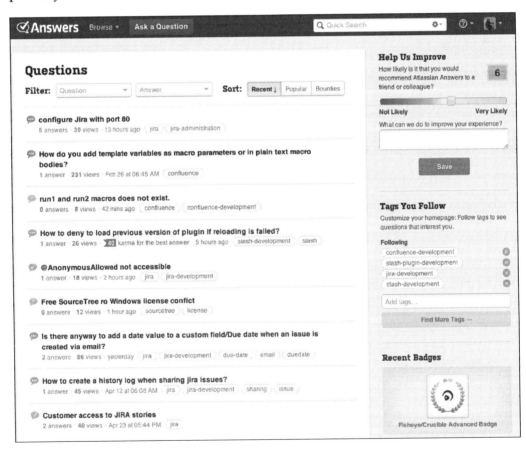

If you can't find an answer to your question on Answers, or you need to share some information about your installation you are not comfortable with, there is always Atlassian Support to help.

Atlassian Support

With a valid license you are entitled to support from Atlassian. To get the most out of the Atlassian Support, it helps to do a preliminary diagnosis on your system using the built-in support tools.

Atlassian Support tools

Confluence provides a built-in log scanner. The scanner will check your Confluence logs for errors and will compare them against a list of know issues in Atlassian's knowledge base and bug tracker. The log scanner is called **Hercules**. Hercules will connect to the Internet to retrieve the last set of known issues; your files will not be sent over the Internet. System administrators can use Hercules to scan logfiles.

To use the log scanner:

1. Browse to the Administration Console (**Administration | Confluence Admin**).

2. Choose **Atlassian Support Tools** in the left-hand side menu.

3. Select the **Log Scanner** below the **Troubleshooting** header.

4. If your logfile is in the default location, click on **Scan**. Otherwise, change the location first.

5. The log scanner will return a list of links pointing to Atlassian's knowledge base or bug tracker.

   ° The last reported problems are displayed first. If you have more than 10 errors matching known issues, click on the **Show All** link that appears on top of the page.

    ◦   Choose a link to check the reported problem and possible solution or workaround.

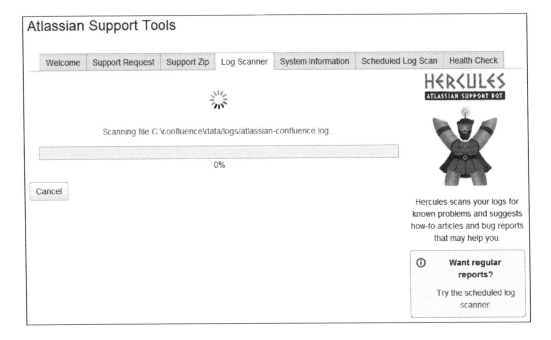

Raising a support ticket

At this point we may have an issue without a known solution, and we have fixed most of the issues resulting from our log scanner diagnosis. This would be a good time to raise a support ticket at Atlassian.

The easiest way to raise a support ticket is directly from the Administration Console. If you are not able to use this method, you have to use the JIRA instance at `https://support.atlassian.com`.

Submitting a support request via Confluence

The advantage of using this method is that all files needed to provide good support are directly added to the support request. Having an SMTP server set up is required for this method.

To submit a support request:

1. Browse to the Administration Console (**Administration | Confluence Admin**).
2. Choose **Atlassian Support Tools** in the left-hand menu.
3. Select **Support Request**.
4. Provide as much information a possible:
    - **Contact email**: This defaults to the logged-in user. The e-mail address is used to find or create an account on `https://support.atlassian.com`. All further notification will be send to this e-mail.
    - **Summary**: A brief description of the problem.
    - **Description**: As much information as you can share, including any error message and steps to reproduce the problem.
5. In the **Support Data to Attach** section, select the types of additional files you want to attach to the request. The more the better in this case, but keep in mind your company's privacy and non-disclosure rules.
6. Choose **Send** to post your request.

Once the support request is received you will receive a notification via e-mail.

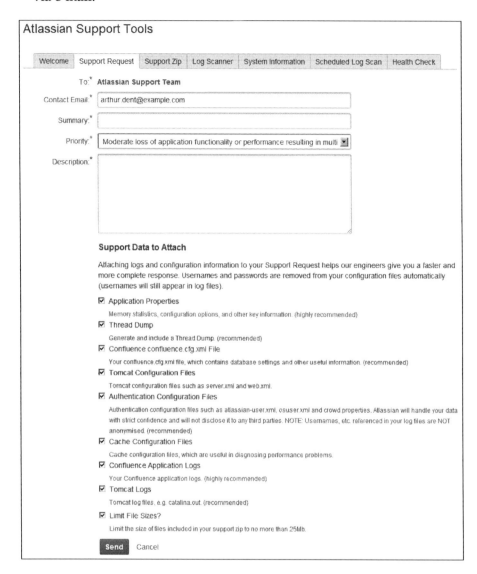

Atlassian experts

Atlassian has over 250 partners, called **experts**, who are dedicated to helping you with specific needs around Confluence and all other products. If you need training, custom add-ons or in-house support setting up your suite, a local expert is there to help you.

Getting an expert in early, to help you setting up Confluence, will pay off in the long term. Experts have seen *many different installations*, use cases and are well aware of the more than 1000 add-ons available to you.

To find a local expert, perform the following steps:

1. Browse to `http://www.atlassian.com/resources/experts/`.

2. Use the filter to specify:

   ° What kind of expert you are looking for (training, tuning, migration)

   ° For what kind of product (Confluence, JIRA)

   ° In which country

3. Click on **Search Experts** to generate a list with experts matching your filter.

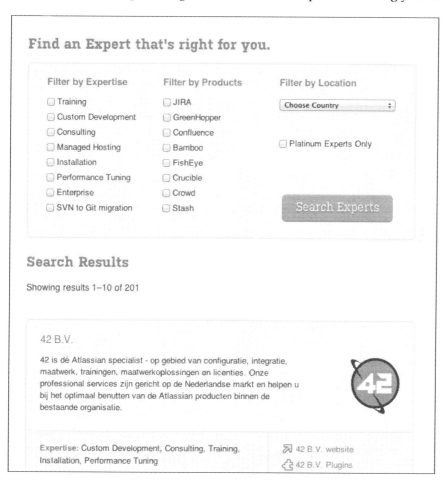

Summary

In this chapter we have learned where we can find add-ons to add new features to Confluence so it will fit all of your needs. The Atlassian Marketplace is a vibrant place, and more and more add-ons are added every day. Browsing through it can be done with ease from within Confluence.

Content is everything, and everything is content, in Confluence. Under normal circumstances, indexing that content works fine, but in some cases we have to help Confluence. We learned about content indexing and how to maintain it if needed.

With application links, it is possible to integrate Confluence with other tools to create a real suite of products. Application links make it possible to get different content from different tools all in one single application. With Application Navigator, it's also very easy to switch between the various tools.

Last but not least, we learned how to get support if we are stuck. There are many online resources available, and the Atlassian Support and experts are there to get you on the road again.

The next chapter will give you a peek into how you can write your own add-ons. This means that some coding is involved. If this is not something you are comfortable with, just give the book to a developer in your company when you're finished; he or she might be able to help you write the add-on you need.

10
Extending Confluence

Not every feature might be available in Confluence out of the box or as add-ons in the marketplace. Confluence is very extendable with custom plugins, and if you are a developer, you can even create your own plugin using the **Atlassian Software Development Kit (SDK)**.

By the end of this chapter, you will have learned about:

- Setting up your development environment
- Using the Atlassian Plugin SDK
- The different extensions points
- How to release your plugin

If you are not a developer yourself, this chapter will probably be difficult to read, but it could give you an insight into what is possible with extending Confluence.

The Atlassian Plugin SDK

Atlassian provides plugin developers with a Software Development Kit (SDK). By using this SDK, developers can create plugins that extend the functionality of all Atlassian products. The SDK allows you to quickly connect and use the plugin development platform.

The Atlassian Plugin SDK makes your life easier by helping to do the following:

- Build plugins for any Atlassian application with a single tool.
- Create a plugin skeleton, specific to the Atlassian application you are developing for.
- Download the application binaries, install your plugin, and start the application.

- Dynamically re-install your plugin after changes during development. No restart required.

- Write quality unit tests and integration tests.

- Speed up the all-important code-deploy-test cycle.

Installing the Atlassian Plugin SDK

Before we can start building our first plugin, we have to install the Atlassian Plugin SDK. We will go through the steps required to install the SDK on a Windows system.

Prerequisites

First we have to make sure our Windows system has the prerequisite software and is configured correctly. The Atlassian SDK relies on Version 1.6.x or higher of the Oracle JDK.

To install the Oracle JDK, perform the following steps:

1. Download the latest JDK from `http://www.oracle.com/technetwork/java/javase/downloads/index.html`.

 At the time of writing the latest version is JDK 7 update 17.

2. Double-click the downloaded installation file to start the installation wizard.

3. Select where you would like to install Java, or simply accept the default values. The location where you install the JDK will be referred to as `JAVA_HOME`.

4. Right-click the Computer icon.

5. Select **Advanced system settings** from the left-hand side menu.

6. Click on the **Environment Variables** button.

7. Create a new environmental variable name `JAVA_HOME` with the value of where you just installed Java as shown:

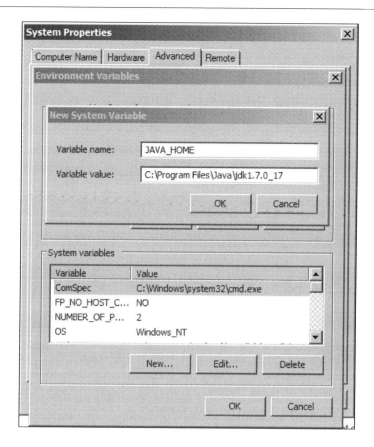

Now that you have the JDK installed on your system, add the JAVA `bin` directory to your path to ensure that you can use Java from the command prompt. Again, we assume a Windows setup.

To add `JAVA_HOME` to your path, perform the following steps:

1. Right-click the Computer icon.
2. Select **Advanced system settings** from the left-hand side menu.
3. Click on the **Environment Variables** button.
4. Locate the **Path** variable under the System variables and click on **Edit...**.
5. Add `;%JAVA_HOME%\bin` to the end of variable value.
6. Save the changes and close all dialogs.

Before we continue, we have to make sure the JDK is installed correctly so that the Atlassian SDK is able to use it.

To verify your JDK installation, perform the following steps:

1. Open a command prompt window in Windows.

2. Type the following command to verify that the `JAVA_HOME` variable is set:

    `echo %JAVA_HOME%`

3. This should return a path, that is `C:\Program Files (x86)\Java\jdk1.7.0_17`.

4. When the variable is set, verify that your **Path** includes the JDK bin directory. Type the following command:

    `java -version`

    This should display the version of Java installed, that is:

    `java version "1.7.0_17"`

    `Java(TM) SE Runtime Environment (build 1.7.0_17-b02)`

    `Java HotSpot(TM) Client VM (build 23.7-b01, mixed mode, sharing)`

5. If you have the JDK installed and your **Path** is configured correctly, you can move forward to the next step.

When building a plugin for Confluence, the application will be running on your desktop. For Confluence to be able to start, it assumes **port 1990** is available. On most machines this would not be an issue.

Verify your port numbers by performing the following step:

1. Open a command prompt window and type the following command:

    `netstat -a | find /I "1990"`

If the preceding command doesn't return anything, the port is available. If the preceding command does return something, port 1990 is already being used by another application. The Atlassian SDK will notice this during startup and assign a different port to Confluence. We will go into this in the *Building, installing, and running your plugin* section.

 If you are developing your plugin on a Linux or Mac, you can follow the online guide for installing the JDK at `https://developer.atlassian.com/display/DOCS/Set+up+the+SDK+Prerequisites+for+Linux+or+Mac`.

Setting up the Atlassian SDK

With all the prerequisites installed, we can download and set up the Atlassian SDK.

1. Download the latest version of the SDK via:
    `https://marketplace.atlassian.com/download/plugins/atlassian-plugin-sdk-windows` (direct download link).

2. Locate the downloaded installer and double-click on the EXE file.

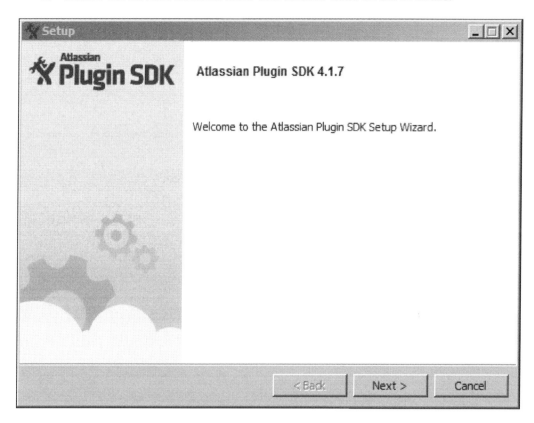

3. Click on **Next** and select a location to install the SDK.
4. Follow the next screens to install the SDK.

The Atlassian Plugin SDK is now installed and we are ready to create our first plugin.

To verify that the SDK is configured correctly, perform the following step:

1. Open a command prompt window and run the following command:

   ```
   atlas-version
   ```

   The system should respond with similar information as follows:

   ```
   ATLAS Version:     4.1.7

   ATLAS Home:        C:\atlassian-plugin-sdk

   ATLAS Scripts:     C:\atlassian-plugin-sdk\bin

   ATLAS Maven Home: C:\atlassian-plugin-sdk\apache-maven

   --------

   Executing: "C:\atlassian-plugin-sdk\apache-maven\bin\mvn.bat"
   --version -gs C:\atlassian-plugin-sdk\apache-maven/conf/settings.
   xml

   Apache Maven 2.1.0 (r755702; 2009-03-18 20:10:27+0100)

   Java version: 1.7.0_17

   Java home: C:\Program Files (x86)\Java\jdk1.7.0_17\jre

   Default locale: en_US, platform encoding: Cp1252

   OS name: "windows server 2008 r2" version: "6.1" arch: "x86"
   Family: "windows"
   ```

Commands

The Atlassian Plugin SDK provides a set of shell scripts for creating, installing, and building plugins for Atlassian products. Let's take a look at some typical tasks and examples of commands in the SDK.

Creating a new plugin

When you want to build a new plugin, you need to create a plugin skeleton. Open a command prompt and run the following command in the location where you want to create the plugin.

```
atlas-create-confluence-plugin
```

Adding a new module to your plugin

If you want to add a new module to your plugin, you could do this via the command line too. Open your command prompt and browse to the location of your plugin. Within your plugin directory run:

```
atlas-create-confluence-plugin-module
```

Running a plugin in an application

If you want to run your plugin in its target application, go to the plugin directory using the command prompt and type:

```
atlas-run
```

The preceding command will start the application specified in your plugin (Confluence, JIRA, and so on) and automatically install your plugin.

Running a specific version of an application

If you are building a plugin that should work for a specific version, or you just want to test your plugin against a new version of the application, you can specify this while starting the application. Run the following commands in your plugin directory:

```
atlas-clean
```
```
atlas-run --version 5.0.1
```

The `atlas-clean` command will clear any previously run version of the plugin. This is only needed if the previous run was a different version.

Using the Maven Command Line Interface (CLI) plugin

The SDK bundles the Maven CLI plugin, allowing you to run a command against a development Confluence installation. To use it with your plugin's host application, go to the plugin's project directory (where you created the plugin) and type:

```
atlas-cli
```

When the command-line interface is started you can use the command `pi` to package your plugin and install it into the running Confluence installation.

Running a standalone application

If you want to quickly test a new version of an application, you can use the standalone command to start that application. You can run this command from anywhere, as there is no plugin required:

```
atlas-run-standalone--product confluence --version 5.0.1
```

The help command

There are more commands available, but these are the most used. If you are ever in doubt how a command is used and which are available, run the following command:

```
atlas-help
```

Maven

When you are building a plugin, you will be using Maven as an underlying library dependency management and build tool. Maven is already bundled with the Atlassian Plugin SDK, so there is no need to install it on your machine. Even if you already have a Maven version installed, you should use the bundled version, as the SDK requires a specific Maven version.

The Atlassian SDK Maven comes with configured settings so that building an Atlassian plugin will be as easy as possible. Using Maven and building your plugin does require an active Internet connection, as Maven will resolve and download all dependencies needed during the build process.

If you are behind a company proxy, make sure to configure Maven accordingly:

1. Open `%USERPROFILE%/.m2/settings.xml` in a text editor. If the file doesn't exist, you can create it.

2. Add the following section to your file and make sure to replace the settings with your proxy settings:

```
<settings>
  <proxies>
    <proxy>
      <active>true</active>
      <protocol>http</protocol>
      <host>proxy.somewhere.com</host>
      <port>8080</port>
      <username>proxyuser</username>
      <password>somepassword</password>
      <nonProxyHosts>
www.google.com|*.somewhere.com
```

```
    </nonProxyHosts>
      </proxy>
    </proxies>
  </settings>
```

3. Save the file.

With a normal Maven installation, or if you have multiple installations, `mvn` would be available via your command prompt. To ensure you use the Atlassian provided version, Maven uses `atlas-mvn` instead.

The pom.xml file

In the root of your plugin, there is a `pom.xml` file; this file is the core of a project's configuration in Maven. In this file, you can define dependencies on other libraries and specify which Confluence version you want to run, but it also holds the name and description of your plugin.

The `pom.xml` file is what is being used when you start your plugin with `atlas-run`.

The plugin descriptor

Every plugin must have a plugin descriptor file. The file, `atlassian-plugin.xml`, describes your plugin to the target application. The Atlassian SDK generates the `atlassian-plugin.xml` file when you create your plugin for the first time. The descriptor is also updated when you use `atlassian-create-confluence-plugin-module` to add a new module.

At some point during the development of you plugin, you will have to update the file manually, so it's a good idea to have a bit of understanding as to what is in the plugin descriptor. The plugin descriptor is located in the directory `<plugin_home>/src/main/resources/`.

A very minimal plugin descriptor's built looks as follows:

```
<atlassian-plugin key="${project.groupId}.${project.artifactId}"
  name="${project.name}" plugins-version="2">
<plugin-info>
<description>${project.description}</description>
<version>${project.version}</version>
<vendor name="${project.organization.name}"
  url="${project.organization.url}" />
</plugin-info>
</atlassian-plugin>
```

This descriptor file mostly contains variables; these are Maven variables and will be replaced with the values from your `pom.xml` file when you build your plugin. The rest of the descriptor file is empty; this plugin does not contain any components, which is very unlikely for a plugin.

We will be adding more modules to this file across this chapter, if you want an overview of the available modules, skip ahead to the *Plugin module types* section.

Using a development environment

When developing your plugin, it is a good idea to use an IDE, short for integrated development environment. A development environment will help you to make fewer mistakes, and can come in very handy when trying to debug your plugin.

Installing Eclipse on Windows

We will be using Eclipse, but if you have a different preference, use your own IDE.

1. Download Eclipse for JAVA EE developers from
   `http://www.eclipse.org/downloads/`.

2. Extract the downloaded ZIP file onto the root of you hard drive. When you are done, if your hard drive root is `C:\`, you will have the following folder on your hard drive:

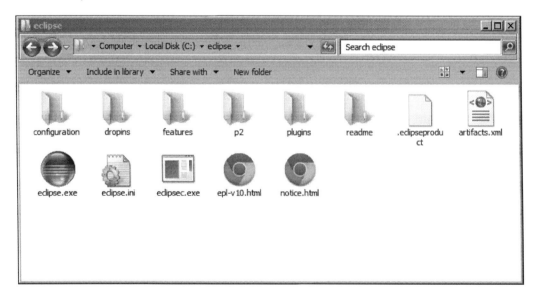

In the next step, we are making sure Eclipse uses the JDK we just installed; this is done by editing the Eclipse initialization file.

1. Make a copy of the original `eclipse.ini` and name it `eclipse.ini.original`.

2. Open the `eclipse.ini` file in Notepad.

3. Add a `-vm` entry before any `-vmargs` entry in the file. The entry should point to the value of your `%JAVA_HOME%/bin`. Eclipse requires that you reverse the slashes to forward slashes. Your file should look similar to this:

```
-startup
plugins/org.eclipse.equinox.launcher_1.3.0.v20120522-1813.jar
--launcher.library
plugins/org.eclipse.equinox.launcher.win32.win32.x86_1.1.200.
v20120913-144807
-product
org.eclipse.epp.package.jee.product
--launcher.defaultAction
openFile
--launcher.XXMaxPermSize
256M
-showsplash
org.eclipse.platform
--launcher.XXMaxPermSize
256m
--launcher.defaultAction
openFile
-vm
C:/Program Files/Java/jdk1.7.0_17/bin
-vmargs
-Dosgi.requiredJavaVersion=1.5
-Dhelp.lucene.tokenizer=standard
-Xms40m
-Xmx512m
```

4. Close and save the file.

5. Start Eclipse and choose a location where Eclipse will store you workspaces.

Installing the Maven Eclipse plugin

We will be using the Maven Eclipse plugin, which will help us with getting the dependencies needed for our Confluence plugins.

1. Select **Help | Install** new Software. Click on the **Add** button to add a new repository.

2. Enter `Sonatype M2Eclipse` in the **Name** field.

3. Enter `http://m2eclipse.sonatype.org/sites/m2e` in the **Location** field.

Extending Confluence

4. Click on **OK** to close the dialog. The system searches the site for the plugin. After a moment, the **Name** field fills with the **Maven Integration for Eclipse** software as the following:

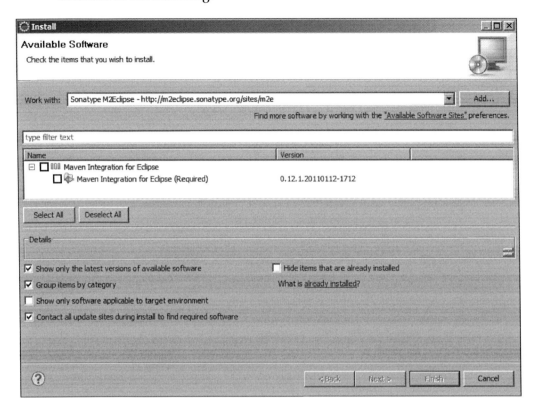

5. Check the checkbox and click on **Next**.
6. Accept the terms of the license agreements and click on **Finish**.
7. Restart Eclipse when prompted.

Configuring the Maven plugin

After Eclipse has restarted, ensure that the Maven plugin is configured correctly.

1. Choose **Window | Preferences** from the eclipse menu bar.
2. Type Maven in the filter text field and select **Installations**.
3. Click on the **Add** button to add a new Maven installation.
4. Browse to your Atlassian SDK installation and select the apache-maven folder.
5. Click on **OK**.

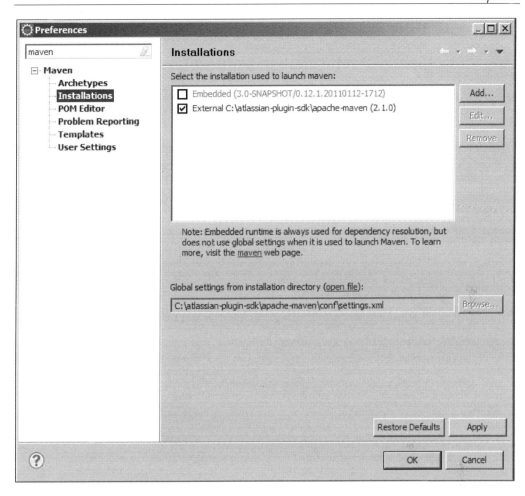

6. Click on **Apply**.

7. Click on the Maven root.

8. Uncheck **Download repository index updates on startup**. This prevents Maven from updating on Eclipse startup, which can be time consuming. The `atlas-` commands will update the repositories for you.

9. Click on **OK** to close the dialog.

Building your first plugin

When you have installed the Atlassian SDK, you can start building your first plugin. We will be building a new Confluence macro, which can be used to format content.

We will take a look at:

- The macro interface, which is the base of all macros
- The xhtml-macro module
- Adding resources, such as a stylesheet, to your plugin

We will be building a macro that displays links as buttons.

Creating the plugin project

First, we have to create our plugin skeleton using the Atlassian SDK and load our new project into Eclipse.

1. Open a command prompt and navigate to the location for you new plugin.
2. Enter the following command to create a new Confluence plugin:

   ```
   atlas-create-confluence-plugin
   ```

3. When prompted, enter the following information to identify your plugin:

groupId	com.example.confluence
artifactId	button-macro
version	1.0-snapshot
package	com.example.confluence.button

4. Confirm your entries when prompted.
5. Start Eclipse.
6. Select **File | Import...** from the Eclipse menu.
7. Type Maven in the filter text field and select **Existing Maven Projects**:

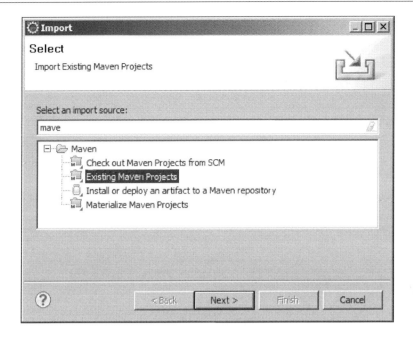

8. Click on **Browse** and browse to the location where you created the plugin.

9. Select the pom.xml file and click on **Finish**. Eclipse will now import your project and download all dependencies if needed. This can take a while.

10. Sometimes an error will occur during this process, if so:

    1. Right-click on the imported project (in the project explorer).

    2. Select **Maven | Update Project Configuration**.

Updating the generated code

When you have just generated a new plugin skeleton, you have to make sure all the details, like the plugin name or description, are correct. In this section, we'll check the Confluence version value and tweak some settings. Open your plugin project in Eclipse and follow along.

Adding plugin metadata to the POM file

The metadata in your POM file will be used when your plugin is built. This would be the place to add your company details and description of the plugin.

1. Edit the `pom.xml` file in the root of your plugin.

2. Add your company or organization details to the `<organization>` element:

```
<organization>
<name>Stefan Kohler</name>
<url>http://www.stefankohler.nl/</url>
</organization>
```

3. Update the `<name>` and `<description>` elements:

```
<name>Confluence Button Macro</name>
<description>Display a link using a nicely formatted button.</
description>
```

4. Save the file.

Verifying your Confluence version

When you generated a new plugin skeleton, a default Confluence version was included in your `pom.xml` file. Before you start building your plugin, make sure this version is up-to-date.

1. Open the `pom.xml` file in Eclipse.

2. Scroll to the bottom of the file.

3. Find the `<properties>` element. This section lists the version of Confluence and other properties of your plugin.

4. Change the Confluence version to `5.1.2`, or a more recent one if available.

5. Save the `pom.xml` file. Eclipse will automatically download the new dependencies for you.

Cleaning up the plugin skeleton

We are building a new macro, and most of the generated code is for a different component. Therefore, we have no use for the generated code. Before we start, let's clean up first.

1. Open `src/main/resources/atlassian-plugin.xml` in Eclipse.

2. Remove the `<web-resource>`, `<component-import>`, and `<component>` sections.

3. Also remove the corresponding files:

    °   `MyPluginComponent.java`

    °   `MyPluginComponentImpl.java`

    °   `MyComponentWiredTest.java`

    °   `MyComponentUnitTest.java`

Adding a new macro module

With our plugin skeleton ready for development, we will be adding some new modules to our plugin descriptor.

1. Open your `atlassian-plugin.xml` file in Eclipse.

2. Add the `xhtml-macro` component to the file:

```
<xhtml-macroname="link-button"
  class="com.example.confluence.button.LinkButton"
  key="link-button">

  <parameters/>
</xhtml-macro>
```

3. The `Class` argument is pointing to an implementation of our macro.

Implementing the macro interface

The macro module we just defined will call the `execute` method of our Java class `com.example.confluence.button.LinkButton`. That class doesn't exist yet, so let's create it.

1. Right-click on the `com.example.confluence.button` package (folder) in your project.

2. Select **New | Class** and enter the following details:

    °   **Package** – `com.example.confluence.button`

    °   **Name** – `LinkButton`

    °   **Interfaces** – Add `com.atlassian.confluence.macro.Macro`

3. Click on **Finish**.

Your new Java class will be generated, and you might notice we have to implement three methods.

Implementing the getBodyType and getOutputType methods

These two methods specify whether the macro has a body (and the type of body if it does have one) and the output type, be it block or inline. The macro we implement will have a body and will have the block output type.

```
@Override
publicBodyTypegetBodyType() {
    returnBodyType.RICH_TEXT;
}

@Override
publicOutputTypegetOutputType() {
    returnOutputType.BLOCK;
}
```

Implementing the execute method

The execute method will determine what the output of our macro will be. I have included an easy template with some HTML to style our button. We will be using the body of our macro and use that as input for our button.

```
@Override
public String execute(Map<String, String> parameters,
    String body, ConversionContext context) throws
MacroExecutionException {

    String template = "<div class=\"aui-button aui-button-primary
link-button\">%s</div>";

    returnString.format(template, body);
}
```

The template we are using makes use of the **Atlassian User Interface (AUI)**, a library with JavaScript, stylesheets, and templates that is included in all Atlassian products. If you use the AUI in your plugin, it will have the same look and feel as Confluence.

More information about the AUI can be found online at `https://developer. atlassian.com/display/AUI/`.

Building, installing, and running your plugin

When we have the basics set for our plugin, it is time to build and run the plugin in Confluence.

1. Save all the changes to your code.

2. Open a command prompt and navigate to the location of your plugin.

3. Run the following command:

    ```
    atlas-run
    ```

    This command will build your plugin, start a Confluence installation, and install your plugin in that Confluence installation. This may take a while. When the process is completed, the last lines of the output should look as follows:

    ```
    [INFO] confluence started successfully in 225s at http://
    localhost:1990/confluence
    ```

    ```
    [INFO] Type Ctrl-D to shutdown gracefully
    ```

    ```
    [INFO] Type Ctrl-C to exit
    ```

    If Confluence couldn't use port 1990 because another application is using it, Confluence will start on a different port and will mention it in these lines.

4. Open your browser at `http://localhost:1990/confluence`.

5. At the Confluence login, enter a username `admin` with the password `admin`.

6. Create a new page with your new macro.

    1. Click on **Create** in the navigation bar.

    2. Select **Insert | Other macros**.

    3. Search for Link Button.

    4. Insert your macro.

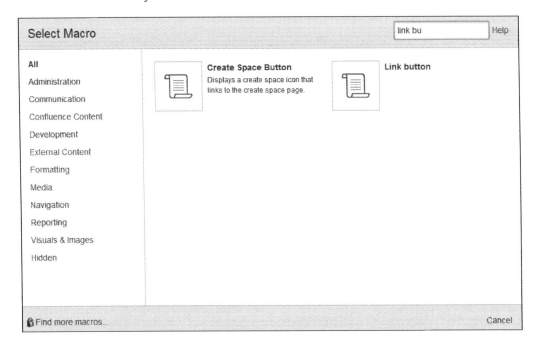

    5. Add a link in the body of your macro as you would normally do in Confluence.

    6. Save the page.

7. Watch how your new macro has formatted your link:

Adding resources

What the preceding screenshot displays is not very user-readable; it would be better if the link itself is white. For this we have to add resources, a CSS file, to our plugin.

In the `atlassian-plugin.xml` file, add the `<web-resources>` element to the file:

```
<web-resource key="link-button-resources"
name="Link Button Resources">

<resource type="download" name="button-macro.css"
location="css/button-macro.css" />

<context>atl.general</context>

</web-resource>
```

The `<resource>` element determines which file will be included with our plugin. The location is relative to the `src/main/resources` folder.

The `<context>` element will tell Confluence when to load these extra resources. In our case, the resources are loaded on every page except for administrative screens.

The following CSS has to be added to our `button-macro.css` class:

```
.aui-button.link-button a {
  color: #ffffff !important;
}
```

After reloading our plugin, the button should now look like this:

Reloading your plugin with FastDev

FastDev is a feature of Atlassian SDK that speeds up plugin development. FastDev will scan your plugin directory for changes, and is able to package and reinstall your plugin directly from Confluence. More information on FastDev at `https://developer.atlassian.com/display/DOCS/Automatic+Plugin+Reinstallation+with+FastDev`.

Releasing your plugin

At a certain point, you are done developing your plugin and you want to deliver the end result to your company or maybe even to the rest of world. The first thing we have to do is release your plugin.

The release process relies heavily on you to have a revision control system for your plugin, like Subversion or GIT. If you don't have such a system in place, you could consider taking a look at `http://bitbucket.org`, which is an online Atlassian tool that offers free source hosting.

Before we can release our plugin, we have to make sure that our `pom.xml` file has all the requirements to do so.

To set the SCM properties, perform the following steps:

1. Open the `pom.xml` file in your plugin.

2. Add the following lines to the file with your SCM information:

```
<scm>
<connection>
scm:git:git@bitbucket.org:stefankohler/plugin-example-button.git
</connection>
<developerConnection>
scm:git:file:///${basedir}
</developerConnection>
url>
https://bitbucket.org/stefankohler/plugin-example-button
</url>
</scm>
```

3. Save the `pom.xml` file.

The `connection` and `developerConnection` tell Maven how to connect to your repository. While `connection` requires read access for Maven to be able to find the source code (for example, an update), `developerConnection` requires a connection that will give write access.

The `url` element is not required, but can be used for a publicly accessible URL to your repository.

Setting distributionManagement

The release process will upload your plugin to a specified location defined by the distributionManagement section in your pom.xml file. This location can be anything from a remote server to your local filesystem. For now, we will set this location to a temp directory on your local machine, as the process requires this setting.

1. Open the pom.xml file in your plugin.
2. Add the following lines to the file:

    ```
    <distributionManagement>
    <repository>
    <id>local-repository</id>
    <url>file:///${basedir}/target</url>
    </repository>
    </distributionManagement>
    ```

3. The variable will be replaced with your own local settings.
4. Save the file.

The next step is to release your plugin:

1. Make sure all changes have been committed.
2. Open a command prompt and navigate to the location of your plugin and run the following command:

    atlas-mvn release:prepare

3. This command will update your pom.xml file with the required version and will make a new tag for the release. During the process you will be asked the release version and the next development version.
4. After the command has finished run the following command:

    atlas-mvn release:perform

    This command will:

    ° Check out the just created tag.
    ° Run all tests.
    ° Compile the code and package it.
    ° Upload your binary to a defined location.

5. After the command is finished, you can find your released plugin in the target directory in your plugin folder. This should be a .jar file, named for your plugin and version, that is button-macro-1.0.jar.

Releasing your plugin without revision control

If you don't have any revision control, the release process of your plugin involves some manual steps.

1. Open the `pom.xml` file in your plugin.

2. Change the `<version></version>` parameter to your release version, that is `1.1`.

3. Save the file.

4. Open a command prompt and go to your plugin location.

5. Run the `atlas-package` command. This command will compile, test, and build your plugin.

6. After the command is finished, you can find your released plugin in the target directory in your plugin folder. This should be a `.jar` file, named for your plugin and version, that is `button-macro-1.1.jar`.

Plugin module types

An Atlassian plugin can specify one or more plugin modules to affect the underlying Atlassian applications. Plugin modules are elements you can add to your plugin and which will be translated by the SDK and the application architecture to something Confluence understands.

We already used the `xhtml-macro` and `web-resource` modules in our first plugin, but there are many more.

Generic module types

These are module types that are available in every application, not just Confluence. If you are building a plugin for multiple applications, stick to only these types.

Module type	Description
component	Adds components to the component system for reuse and autowiring. Think of your own services.
component-import	Imports components from other add-ons so that they are available in your own add-on.
module-type	Adds new plugin modules to the plugin framework. Useful when building for, or on top of other add-ons.
path-converter	Enables you to create custom URL schemes for your add-on, that is you can have SEO-friendly URL schemes.
rest	Makes services and resources available as REST API.
servlet	Deploys a standard Java servlet within a Confluence add-on.
servlet-context-listener	Deploys a Java servlet context listener as a part of your add-on.
servlet-context-param	Adds parameters in the Java Servlet context shared by your add-on's servlets, filters, and listeners.
servlet-filter	Adds a Java servlet filter to your add-on. Don't forget to specify the location and ordering of your filter.
velocity-context-item	Adds helper objects to your Velocity context, which can be used in templates.
web-item	Adds links and tabs to the Confluence UI.
web-resource	Enables you to include stylesheets and JavaScript to your add-on.
web-resource-transformer	Allows you to manipulate web resources before they are send to the browser.
web-section	Adds sections of links to the Confluence UI.

Confluence-specific module types

Each Atlassian application has it own modules, as does Confluence. The following are the module types supported by Confluence:

Module type	Description
codeformatter	Adds new code languages to the {code} macro.
colour-scheme	Adds a color scheme to a theme.
decorator	Adds a decorator (layout) to your add-on for usage without a theme.
device-type-renderer	Adds a renderer for a specified (mobile) device type.
extractor	Allows you to extract data and put this in the Confluence indexer.
job	Adds a repeatable job, like a scheduled service to Confluence.
keyboard-shortcut	Defines a new keyboard shortcut within Confluence.
language	Provides a new language translation to Confluence.
layout	Adds a layout (decorator) to your add-on for usage with a theme.
lifecycle	Can be used to schedule tasks during application startup and shutdown.
listener	A special component that will respond to certain events in Confluence.
xhtml-macro	Adds a new macro to the WYSIWYG editor. Should output HTML that can be embedded in a page.
rpc-soap	Adds a SOAP service to Confluence.
rpc-xmlrpc	Adds an XML-RPC service to Confluence.
theme	Creates a new theme (look and feel) for Confluence or a single space.
trigger	Adds a trigger that schedules jobs.
xwork	Adds new actions and views to an add-on, enabling user interaction.

The plugin module types in detail

The preceding list is pretty comprehensive and there is so much to choose from. In this section, I will explain in detail some plugin module types that you will almost certainly use in most of your plugins.

XWork

If you want to add an action or screen to Confluence, like a configuration screen, there are two options. The first is building a standard Java servlet, the second is making use of XWork/WebWork.

The module descriptor

The syntax of an XWork module is as follows

```
<xwork name="plugin-actions" key="plugin-actions">
<package name="configure" extends="default"
namespace="/plugins/config">

<default-interceptor-ref name="defaultStack" />

<action name="alpha"
class="com.example.action.AlphaConfigAction"
method="view">

<result name="success"type="velocity">
        /templates/alpha-config-action.vm
</result>

</action>
</package>
</xwork>
```

Let's go quickly over the XML to explain what we just defined:

```
<xwork name="plugin-actions" key="plugin-actions">
```

defines the XWork module, both the name and key attributes are for identification only.

```
<package name="configure" extends="default"
namespace="/plugins/config">
```

Packages are used to group actions, and your XWork module can have more than one. name is the only required attribute and identifies the package. extends specifies if the package inherits behavior from other packages; in this case we use the Confluence default. With namespace, you can define under which URL the actions are available.

```
<action name="alpha"
class="com.example.action.AlphaConfigAction"
method="view">
```

The action element is the basic unit of work and defines an action, which in most cases is a URL. The name attribute completes the URL, as the preceding action is available at /plugins/config/alpha.action. An action always has a class, which will extend ConfluenceActionSupport. With method, it is possible to specify the method in the class responsible for this action.

```
<result name="success"type="velocity">
/templates/alpha-config-action.vm
</result>
```

The result element will map the result of an action to a template. In the preceding example, the velocity template alpha-config-action.vm will be rendered if our AlphaConfigAction returns success.

The action class

Every action should have an implementation that extends the ConfluenceActionSupport class. Actions can use the same implementation if that makes sense for your plugin.

Our AlphaConfigAction class should look something like this:

```
public class AlphaConfigAction extends ConfluenceActionSupport {

public String view() {
if (condition == true) return SUCCESS;
  return ERROR;
    }

public String getViewMessage() {
return "Don't forget a towel";
    }

}
```

Based on our action configuration, the method `view()` is called and based upon the return the success or error template is rendered.

This is of course a simple example, but you can do much more in this action class. The action class is also available in your template, so if you want to render certain information via that template, make sure there is a `get` method available, just like `#getViewMessage()`.

Web Sections

Web Sections allows your plugin to add new sections to existing menus; each section can contain one or more links, which are defined as Web Items. We can use Web Sections to add a new section to the Confluence administration for our plugin configuration.

The module descriptor

The syntax of a Web Section is as follows:

```
<web-section key="plugin-admin-section" location="system.admin"
weight="1000">

<label key="plugin.menu.section" />

<condition class="com.atlassian.confluence.plugin.descriptor.web.
conditions.SystemAdministratorCondition" />

</web-section>
```

Let's break down this definition:

```
<web-section key="plugin-admin-section" location="system.admin"
weight="1000">
```

A web-section element requires a `key`, which is a unique identifier for this component. `location` relates to the menu this section needs to be added to and the `weight` determines at which position it needs to be added to.

`location` menus can be difficult to find if you are not familiar with the source code of Confluence itself. More `location` menus are documented on `https://developer.atlassian.com/display/CONFDEV/Web+UI+Modules`. A few that are commonly used are:

Location	Description
`system.profile`	The tabs above the user profile view.
`system.user`	The drop-down menu when you click the user avatar in the top-right corner.
`system.admin`	The links in the left-hand side menu in the Administrator Console.

The `label` element is the only required element in the web-section plugin. It looks up for the `label` in your plugin properties file and uses it in the menu section header.

```
<label key="plugin.menu.section" />
```

You can add one or more conditions to a web panel or item. The implementation of these conditions must return `true` in order for the section to display in the interface. This can be used the make sure the links are only available for administrators.

```
<condition class="com.atlassian.confluence.plugin.descriptor.web.
conditions.SystemAdministratorCondition" />
```

Web Items

With Web Items you can add links to Confluence via your plugin. If you build a screen you probably want users to find it; adding a web items to your plugin should make this possible.

The module descriptor

A common Web Item will be configured similar to this:

```
<web-item key="config-link" name="Plugin Configuration"
section="system.admin/plugin-admin-section" weight="10">

<label key="plugin.menu.config" />

<linklinkId="config-link">/plugins/config/alpha.action</link>

<icon height="16" width="16">
<link>/images/icons/config.gif</link>
</icon>
</web-item>
```

I'll explain this example a bit more in detail:

```
<web-item key="config-link" name="Plugin Configuration"
section="system.admin/plugin-admin-section" weight="10">
```

The `web-item` attribute knows a `section` argument instead of a location, as Web Items must be placed in sections. In our example, I'm placing this Web Item in the section we have defined earlier.

```
<linklinkId="config-link">/plugins/config/alpha.action</link>
```

The `link` element will determine where the user will go after clicking on the menu item. The `linkId` argument is optional and will provide an HTML ID when rendered. The link can either be relative to the Confluence server or absolute, pointing to any website you wish.

```
<icon height="16" width="16">
<link>/images/icons/config.gif</link>
</icon>
```

Web Items can contain icons that will be placed before the their `label` elements. The icon can have a `width` and a `height` attribute. The location of the image is defined by the `link` element.

Just like Web Sections can, Web Items can contain conditions to determine when a link is shown and to who.

Online resources

This chapter gives you only a small insight into the possibilities on extending Confluence and writing your own plugins. There are many online resources available to move you forward from this point.

All developer documentation is bundled and located at `https://developer.atlassian.com`.

- **The Confluence module types**: For more details about the available modules and which arguments and elements they accept, visit `https://developer.atlassian.com/display/CONFDEV/Confluence+Plugin+Module+Types`.
- **Confluence Plugin Tutorials**: Various Confluence tutorials from beginner to advanced developer are available at `https://developer.atlassian.com/display/CONFDEV/Confluence+Tutorials`.

- **Atlassian Design Guidelines and User Interface**: Atlassian provides a toolkit for you to help you create beautiful features for their products at `https://developer.atlassian.com/display/AUI/`.

- **The Marketplace**: Everything you need to get your plugin Marketplace-ready is available at `https://developer.atlassian.com/display/MARKET/Atlassian+Marketplace`.

Get the sources

If you have a valid license for Confluence, you can download the sources via `https://my.atlassian.com`. If you are building your plugin, these sources are sometimes the best documentation available.

When you are stuck, search the source code for similar situations and take a look at how Atlassian solved those problems.

Summary

We have taken a look at how to extend Confluence with a plugin. We have learned how to set up our IDE and build our first plugin, creating a new Confluence macro.

We have also seen that Confluence has over 30 extension points that you can use enhancing Confluence with your features. This chapter should give you a head start when you start building your own plugin and a general sense about the possibilities.

With that, you have all the essentials to work with Confluence and make the tool essential to your company. If you are ever stuck, you'll find me, and many others in the community, on Atlassian Answers (`https://answers.atlassian.com`).

Index

Symbols

*.atlassian.com 238
#dashboardlink () macro 207
#includePage (pageTitle) macro 207
@mention notifications 138
#searchbox () macro 207
.vmd file 207

A

access
  limiting, to Confluence administration
    178-180
add-ons
  installing, by file upload 243
  installing, via Marketplace 242
  searching, Advanced Search used 236, 237
  searching, steps 241, 242
  updating, steps 244
  user request 247
  working with 235
administration roles
  comparing 165, 166
administrator roles
  Confluence administrator 160
  super user 160
  system administrator 160
administrator sessions
  securing 175
advanced customization, Confluence
  about 201
  custom HTML 202
  custom stylesheets 203
  default space content 201
  site layouts 206

Advanced Search
  used, for searching add-ons 236, 237
advanced settings, Crowd directory 59
advanced settings, JIRA 61
advanced settings, LDAP directory 54
anchor
  link, creating to 96
anonymous users
  permissions, assigning to 170
application links
  about 251
  adding 252-254
  authentication, configuring 257
  editing 255
Application Navigator
  about 261
  links, adding 262
  links, managing 262, 263
application servers 12
architecture, Confluence 7
Atlassian
  about 7
  URL, for online documentation 264
Atlassian Answers 264
Atlassian Design Guidelines and User
    Interface
  URL 302
Atlassian experts 268
Atlassian Marketplace
  about 236
  URL 236
Atlassian Plugin SDK
  about 271
  commands 276
  functions 271, 272
  installing 272

prerequisites 272-274
setting up 275
Atlassian security advisory 176, 178
**Atlassian Software Development Kit (SDK)
271**
Atlassian Support
about 265
ticket, raising 266
Atlassian Support tools 265
Atlassian User Interface (AUI) 289
attached image, displaying
about 89
on different page 90
on remote web page 90
attachments
about 83
downloading 85
embedding 85
labels, adding to 117
Attachments/ directory 10
attachment version management 84
authentication
about 33
password authentication 34
Seraph 34
autocomplete
link, creating to Confluence pages 94
autocomplete, Confluence editor 71
autoconverting, Confluence editor 72
autoformatting, Confluence editor 71
autowatch 123

B

Backups/ directory 10
basic HTTP authentication
about 257, 260
configuring 261
best practices, Confluence security 180, 181
blog posts
about 64
versus pages 65
watching 125, 126
browser requisites, Confluence 5.1
about 8
Google Chrome (Windows and Mac) 9
Microsoft Internet Explorer (Windows) 9
Mobile Safari (iOS) 9
Mozilla Firefox (all platforms) 9
Safari (Windows and Mac) 9
Bundled-plugins/ directory 10

C

CA certificate 21
category
adding, to space 119
certificate
generating 21, 22
collaboration tool
about 33, 137
content sharing 139
likes 140
mentions 138
status updates 140
color scheme
about 200
modifying, of space 200
Column macro
adding, to page 80
Column Width parameter 81
commands, Atlassian Plugin SDK
about 276
help command 278
Maven CLI plugin, using 277
module, adding to plugin 277
plugin, creating 276
plugin, running in application 277
specific version, running of application 277
standalone application, running 278
comments 65
Common Vulnerability Scoring System. *See*
CVSS
CONF_HOME directory
about 9
Attachments/ directory 10
Backups/ directory 10
Bundled-plugins/ directory 10
Config/ directory 10
confluence.cfg.xml file 10
Index/ directory 10
Logs/ directory 10
Plugins-osgi-cache/ directory 10
Temp/ directory 10

Thumbnails/ directory 10
Config/ directory 10
**configuration, basic HTTP authentication
 261**
configuration, Confluence Home 19
configuration, default theme 191, 192
**configuration, Documentation Theme
 193-195**
configuration, e-mail JNDI resource 20
configuration, HTTPS 21
configuration, Maven plugin 282, 283
configuration, OAuth authentication 260
configuration, Tomcat 22
**configuration, trusted applications
 authentication 258**
configuration, workbox notifications 146
CONF_INSTALL directory 9
Confluence
 about 7, 160, 235
 advanced customization 201
 architecture 7
 configuring, as Windows service 23
 connecting, to JIRA 252-254
 customizing 183, 196
 custom stylesheets, adding to 204
 database, creating 17, 18
 data storage 9
 e-mail server, setting up 30, 32
 high-level architecture 8
 home directory 9, 10
 installation directory 9
 installation options 11
 installation wizard 26-30
 installing 12, 13, 18
 Office file, displaying 87
 on mobile device 152
 pages, adding 67
 starting 25
 supported browsers 8
 support request, submitting 267
 technical components 8
 unpacking 18
 user, creating 16, 17
 user management 33
Confluence administration
 access, limiting to 178-180
Confluence administrator 160

confluence.cfg.xml file 10
Confluence dashboard
 about 183
 home page 184
 welcome message 184
Confluence editor
 about 69
 autocomplete 71
 autoconverting 72
 autoformatting 71
 drag-and-drop feature 73
 toolbar 70
Confluence Home
 configuring 19
Confluence Home directory. *See* **also**
 CONF_HOME directory 9
Confluence home page
 about 184
 modifying 184
Confluence Installation directory. *See* **also**
 CONF_INSTALL directory 9
Confluence Like Plugin 140
Confluence logo 196, 197
Confluence pages
 link, creating to 94-96
Confluence Plugin Tutorials
 URL 301
Confluence security
 about 174
 administrator sessions, securing 175
 Atlassian security advisory 176, 177
 best practices 180, 181
Confluence server
 notifications, sending to 148, 149
Confluence-specific module types
 codeformatter 296
 colour-scheme 296
 decorator 296
 device-type-renderer 296
 extractor 296
 job 296
 keyboard-shortcut 296
 language 296
 layout 296
 lifecycle 296
 listener 296
 rpc-soap 296

rpc-xmlrpc 296
theme 296
trigger 296
xhtml-macro 296
xwork 296
Confluence version
verifying 286
content
accessing 159, 160
adding 73
adding, to templates 213
displaying, labels used 120
exporting 107
importing 103
notification options, editing 123
tracking 123
watching 123
Content by Label macro
about 120
adding, to page 121
properties 121, 122
Content By Label macro, properties
Author(s) 121
Display Excerpts 122
Include this Content Type Only 122
Label(s) 121
List Title 122
Maximum Pages 122
Operator 122
Restrict to Spaces 122
Reverse Sort 122
Show Labels for Each Page 122
Show Space Name for Each Page 122
Sort By 122
content history
working with 101
content indexing 249
content labels 116
content layouts 206
content sharing 139
copy and paste
link, creating to Confluence pages 96
Crowd directory
connecting, to Confluence 57
Crowd directory connection
about 57, 58
advanced settings 59

permissions 59
server settings 58
customer details pages
creating, steps 229, 230
custom HTML
about 202
inserting, steps 203
custom stylesheets
about 203
adding, to Confluence 204
enabling, for spaces 204
example 204
CVSS
URL 176

D

dashboard
favorites, viewing via 129
database
creating, for Confluence 17, 18
data storage, Confluence 9
decorator files
about 206
editing 206
default content, modifying
of global space 202
of personal space 202
default space content 201, 202
default space logo
setting 198
default space permissions
setting 170, 171
default theme
about 190, 191
configuring 191, 192
space logo, modifying with 198
descriptive header, user macro template 223
development environment
Eclipse, installing on Windows 280, 281
Maven Eclipse plugin, installing 281, 282
Maven plugin, configuring 282, 283
using 280
Did you mean feature 132, 249
Documentation Theme
about 192, 193
configuring, steps 193-195

space logo, modifying with 199
dq1dnt4af4eyy.cloudfront.net 238
draft
  edit proces, resuming 99, 100
  unsaved changes, viewing 100
draft interval
  modifying 99
drafts 98, 99
drag-and-drop feature
  files, attaching to page 83
  used, for embedding Office files 88
  used, for reordering pages 112
drag-and-drop feature, Confluence editor 73

E

Eclipse
  installing, on Windows 280, 281
e-mail JNDI resource
  configuring 20
e-mail server, Confluence
  setting up 30-32
execute method
  implementing 288
export layouts 206
external user directories
  about 49
  Crowd directory 57
  directory order, effects 50
  JIRA directory 59
  LDAP directory 52
  limitations 51

F

favorites
  about 127
  page, adding as 127
  space, adding as 128
  viewing 128
  viewing, via dashboard 129
files
  attaching, to page 83
  attaching, via classic upload approach 84
filter options
  using 132
full search
  about 131

performing 131
functions, Atlassian Plugin SDK 271, 272

G

gallery
  images, displaying in 93
Gallery macro
  features 93
generated code
  updating 285
generic module types
  about 294
  component 295
  component-import 295
  module-type 295
  path-converter 295
  rest 295
  servlet 295
  servlet-context-listener 295
  servlet-context-param 295
  servlet-filter 295
  velocity-context-item 295
  web-item 295
  web-resource 295
  web-resource-transformer 295
  web-section 295
getBodyType method
  implementing 288
getOutputType method
  implementing 288
global color scheme
  modifying 200
global Confluence theme
  modifying, steps 189
global permissions
  about 160
  Attach Files to User Profile 165
  can use 165
  Confluence Administrator 165
  Create Space(s) 165
  notes 167
  overview 164, 165
  Personal Space 165
  System Administrator 165
  Update User Status 165
  updating 163

viewing 162
global spaces
  about 63
  adding, steps 65, 66
  default content, modifying of 202
global templates
  about 211, 212
  creating 212
groups
  confluence-administrators 39
  confluence-users 39
  creating 39
  group membership, editing from user
    details screen 40
  group membership, editing via group
    management screen 41
  managing 39
  permissions, assigning to 169
  permssions, adding for 163
  permssions, editing 163
  users, adding 40
group schema settings, LDAP directory 56

H

heading
  link, creating to 98
heat map 120
help command 278
Hercules 265
high-level architecture, Confluence 8
HSQLDB database 12
HTTPS
  configuring 21
  traffic, redirecting to 23

I

image effects
  using 91
images
  about 89
  aligning 92
  appearance, modifying 91
  displaying, in gallery 93
  link, adding to 92
import user macros
  selecting 218

included notifications 145, 146
Index/ directory 10
indexes
  rebuilding 249-251
indexing language
  modifying 251
Insert Link dialog
  link, creating to Confluence pages 94
installation, add-ons
  about 242
  by file upload 243
  via Marketplace 242
installation, Atlassian Plugin SDK 272
installation, Confluence
  about 12, 13
  Confluence Home, configuring 19
  Confluence, unpacking 18
  e-mail JNDI resource, configuring 20
  HTTPS, configuring 21
  port, configuring 19, 20
installation, Java 13, 14
installation, Maven Eclipse plugin 281, 282
installation options, Confluence
  about 11
  application servers 12
  databases 12
  operating systems 11
  standalone distributions 11
  WAR distributions 11
installation, PostgreSQL 15
installation wizard, Confluence 26-30
installed add-ons
  removing, steps 245, 246
installed template bundles
  verifying 217
Instant Camera effect 92
instructional text 214

J

Java
  installing 13, 14
JAVA_HOME
  adding, to path 273
JIRA
  Confluence, connecting to 252-254
  notifications, including from 148

JIRA project
space, linking to 256
JIRA server connection
about 59
advanced settings 61
performing 60
permissions 61
server settings 61

K

Karma 264
keyboard shortcuts, tables 82

L

labels
about 116
adding, to attachments 117
advantages 116
removing 117
searching 133, 134
used, for displaying content 120
using, for reviews 120
viewing 119
labels view
features 119
LDAP directory
connecting, to Confluence 52
LDAP directory connection
about 52
advanced settings 54
group schema settings 56
membership schema settings 57
permissions 53
schema settings 53
server settings 52
user schema settings 55
likes 140
limitations, external user directories
build-in user management 51
directories, editing 51
link
about 94
adding, to image 92
link, Application Navigator
adding 262
managing 262, 263

links, creating
to anchor 96
to Confluence pages 94-96
to heading 98
to undefined page 98
to web pages 96
location
setting, of page 68
Logs/ directory 10

M

macro browser 76
macro interface
implementing 287
macro keyboard shortcut 78
macro module
adding 287
macros
about 75
editing 76, 77
Maven
about 278
pom.xml file 279
Maven CLI plugin
using 277
Maven Eclipse plugin
installing 281, 282
Maven plugin
configuring 282, 283
membership schema settings, LDAP
directory 57
mentions 138
metadata details macro. *See* **Page Properties**
macro
mobile device, Confluence
about 152
interface 153, 154
notifications 156
searching 156
tasks 156
user profiles 155
mobile interface 153-156
multimedia files
embedding, within Multimedia macro 86
Multimedia macro
inserting 86

multimedia files, embedding within 86
MySQL 12

N

notification options
  editing 123
notifications
  about 143, 156
  included notifications 145, 146
  including, from JIRA 148
  managing 144
  sending, to Confluence server 148, 149
  workbox notifications 146

O

OAuth 257, 260
OAuth authentication
  configuring 260
Office file
  about 87
  displaying, in Confluence 87
offline mode, Universal Plugin Manager
    (UPM) 240
online mode, Universal Plugin Manager
    (UPM) 238, 239
online resources
  about 301
  Atlassian Design Guidelines and User
    Interface 302
  Confluence module types 301
  Confluence Plugin Tutorials 301
  The Marketplace 302
Oracle 12
Oracle JDK
  installing 272
orphaned page
  about 113, 114
  viewing 113

P

page
  about 64
  adding 66
  adding, as favorites 127
  adding, to Confluence 67

Column macro, adding 80
Content by Label macro, adding to 121
creating, from another page 68
files, attaching to 83
location, setting for 68
Panel macro, adding to 75
reordering, drag-and-drop used 112
Section macro, adding 80
tasklists, adding 151
tasks, managing on 152
versus blog posts 65
watching 125
Word document, importing into 106
page family 111
page history
  viewing 101, 102
page layouts
  about 78
  selecting 79
  using 79
page order
  modifying 111, 112
  setting, to alphabetical 113
Page Properties macro 228-230
page restriction hierarchy
  about 171
  inheritance 172
page restrictions
  about 171
  hierarchy 171
  managing 172, 173
  removing 173, 174
page structure
  adding 78
Panel macro
  about 78
  adding, to page 75
  storage format, obtaining 227
password authentication 34
permissions
  adding, for group 163
  adding, for user 163
  assigning, to anonymous users 170
  assigning, to groups 169
  assigning, to users 170
permissions, Crowd directory 59
permissions, JIRA 61

permissions, LDAP directory 53
personal space
  about 64
  default content, modifying of 202
personal tasks 149
pgAdmin III administration tool 16
plugin
  about 236
  building 284, 289
  distribution management, setting 293
  releasing 292
  releasing, without revision control 294
  running 289
plugin descriptor 279, 280
plugin metadata
  adding, to POM file 286
plugin module types
  about 294
  Confluence-specific module types 296
  generic module types 294, 295
  Web Items 300
  Web Sections 299
  XWork 297
plugin project
  creating 284, 285
plugin skeleton
  cleaning up 286
Plugins-osgi-cache/ directory 10
POM file
  plugin metadata, adding to 286
pom.xml file 279
port
  configuring 19, 20
PostgreSQL
  about 12
  installing 15
  URL, for downloading 15
project links 256
public signup
  enabling 47, 48

Q

quick navigation aid
  about 129
  facts 130

  using 129
quick search 129

R

results
  filtering 132

S

schema settings, LDAP directory 53
search fields
  created 134
  creatorName 133
  filename 134
  lastModifiers 133
  macroName 133
  spacekey 133
  URL 134
search syntax 134, 135
Section macro
  adding, to page 80
  Show Border parameter 81
sections 78
secure administrator sessions
  configuring 175
Seraph
  about 34
  URL 34
server settings, Crowd directory 58
server settings, JIRA 61
server settings, LDAP directory 52
shortcut links
  about 231
  creating 231, 232
  using 232
single page
  exporting 107
  Word document, importing as 104, 105
Single sign-on (SSO) system 34
site layouts 206
space
  adding, as favorites 128
  archiving 114-116
  category, adding to 119
  exporting 107, 108

linking, to JIRA project 256
watching 125
space category
about 118
using 118
space logo
about 198
modifying, with default theme 198
modifying, with Documentation Theme
199
space permissions
about 167
Attachments - Add 167
Attachments - Remove 168
Blog - Add 167
Blog - Remove 167
Comments - Add 167
Comments - Remove 167
Mail - Remove 168
managing 168
overview 167
Pages - Add 167
Pages - Remove 167
Pages - Restrict 167
Space - Admin 168
Space - Export 168
View 167
space permission screen
anonymous access section 168
groups section 168
individual users section 168
space project links 256
spaces
about 63
custom stylesheets, enabling for 204
organizing 111
space templates
about 211, 212
creating 212
space theme
modifying, steps 190
status
updating 141
status updates
about 140
displaying 142
managing 142

storage format
obtaining, for panel macro 227
Storage Format tool 227
styling 73
super user 160
Support Entitlement Number (SEN) 239
support request
submitting, via Confluence 267
support ticket
raising 266
system administrator 160

T

tables
about 81
creating 81
editing 82
keyboard shortcuts 82
sorting 83
tasklists
about 151
adding, on page 151
tasks
about 149, 156
completing 150
creating 149
managing, on page 152
priority, modifying 150
Team Calendars 235
Temp/ directory 10
template code, user macro template 226
templates
about 209
content, adding to 213
creating 211
importing 217, 218
tips, for creating 213-215
using 210
variables, inserting into 215
The Confluence module types
URL 301
The Marketplace
URL 302
themes 188
Thumbnails/ directory 10

Tomcat
  configuring 22
Tomcat 6.0 12
toolbar, Confluence editor
  about 70
  benefits 70
traffic
  redirecting, to HTTPS 23
trusted applications 257
trusted applications authentication
  about 257
  configuring 258

U

undefined link 98
undefined page
  link, creating to 98
Universal Plugin Manager (UPM)
  about 238
  offline mode 238-240
  online mode 238, 239
user administration
  about 42
  membership search, using 43
  password, resetting 46
  simple user search, using 43
  user details, editing 44, 46
  users, searching 42
user directory 49
user macros
  editing 219
  managing 218, 219
  removing 219
  writing 220-222
user macro template
  about 223
  descriptive header 223
  parameters 224, 225
  template code 226
  writing 223
user management
  authentication 33
  external user directories 49
  groups, managing 39
  public signup, enabling 47
  user, adding 34

users, administrating 42
user profiles 155
user request, add-ons
  about 247
  disabling 248, 249
  viewing 247, 248
users
  adding 34
  adding, manually 35, 36
  creating, for Confluence 16, 17
  invites, sending 38
  open registration, enabling 37
  permssions, assigning to 170
  permssions, adding for 163
  permssions, editing 163
  registering 37
user schema settings, LDAP directory 55, 56

V

variables 214
  inserting, into template 215
variable type
  list 216
  multi-line text 216
  text 216

W

WAR distribution 11
watches
  managing 126, 127
Web Items, plugin module types
  about 300
  module descriptor 300, 301
web pages
  link, creating to 96
Web Sections, plugin module types
  about 299
  module descriptor 299, 300
WebSudo 30, 175
welcome message, Confluence dashboard
  about 184
  content, including from another page
      187, 188
  editing 185
  Get Started text, removing 186
  restoring 185, 186

wiki markup 71

Windows

Eclipse, installing on 280, 281

Windows service

Confluence, configuring as 23

Word document

importing 103

importing, as single page 104, 105

importing, into multiple pages 106

workbox notifications

configuring 146

enabling 146, 147

X

xhtml-macro module 284

XWork, plugin module types

about 297

action class 298, 299

module descriptor 297

Thank you for buying
Atlassian Confluence 5 Essentials

About Packt Publishing

Packt, pronounced 'packed', published its first book "Mastering phpMyAdmin for Effective MySQL Management" in April 2004 and subsequently continued to specialize in publishing highly focused books on specific technologies and solutions.

Our books and publications share the experiences of your fellow IT professionals in adapting and customizing today's systems, applications, and frameworks. Our solution based books give you the knowledge and power to customize the software and technologies you're using to get the job done. Packt books are more specific and less general than the IT books you have seen in the past. Our unique business model allows us to bring you more focused information, giving you more of what you need to know, and less of what you don't.

Packt is a modern, yet unique publishing company, which focuses on producing quality, cutting-edge books for communities of developers, administrators, and newbies alike. For more information, please visit our website: www.packtpub.com.

About Packt Enterprise

In 2010, Packt launched two new brands, Packt Enterprise and Packt Open Source, in order to continue its focus on specialization. This book is part of the Packt Enterprise brand, home to books published on enterprise software – software created by major vendors, including (but not limited to) IBM, Microsoft and Oracle, often for use in other corporations. Its titles will offer information relevant to a range of users of this software, including administrators, developers, architects, and end users.

Writing for Packt

We welcome all inquiries from people who are interested in authoring. Book proposals should be sent to author@packtpub.com. If your book idea is still at an early stage and you would like to discuss it first before writing a formal book proposal, contact us; one of our commissioning editors will get in touch with you.

We're not just looking for published authors; if you have strong technical skills but no writing experience, our experienced editors can help you develop a writing career, or simply get some additional reward for your expertise.

JIRA 4 Essentials

ISBN: 978-1-84968-172-8   Paperback: 352 pages

Track bugs, issues, and manage your software
development projects with JIRA

1. Successfully manage issues and track your
    projects using JIRA

2. Model business processes using JIRA
    Workflows

3. Ensure only the right people get access to your
    data, by using user management and access
    control in JIRA

Mastering Redmine

ISBN: 978-1-84951-914-4   Paperback: 366 pages

A comprehensive guide with tips, tricks and best
practices, and an easy-to-learn structure

1. Use Redmine in the most effective manner and
    learn to master it

2. Become an expert in the look and feel with
    behavior and workflow customization

3. Utilize the natural flow of chapters, from initial
    and simple topics to advanced ones

Please check **www.PacktPub.com** for information on our titles

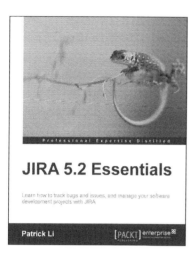

JIRA 5.2 Essentials

ISBN: 978-1-78217-999-3   Paperback: 396 pages

Learn how to track bugs and issues, and manage your software development projects with JIRA

1. Learn how to set up JIRA for software development

2. Effectively manage and handle software bugs and issues

3. Includes updated JIRA content as well as coverage of the popular GreenHopper plugin

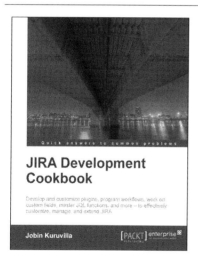

JIRA Development Cookbook

ISBN: 978-1-84968-180-3   Paperback: 476 pages

Develop and customize plugins, program workflows, work on custom fields, master JQL functions, and more—to effectively customize, manage, and extend JIRA

1. Extend and Customize JIRA—Work with custom fields, workflows, Reports & Gadgets, JQL functions, plugins, and more

2. Customize the look and feel of your JIRA User Interface by adding new tabs, web items and sections, drop down menus, and more

3. Master JQL - JIRA Query Language that enables advanced searching capabilities through which users can search for issues in their JIRA instance and then exploit all the capabilities of issue navigator

Please check **www.PacktPub.com** for information on our titles

34176483R00189

Made in the USA
Lexington, KY
26 July 2014